ISBN 978-0-331-60318-7
PIBN 10636900

THE

SACRED BOOKS OF THE HINDUS

Translated by various Sanskrit Scholars

EDITED BY

MAJOR B. D. BASU, I.M.S. (*Retired*)

VOL. XI.

SAMKHYA PHILOSOPHY

PUBLISHED BY

THE PÂṆINI OFFICE, BHUVANEŚWARI ÂŚRAMA, BAHADURGANJ

Allahabad

PRINTED BY APURVA KRISHNA BOSE, AT THE INDIAN PRESS

1915

THE SAMKHYA PHILOSOPHY

CONTAINING

(1) SÂMKHYA-PRAVACHANA SÛTRAM, WITH THE VRITTI OF ANIRUDDHA, AND THE BHÂṢYA OF VIJNÂNA BHIKṢU AND EXTRACTS FROM THE VRITTI-SÂRA OF MAHÂDEVA VEDANTIN;
(2) TATVA SAMÂSA; (3) SÂMKHYA KÂRIKÂ;
(4) PANCHAŚIKHÂ SÛTRAM.

TRANSLATED BY

NANDALAL SINHA, M.A., B.L., P.C.S.
DEPUTY MAGISTRATE, DALTONGANJ.

PUBLISHED BY
SUDHINDRA NATH VASU,
THE PÂṆINI OFFICE, BHUVANEŚWARÎ ÂŚRAMA, BAHADURGANJ,
Allahabad
PRINTED BY APURVA KRISHNA BOSE, AT THE INDIAN PRESS
1915

PREFACE.

The present volume of the *Sacred Books of the Hindus* which bears the modest title of the *Sâṃkhya-Pravachana-Sûtram*, is, in reality, a collection of all the available original documents of the School of the Sâṃkhyas, with the single exception of the commentary composed by Vyâsa on the *Sâṃkhya-Pravachana-Yoga-Sûtram* of Patañjali. For it contains in its pages not only the *Sâṃkhya-Pravachana-Sûtram* of Kapila together with the *Vṛitti* of Aniruddha, the *Bhâṣya* of Vijñâna Bhikṣu, and extracts of the original portions from the *Vṛittisâra* of Vedântin Mahâdeva, but also the *Tattva-Samâsa* together with the commentary of Narendra, the *Sâṃkhya-Kârikâ* of Îśvarakṛiṣṇa with profuse annotations based on the *Bhâṣya* of Gauḍapâda and the *Tattva-Kaumudî* of Vâchaspati Miśra, and a few of the Aphorisms of Pañchaśikha with explanatory notes according to the *Yoga-Bhâṣya* which has quoted them. An attempt, moreover, has been made to make the volume useful in many other respects by the addition, for instance, of elaborate analytical tables of contents to the *Sâṃkhya-Pravachana-Sûtram* and the *Sâṃkhya-Kârikâ*, and of a number of important appendices.

The Contents of the Volume.

In the preparation of this volume, I have derived very material help from the excellent editions of the *Vṛitti* of Aniruddha and the *Bhâṣya* of Vijñâna Bhikṣu on the *Sâṃkhya-Pravachana-Sûtram* by Dr. Richard Garbe, to whom my thanks are due. And, in general, I take this opportunity of acknowledging my indebtedness to all previous writers on the Sâṃkhya, living and dead, from whose writings I have obtained light and leading in many important matters connected with the subject.

An introduction only now remains to be written. It is proposed, however, to write a separate monogram on the Sâṃkhya Darśana, which would be historical, critical and comparative, in its scope and character. In this preface, therefore, only a very brief account is given of some of the cardinal doctrines of the Sâṃkhya School.

The Law of the Identity of Cause and Effect.

The first and foremost among these is the *Sat-Kârya-Siddhânta* or the Established Tenet of Existent Effect. It is the Law of the Identity of Cause and Effect: what is called the cause is the unmanifested state of what is called the effect, and what is called the effect is only the manifested state of what is called the cause; their substance is one and the same; differences of manifestation and non-manifestation give rise to the distinctions of Cause and Effect. The effect, therefore, is never non-existent; whether before its production, or whether after its destruction, it is always existent in the cause. For, nothing can come out of nothing, and nothing can altogether vanish out of existence.

Definition of Cause and Effect.

This doctrine would be better understood by a comparison with the contrary views held by other thinkers on the relation of cause and effect. But before we proceed to state these views, we should define the terms "cause" and "effect." One thing is said to be the cause of another thing, when the latter cannot be without the former. In its widest sense, the term, Cause, therefore, denotes an agent, an act, an instrument, a purpose, some material, time, and space. In fact, whatever makes the accomplishment of the effect possible, is one of its causes. And the immediate result of the operation of these causes, is their effect. Time and Space, however, are universal causes, inasmuch as they are presupposed in each and every act of causation. The remaining causes fall under the descriptions of "Material," "Efficient," "Formal," and "Final."

Aristotelian Division of Causes.

The Sâṃkhya Division.

The Sâṃkhyas further reduce them to two descriptions only, *viz.*, *Upâdâna*, *i.e.*, the material, which the Naiyâyikas call *Samavâyi* or Combinative or Constitutive, and *Nimitta*, *i. e.*, the efficient, formal, and final, which may be variously, though somewhat imperfectly, translated as the instrumental, efficient, occasional, or conditional, because it includes the instruments with which, the agent by which, the occasion on which, and the conditions under which, the act is performed.

Causes *Upâdâna* and *Nimitta* distinguished.

Obviously, there is a real distinction between the *Upâdâna* and the *Nimitta*: the *Upâdâna* enters into the constitution of the effect, and the power of taking the form of, in other words, the potentiality of being re-produced as, the effect, resides in it; while the *Nimitta*, by the exercise of an extraneous influence only, co-operates with the power inherent in the material, in its re-production in the form of the effect, and its causality ceases with such re-production. To take the case of a coin, for example: the material causality was in a lump of gold; it made possible the modification of the gold into the form of the coin, it will remain operative as long as the coin will last as a coin, and after its destruction, it will pass into the potential state again; but the operation of the *Nimittas* came to an end as soon as the coin was minted.

Similarly, the Sâṃkhyas distinguish the Effect under the twofold aspect of simple manifestation and of re-production. Thus, the coin is an instance of causation by re-production, while the production of cream from milk is an instance of causation by simple manifestation.

Theories of the Origin of the World.

Now, as to the origin of the world, there is a divergence of opinion among thinkers of different Schools: Some uphold the Theory of Creation, others maintain the Theory of Evolution. Among the Creationists are counted the Nâstikas or Nihilists, the Buddhists, and the Naiyâyikas; and among the Evolutionists, the Vedântins and the Sâṃkhyas. The Nâstikas hold that the world is non-existent, that is, unreal, and that it came out of what was not; the Buddhists hold that the world is existent, that is, real, and that it came out of what was not; the Naiyâyikas hold that the world is non-existent, that is, non-eternal, perishable, and that it came out of the existent, that is, what is eternal, imperishable; the Vedântins hold that the world is non-existent, that is, unreal, and that it came out of what was existent, that is, real, namely, *Brahman*; and the Sâṃkhyas hold that the world is existent, that is, real, and that it came out of what was existent, that is, real, namely, the *Pradhâna*. Thus, there are the *A-Sàt-Kârya-Vâda* of the Nâstikas that a non-existent world has been produced from a non-existent cause, and of the Buddhists that an existent world has been produced from a non-existent cause, the *Abhâva-Utpatti-Vâda* of the Naiyâyikas that a non-eternal world has been produced from an eternal cause, the *Vivarta-Vâda* of the Vedântins that the world is a re-volution, an illusory appearance, of the one eternal reality, *viz.*, *Brahman*, and the *Sat-Kârya-Vâda* of the Sâṃkhyas that an existent world has been produced from an existent cause.

Arguments which establish the Sâṃkhya Theory.

Against the theories of *A-Sat-Kârya*, *Abhâva-Utpatti*, and *Vivarta*, and in support of their theory of *Sat-Kârya*, the Sâṃkhyas advance the following arguments:

I. There can be no production of what is absolutely non-existent; *e.g.*, a man's horn.

II. There must be some determinate material cause for every product. Cream, for instance, can form on milk only, and never on water. Were it as absolutely non-existent in milk as it is in water, there would be no reason why it should form on milk, and not equally on water.

III. The relation of cause and effect is that of the producer and the produced, and the simplest conception of the cause as the producer is that it possesses the potentiality of becoming the effect, and this potentiality is nothing but the unrealised state of the effect.

IV. The effect is seen to possess the nature of the cause, *e.g.*, a coin still possesses the properties of the gold of which it is made.

V. Matter is indestructible; "destruction" means disappearance into the cause.

It follows, therefore, that cause and effect are neither absolutely dissimilar nor absolutely similar to each other. They possess *essential* similarities and *formal* dissimilarities. Such being the relation between cause and effect, the world cannot possibly have come out of something in which it had been absolutely non-existent, and which accordingly was, in relation to it, as good as non-existent. For the world is neither absolutely unreal nor absolutely real. The test of objective reality is its opposition to consciousness. It is distinguished as *Prâtibhâsika* or apparent, *Vyâvahârika* or practical or phenomenal, and *Pâramârthika* or transcendental. Of these, the world possesses phenomenal reality, and must, therefore, have a transcendental reality as its substratum. Thus is the Doctrine of *Sat-Kârya* established.

The World possesses Phenomenal reality.

A natural corollary from the above doctrine is the other doctrine of *Pariṇâma* or transformation. It is the doctrine that, as all effects are contained in their causes in an unmanifested form, the "production" of an effect is nothing but its manifestation, and that, as cause and effect are essentially identical, an effect is merely a transformation of the cause.

The Doctrine of Transformation.

Now, the question arises, whether the cause of the world be a single one, or whether it be manifold. Some think that, according to the Naiyâyikas, who declare the existence of *Parama-Aṇus* or the ordinary Atoms of Matter, the world has sprung from a plurality of causes. This is, however, to take a very superficial view of the Nyâya-Vaiśeṣika Darśana. The Naiyâyikas were certainly not timid explorers of metaphysical truths; there is absolutely no reason for supposing that they either would not or could not penetrate behind and beyond the ordinary Atoms of Matter. As I have elsewhere pointed out, it would be a mistake to treat the six Darśanas as each being a complete and self-contained system of thought; in respect of their scope and purpose, they bear no analogy to the philosophies of the West. They are singly neither universal nor final; but they mutually supplement one another. Their Ṛisis address themselves to particular sets of people possessing different degrees of mental and spiritual advancement. They reveal

The Cause of the World, one or manifold?

The Position of the Naiyâyikas explained.

and explain the truths embodied in the Vedas to them from their point of view and according to their competence, and thus help them in realising the truths for themselves and thereby in progressing towards Self-realisation. If the Naiyâyikas, therefore, do not carry their analysis of the world further than the ordinary Atoms of Matter, it must not be assumed that they teach a sort of atomic pluralism as the ultimate theory of the origin of the world, and are in this opposed to the authors of the other Śâstras which teach a different origin. The right explanation is that they make but a partial declaration of the Vedic truths and cut short the process of resolution at the ordinary Atoms of Matter, because they address themselves to a class of students who do not possess the mental capacity to grasp subtler truths.

Unity of the Cause of the World.

For the sense of unity which has found expression in the Law of Parsimony, points to a single original of the world or material manifestation, as revealed in the Vedas. And the Sâṃkhya makes its students acquainted with this. It is called the Root, and is described as the *Pradhâna*, that in which all things are contained, and as *Prakriti*, the mother of things.

The Scope of the Sâṃkhya.

It is a long way from the ordinary Atoms of Matter to the Pradhâna or Primordial Matter. The Sâṃkhya undertakes to declare and expound the successive transformations of the Pradhâna down to the Gross Matter, with the object of accomplishing the complete isolation of the Self from even the most shadowy conjunction with the Pradhâna.

Definition of Prakṛiti.

The definition of Prakṛiti is that it is the state of equilibrium of Sattva, Rajas, and Tamas, called the Guṇas. It is the genus of which the Guṇas are the species. Their state of equilibrium is their latent, potential, or inactive state, the state of not being developed into effects. The Guṇas are extremely fine substances, and are respectively the principles of illumination, evolution, and involution, and the causes of pleasure, pain, and dullness. For, Sattva is light and illuminating, Rajas is active and urgent, and Tamas is heavy and enveloping. They are in eternal and indissoluble conjunction with one another, and, by nature, mutually overpower, support, produce, and intimately mix with, one another.

The Doctrine of the Three Guṇas.

This doctrine of the Three Guṇas is the very foundation of the Sâṃkhya Tantra. It is explained in the following manner: (1) Everything in the world, external as well as internal, is in constant change; and there can be no change, whether it be movement in space, or whether it be movement in time, without rest. Side by side, therefore, with the principle of mutation, there must be a principle of conservation. And, as Berkeley tells us, existence is perception,--whatever is not manifested to Consciousness, individual or universal, does not exist. Another principle is, therefore, required which would make the manifestation of the other two principles and of their products, (as also of itself and of its own), to Consciousness possible. Thus, at the origin of the world, there must be a principle of conservation, a principle of mutation, and a principle of manifestation. (2) Similarly, an examination of the intra-organic energies would disclose the existence of three distinct principles behind them. These energies are the eleven Indriyas or Powers of Cognition and Action, and Prâṇa or Vital Force. Among them, the Powers of Cognition, *e.g.*, Seeing, Hearing, etc., cause manifestation of objects, the Powers of Action, *e.g.*, seizing by the hand, etc., produce change, and Prâṇa conserves and preserves life. (3) In the mind, again, modifications of three distinct characters take place; *viz.*, cognition, conation, and retention; and these could not be possible without there being a principle of manifestation, a principle of mutation, and a principle of conservation respectively. (4) Likewise, a psycho-æsthetic analysis of our worldly experience yields the result that everything in the universe possesses a threefold aspect, that is, it may manifest as agreeable, or as disagreeable, or as neutral, *i.e.*, neither agreeable nor disagreeable. It must then have derived these characteristics from its cause; for nothing can be in the effect which was not in the cause. The principles of manifestation, mutation, and conservation, therefore, which are operative in the change of the states of agreeable, disagreeable, and neutral, must also possess the nature of being pleasant (śânta), unpleasant (ghora), and dull (mûḍha).

It is these principles of manifestation, mutation, and conservation, possessing the nature of pleasure, pain, and dullness, that are respectively the Guṇas, Sattva, Rajas, and Tamas, of the Sâṃkhyas. They are the constitutive elements of Prakṛiti. They are Guṇas in their manifested forms; they are Prakṛiti in their unmanifested form.

The Transformations of Prakṛiti enumerated and distinguished.

The transformations of Prakṛiti are either *prakṛiti-vikṛiti*, original or evolvent as well as modification or evolute, or *vikṛiti*, modification or evolute merely. The former are themselves transformations of their antecedents, and, in their turn, give rise to subsequent transformations. They are Mahat, Ahaṃkâra, and the five Tan-mâtras. The latter are the eleven Indriyas and the five gross Elements. The transformation of Prakṛiti ceases with them. Of course, the gross Elements combine and evolve the material world ; but the world is not a different Tattva or principle from the Elements, because it does not develop a single attribute which is not already possessed by them. For the test of a Tattva or original or ultimate principle is that it possesses a characteristic property which is not possessed by any other Tattva.

The Objective World consists of Twenty-four Tattvas.

The objective world thus contains twenty-four Tattvas, namely, Prakṛiti, Mahat, Ahaṃ-kâra, Manas, the five Indriyas of Cognition, the five Indriyas of Action, the five Tan-mâtras, and the five gross Elements.

The Transformation of Prakṛiti is Mahat or Buddhi.

At the beginning of creation, there arises in Prakṛiti *Spandana* or cosmic vibration which disturbs its state of equilibrium, and releases the Guṇas from quiescence. Rajas at once acts upon Sattva and manifests it as Mahat. Mahat denotes Buddhi, the material counterpart and basis of what we term Understanding or Reason. Buddhi is called Mahat, great, because it is the principal among the Instruments of Cognition and Action. Mahat also means "light"; it is derived from the Vedic word *Mahas* or *Maghas*, meaning light. And Buddhi is called Mahat, because it is the initial transformation of Sattva which is the principle of manifestation. Or, Buddhi which is the first manifestation of the Guṇas and which is the material cause of the world, is called Mahat, in order to distinguish it from individual or finite Buddhis which are its parts. For "what is the Buddhi of the first-born golden-egged (Brahmâ), the same is the primary basis of all Buddhis; it is here called the 'great self.'"

Universal and Individual Buddhis distinguished.

Definition of Buddhi.

The function of Buddhi is *Adhyavasâya* or certainty leading to action. It manifests in eight forms; *viz.*, as virtue, knowledge, dispassion and power, while Sattva is predominant in it, and as vice, ignorance, passion, and weakness, while Tamas is predominant in it. And these, again, are modified into innumerable forms, which are classified as Error, Incapacity, Complacency, and Perfection. Such is Pratyaya-sarga or the creation of Buddhi or intellectual creation as contra-distinguished from elemental creation.

The Transformation of Buddhi is Ahaṃ-kâra.

From Buddhi springs Ahaṃ-kâra: from "*cogito*," I think, "*sum*," I am. Ahaṃ-kâra is literally the I-maker. It is the material counterpart and basis of what we term egoism, and causes modifications of Buddhi in the forms of "I am," "I do," etc., etc. It is the principle of personal identity and of individuation. Its function is *Abhimâna*, conceit, thinking with reference to itself, assumption of things to itself. But it is not a mere function; it is a substance in which reside *Vâsanâs* or the resultant tendencies of accumulated experience, and which is capable of modification into other and grosser forms.

This Aham-kâra, which is the first transformation of Buddhi, is the cosmic Aham-kâra, the Upâdhi or adjunct of the golden-egged Brahmâ, the Creator. It is the infinite source of the finite Aham-kâras of individual Jîvas.

Universal and Individual Aham-kâras distinguished.

The modification of Aham-kâra is twofold, according as it is influenced by Sattva or by Tamas. The Sâttvic modifications are the eleven Indriyas, that is, the five Indriays of Cognition, *viz.*, the powers located in the Eye, Ear, Nose, Tongue, and Skin, the five Indriyas of Action, *viz.*, the powers located in the voice, hand, feet, and the organs of generation and of excretion, and Manas. Manas is both a power of cognition and a power of action. Assimilation and differentiation are its distinctive functions.

The Transformations of Aham-kâra are: The Indriyas.

The Tâmasic modifications of Aham-kâra are the five Tan-mâtras, *viz.*, of Sound, Touch, Form, Flavour and Smell. They are pure, subtle or simple elements, the metaphysical parts of the ordinary Atoms of Matter. They are "fine substances," to quote from Vijñâna Bhikṣu, "the undifferentiated (a-viśeṣa) originals of the Gross Elements, which form the substratum of Sound, Touch, Form, Flavour and Smell, belonging to that class (that is, in that stage of their evolution) in which the distinctions of Śânta (pleasant), etc., do not exist." The process of their manifestation is as follows: The Tan-mâtra of Sound, possessing the attribute of Sound, is produced from Aham-kâra; then, from the Tan-mâtras of Sound, accompanied by Aham-kâra, is produced the Tan-mâtra of Touch, possessing the attributes of Sound and Touch. In a similar manner, the other Tan-mâtras are produced, in the order of their mention, by the addition of one more attribute at each successive step.

And the Tan-mâtras.

The transformations of the Tan-mâtras are the Gross Elements of Ether, Air, Fire, Water, and Earth,—the ordinary Atoms of Matter, in which appear for the first time the distinctions of being pleasant, painful, and neutral. All Bodies, from that of Brahmâ down to a stock, are formed of them.

The Transformations of the Tan-mâtras are the Gross Elements.

Now, all this objective world is non-intelligent, because its material cause, Prakṛiti, is non-intelligent. It does not, therefore, exist or energise for its own sake. There must be some one else of a different nature,

How the Existence of a Subjective Principle, Puruṣa, is explained.

some intelligent being, for whose benefit, *i.e.*, experience and freedom, all this activity of Prakṛiti is. Thus do the Sâṃkhyas explain the existence of Puruṣa.

The Twentyfive Tattvas.

To classify the Tattvas logically, they may be exhibited thus :

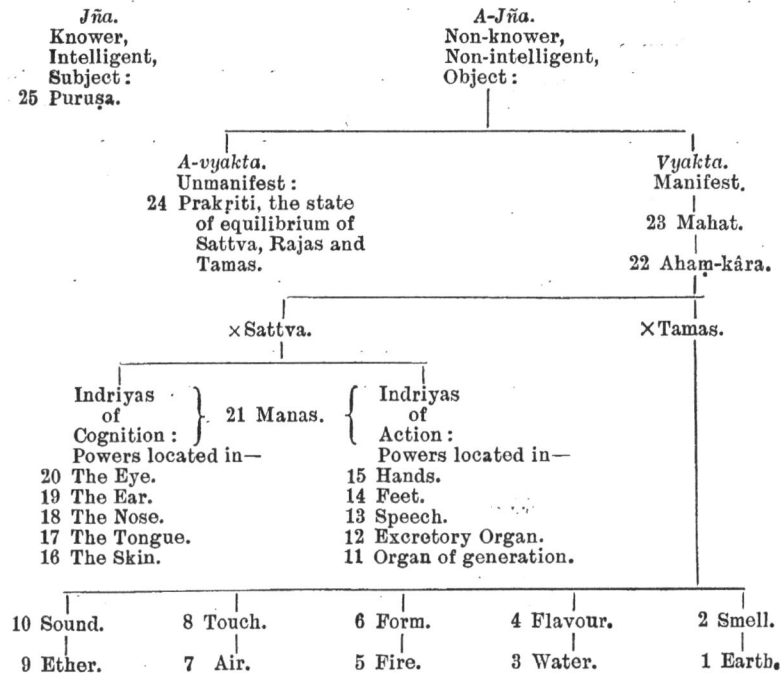

- *Jña.* Knower, Intelligent, Subject: 25 Puruṣa.
- *A-Jña.* Non-knower, Non-intelligent, Object:
  - *A-vyakta.* Unmanifest: 24 Prakṛiti, the state of equilibrium of Sattva, Rajas and Tamas.
  - *Vyakta.* Manifest.
    - 23 Mahat.
      - 22 Aham-kâra.
        - × Sattva.
          - Indriyas of Cognition: Powers located in— 20 The Eye. 19 The Ear. 18 The Nose. 17 The Tongue. 16 The Skin.
          - 21 Manas.
          - Indriyas of Action: Powers located in— 15 Hands. 14 Feet. 13 Speech. 12 Excretory Organ. 11 Organ of generation.
        - × Tamas.
          - 10 Sound. — 9 Ether.
          - 8 Touch. — 7 Air.
          - 6 Form. — 5 Fire.
          - 4 Flavour. — 3 Water.
          - 2 Smell. — 1 Earth.

Of these, Puruṣa is the principle of Being, Prakṛiti is the principle of Becoming: Puruṣa eternally is, never becomes, while Prakṛiti is essentially Movement; even during *Pralaya* or Cosmic Dissolution, its activity does not altogether cease; it then undergoes homogeneous transformation: Sattva modifying as Sattva, Rajas modifying as Rajas, and Tamas modifying as Tamas. Purusa, on the other hand, is eternal consciousness undisturbed. Nothing can come into him, nothing can go out of him; he is *Kûṭa-stha*, dwelling in the cave. And these two eternal co-ordinate principles are in eternal conjunction with each other. But conjunction as such does not set Prakṛiti in movement. Creation is caused by *Râga* or Passion. *Râga* is a change of state which spontaneously takes place in the Rajas of Buddhi, through the influence of Dharma and A-dharma. These are the natural consequences of the previous changes in the transformations of Prakṛiti,

Puruṣa and Prakṛiti contrasted.

The Spontaneity of Prakṛiti.

and they reside in Ahaṃ-kâra in the form of *Vâsanâ* or tendency, and render impure the Sattva of Buddhi. The activity of Prakṛiti, in the form of the disturbance of its Rajas element, is spontaneously evoked for the purpose of working out and exhausting the stored up Vâsanâ; its successive transformation is really a process of purification of the Sattva of Buddhi. This spontaneous tendency towards purification is due to the vicinity of Puruṣa.

The Nature of Puruṣa.

The Sâṃkhyas constantly hammer on the theme that no pain, no suffering, no bondage ever belongs to Puruṣa. Puruṣa is eternally free, never bound, never released. And because they thus thoroughly reveal the nature of Puruṣa, their doctrine is described as the Sâṃkhya, thorough-revealer.

The Meaning of the word, Sâṃkhya.

The "Bondage" of Puruṣa:

The "experience" of Puruṣa consists in his being the indifferent spectator of the changes that take place in Buddhi; his "bondage" is nothing but the reflection on him of the bondage, that is, the impurities, of Buddhi; his "release" is merely the removal of this reflection which, again, depends upon the recovery by Buddhi of its state of pristine purity, which means its dissolution into Prakṛiti. To say that the activity of Prakṛiti is for the benefit of Puruṣa is, therefore, a mere figure of speech. It is really for the purification of the Sattva of Buddhi.

Is due to A-vivaka.

To think, as people generally do, that pleasure and pain, release and bondage really belong to Puruṣa, is a mistake pure and simple. It is *A-vidyâ*. *A-viveka* is the cause of *A-vidyâ*. And *A-viveka*, non-discrimination, is the failure to discriminate Puruṣa from Prakṛiti and her products. Many are ignorant of the very existence of Puruṣa. Many are ignorant of his exact nature: some identify him with Prakṛiti, some with Maḥat, some with Ahaṃ-kâra, and so on. Many, again, know the Tattvas in some form or other, but they know them not: knowledge, in the sense of mere information, they have, but no realisation, and it is realisation which matters. The Sâṃkhyâ, for this reason, enters into a detailed examination of the *Tattvas*, their number, nature, function, effect, inter-relation, resemblance, difference, etc., and insists on *Tattva-abhyâsa* or the habitual contemplation of the *Tattvas*, so that they may be *Sâkṣât-kṛita* or immediately known or realised. The way is also shown as to how, and the means, too, whereby, to discriminate, on the one hand, the gross Elements from the Tan-mâtras, the Tan-mâtras from the Indriyas, and both from Ahaṃ-kâra, Ahaṃ-kâra from Buddhi, and Buddhi

The Aim of the Sâṃkhya.

from Puruṣa, and, on the other hand, to discriminate Puruṣa from the gross and subtle Bodies and to prevent their further identification.

The Relation of the Yoga to the Sâṃkhya is that of Practice to Theory.

The Yoga which is the practice of the Sâṃkhya, which is the theory, takes up, and starts from, these central teachings of its predecessor, *viz.* (1) All activity—all change—is in and of Prakṛiti. (2) No activity—no change—is in Puruṣa. (3) The modifications of the mind are reflected in Puruṣa, and make him look like modified. (4) When the mind is calm and purified, Puruṣa shines as he really is. (5) Save and except these, reflection and its removal, bondage and release do not belong to Puruṣa. (6) Bondage and release are really of Prakṛiti, or, more strictly speaking, of the individualised form of its first transformation, *viz.*, Buddhi. From the point of view of the philosophy of the history of the Darśanas, these are the last words of the Sâṃkhya.

The Doctrine of the Subtle Body.

The Sâṃkhya also has brought the doctrine of Sûkṣma or Liṅga Śarîra, the Subtle Body, prominently to the fore. For, the purification of the Sattva of Buddhi may not be, and, as a general rule, is not, possible in one life, nor in one region of the Universe. But death seems to put an untimely end to the process of purification, by destroying the gross Body. How then can the process of purification be continued in other lives and in other regions? The Sâṃkhya replies that it can be and is so continued by means of the Subtile Body. It is composed of the seventeen *Tattvas,* beginning with Buddhi and ending with the Tan-mâtras. It is produced, at the beginning of Creation, one for each Puruṣa, and lasts till the time of Mahâ-Pralaya or the Great Dissolution. It is altogether unconfined, such that it may ascend to the sun dancing on its beams, and can penetrate through a mountain. And it transmigrates from one gross Body to another, from one region of the Universe to another, being perfumed with, and carrying the influence of, the *Bhâvas* or dispositions of Buddhi characterised as virtue, knowledge, dispassion, and power, and their opposites.

The Plurality of Puruṣas.

The Sâṃkhyas, again, teach a plurality of Puruṣas. This topic has been very fully discussed in the *Sâṃkhya-Pravachana-Sûtram,* I. 149-159, and the commentaries. Therein Vijñâna Bhikṣu has mercilessly criticised the doctrine of Non-duality maintained by some of the Vedântins, and has sought to establish the plurality of Puruṣas. And Garbe, in his characteristic style, contents himself with a flippant criticism of Vijñâna Bhikṣu's explanations. But Vijñâna Bhikṣu's criticisms are not aimed principally against the unity of Puruṣas, but at those interpretations of it, according to which the empirical Puruṣas, that is, mundane Puruṣas, the plurality of whom is established by irrefutable arguments, as in the Sâṃkhya Śâstra, are reduced to mere shadows without substance. He does not so much attack the unadulterated *A-Dvaita* of the Vedas and the Upaniṣats as its later developments. He was fully aware of the fact that none of the six Darśanas, for example, was, as we have hinted more than once, a complete system of philosophy in the Western sense, but merely a catechism explaining, and giving a reasoned account of, some of the truths revealed in the Vedas and Upaniṣats, to a particular class of students, confining the scope of its enquiry within the province of Creation, without attempting to solve to them the transcendental riddles of the Universe, which, in their particular stage of mental and spiritual development, it would have been impossible for them to grasp. Similarly, Garbe is wrong in thinking that Vijñâna Bhikṣu "explains away the doctrine of absolute monism." It is only a matter of interpretation and of stand-point; compare Râmânuja, Madhva, etc. For Vijñâna does not hesitate to do away even with the duality of Prakṛiti and Puruṣa when he observes that all the other *Tattvas* enter into absorption in Puruṣa and rest there in a subtle form, as does energy in that which possesses it. (*Vide* his Commentary on S-P-S., I. 61). For an explanation, therefore, of the apparent contradictions in the Darśanas, one must turn to the Vedas and Upaniṣats and writings of a similar scope and character. The Bhagavat-Gitâ, for instance, declares:—

द्वाविमौ पुरुषौ लोके क्षरश्चाक्षर एव च ।
क्षरः सर्वाणि भूतानि कूटस्थोऽक्षर उच्यते ॥ १५ । १६ ॥
उत्तमः पुरुषस्त्वन्यः परमात्मेत्युदाहृतः ।
यो लोकत्रयमाविश्य विभर्त्यव्यय ईश्वरः ॥ १५ । १७ ॥

In the world there are these two Puruṣas only, the mutable and the immutable. The mutable is all created things; the intelligent experiencer is said to be the immutable.—XV. 16.

While the highest Puruṣa is a different one, who (in the Upaniṣats) is called the Parama-Âtmâ, the Supreme Self, and who, presiding over the three worlds, preserves them, as the undecaying, omniscient, omnipotent Îśvara.—XV. 17.

Along such lines the so-called contradictions of the Darśanas find their reconciliation and true explanation in the higher teachings of the Upaniṣats.

The Sâmkhya does not deny the Existence of God.

It will probably be contended that, in the case in question, such reconciliation is impossible in view of "one of the fundamental doctrines of the genuine Sâṃkhya, which is the denial of God" (Garbe). No graver blunder has ever been committed by any student of the Sâṃkhya! The genuine Sâṃkhya no more denies the existence of God than does Garbe's illustrious countryman, Emmanuel Kant, in his *Critique of Pure Reason*. To make this position clear, let us paraphrase the *Sâṃkhya-Pravachana-Sûtram* on the subject. Thus, Îśvara is not a subject of proof (I. 92). For, we must conceive Îśvara as being either *Mukta*, free, or *Baddha*, bound. He can be neither free nor bound; because, in the former case, being perfect, He would have nothing to fulfil by creation, and, in the latter case, He would not possess absolute power (I.93-94). No doubt, in the *Śrutis*, we find such declarations as "He is verily the all-knower, the creator of all," and the like; these, however, do not allude to an eternal, uncaused Îśvara (God), but are only eulogies of such Jîvas or Incarnate Selves as are going to be freed, or of the Yogins, human as well as super-human, who have attained perfection by the practice of Yoga (I. 95). Some say that attainment of the highest end results through absorption into the Cause (III. 54). But this is not so, because, as people rise up again after immersion into water, so do **Puruṣas**, merged into Prakṛiti at the time of *Pralaya*, appear, again, at the next Creation, as Îśvaras (III. 54-55). The Vedic declarations, *e.g.*, "He is verily the all-knower, the creator of all," refer to such Highest Selves (III. 56). Neither is the existence of God as the moral governor of the world, proved; for, if God Himself produce the consequences of acts, He would do so even without the aid of Karma; on the other hand, if His agency in this respect be subsidiary to that of Karma, then let Karma itself be the cause of its consequences; what is the use of a God? Moreover, it is impossible that God should be the dispenser of the consequences of acts. For, His motive will be either egoistic or altruistic. But it cannot be the latter, as it is simply inconceivable that one acting for the good of others, should create a world so full of pain. Nor can it be the former; because (1) in that case, He would possess unfulfilled desires, and, consequently, suffer pain and the like. Thus your worldly God would be no better than our Highest Selves. (2) Agency cannot be established in the absence of desire, for, behind every act, there lies an intense desire. And to attribute intense desire to God would be to take away from his eternal freedom. (3) Further, desire is a particular product of Prakṛiti. It cannot, therefore, naturally grow within the Self, whether it be God or the Jîva; it must come from the outside. Now, it cannot be said that desire, which is an evolute of Prakṛiti, directly has connection with the Self, as it would contradict hundreds of

Vedic declarations to the effect that the Self is *Asaṅga*, absolutely free from attachment or association. Neither can it be maintained that Prakṛiti establishes connection of desire with the Self by induction, as it were, through its mere proximity to it; as this would apply equally to all the Selves at the same time (V. 2-9). Furthermore, the above arguments might have lost their force or relevancy, were there positive proof of the existence of God; but there is no such proof. For, proof is of three kinds, *viz.*, Perception, Inference and Testimony. Now, God certainly is not an object of perception. Neither can He be known by Inference; because there is no general proposition (Vyâpti) whereby to infer the existence of God, inasmuch as, Prakṛiti alone being the cause of the world, the law of causation is of no avail here. And the testimony of the Veda speaks of Prakṛiti as being the origin of the world, and hence does not prove the existence of God (V. 10-12).

Thus the Sâṃkhyas maintain that it cannot be proved by evidence that an eternal, self-caused God exists; that the ordinary means of proof, Perception, Inference and Testimony, fail to reach Him; and that there is no other means of correct knowledge on our plane of the Universe. And when, therefore, Kapila thus declares that the various objective arguments for the establishment of theism, *viz.*, the ontological, the cosmological, the teleological, and the moral, cannot stand, and pronounces the verdict of 'non-proven' in regard to the existence of God, he takes up the right philosophical attitude, and there is absolutely no justification for branding his doctrine as atheistical merely on this score. "The notion that the existence of God is susceptible of dialectic demonstration has been surrendered, in later times," as Mr. Fitz-Edward Hall remarks, "by most Christian theologians of any credit: it now being, more ordinarily, maintained that our conviction of deity, on grounds apart from revelation, reposes solely on original consciousness, antecedent to all proof."

Nir-Îśvara and Nâstika are not convertible terms.

Thus the Sâṃkhya is *Nir-Îśvara*, but not *Nâstika*. It is not *Nâstika*, atheistical, because it does not deny the existence of God. It is *Nir-Îśvara, lit.* god-less, as it explains all and every fact of experience without reference to, and without invoking the intervention of, a divine agency. Those who imagine that, in the Sâṃkhya, there is a denial of God, obviously fail to recognize the distinction between the two words, *Nâstika* and *Nir-Îśvara*. They, further, fail to bear in mind that the Sanskrit *Îśvara* and the English *God* are not synonymous terms. For, the opposite of *Nâstika* is *Âstika* (believer), one who believes in the existence of God, the authority of the

February, 1915. N. SINHA

TABLE OF CONTENTS.

INTRODUCTORY.

	PAGES.
The Sâṃkhya Śâstra presupposes Vairâgya or Dispassion ...	1
The origin and development of Vairâgya	1
Mokṣa or Release is achieved through Para Vairâgya or Higher Dispassion	1
The Sâṃkhya is a Mokṣa Śâstra and teaches Para Vairâgya ...	1
The term "A-Dvaita" or Non-Dualism explained	2
Kapila, the father of the Sâṃkhya, is an Avatâra of Viṣṇu ...	2
Loss of the original Sâṃkhya Sûtras	3
The Sâṃkhya is the only true A-Dvaita Śâstra	3
It is not in conflict with the Veda	3
The Sâṃkhya *versus* the Nyâya and the Vaiśeṣika : The latter deals with Vyavahârika or practical reality, while the former deals with Paramârthika or ultimate reality ; hence neither is there opposition between them, nor is the Sâṃkhya superfluous	4-5
The Sâṃkhya *versus* the Vedânta and the Yoga : The exclusion of Îśvara from the Sâṃkhya,—possible reasons for	5-10
The Sâṃkhya is concerned primarily with Puruṣa-Prakṛiti-Viveka or Discrimination between Puruṣa and Prakṛiti, while the Vedânta is concerned primarily with Îśvara	7
The Sâṃkhya Plurality of Self *versus* the Vedânta Unity of Self : does not necessarily imply a conflict...	10
The Sâṃkhya-Pravachana is an elaboration of the Tattva-Samâsa	11
The name "Sâṃkhya" explained	11-12
The Divisions of the Sâṃkhya Śâstra	12

BOOK I : OF TOPICS.

The Supreme Good defined	12
and explained	13-14
"Threefold pain" explained	13-14
Proof of "Duḥkham aṇâgatam," pain not-yet-come	15
Jîvan-Mukti-Daśâ and Videha-Kaivalya compared	16
How "cessation of pain" is an object of desire to Puruṣa ...	16-18

PAGES.

Puruṣa is associated with pain in the form of a reflection ... 17

This view is supported by the Vedânta: the Vedânta Theory of Adhyâsa is the same as the Sâṃkhya Theory of Reflection ... 18

Cessation of pain is not in itself the end, but cessation of the experience of pain is 18

Ordinary means are inadequate to accomplish the Supreme Good 19

They have no doubt their own uses 20

But these must be rejected by reasonable men 21

Also because Mokṣa *or Release is the Good* par excellence ... 22

Scriptural means are equally inadequate 23

Sacrifice is stained with the sin of killing 24

Immortality obtained by the drinking of the Soma juice is not eternal 25-26

Bondage is not natural to Puruṣa 26

Viveka or Discrimination is the means of Release:

A-Viveka or Non-Discrimination, the cause of Bondage, *i.e.*, the experience of pain 26-27

Because were Bondage natural, it would be unchangeable and consequently there can be no Release 28

The scriptures do not lay down precepts for the accomplishment of the impossible 28

The analogy of the "white cloth" and the "seed" 29

is inadmissible 30

Defect of the theory that mere disappearance of the power of pain is Release, pointed out 30-31

Theories of Naimittika or conditional Bondage considered:

Bondage is not conditioned by Time 31

Neither by Space 32

Nor by organisation 33

Because organisation is of the Body and not of Puruṣa ... 33

Puruṣa *is free from Saṅga or intimate association with anything* 34

Bondage is not conditioned by Karma 34-36

How Puruṣa becomes aware of the modifications of the Chitta ... 36

Scripture on Bondage and Release appertaining to the Chitta and not Puruṣa, explained 36

Nor is Prakṛiti *the cause of Bondage to* Puruṣa ... 37

No Bondage without conjunction of Prakṛiti 37-43

Bondage is not the effect of, but the very same as, the conjunction of Prakṛiti 38

PAGES.
Bondage is Aupâdhika or adventitious, and not real ... 39
The Vaiśeṣika theory criticised and the real character of Puruṣa explained 39-40
The Sâṃkhya Theory of Bondage supported by Yoga-Sûtram, Gîtâ, and Kaṭha-Upaniṣat 41
By "conjunction of Prakṛiti" is meant the conjunction of individual Buddhis to individual Puruṣas 41
"Conjunction" distinguished from Non-Discrimination, Transformation, and Intimate Association 42
How conjunction of Prakṛiti with Puruṣa takes place ... 43
Another interpretation of "Conjunction" criticised and the Sûtrakâra's meaning established 43
Nâstika Theories of Bondage criticised:
Bondage is not caused by A-Vidyâ, *as is asserted by the* Bauddhas 44-45
Bondage is not unreal 44
A-Vidyâ *cannot be an entity* 45-46
Genuine, distinguished from spurious, Vedânta: the Mâyâ-Vâdins are really a branch of the Vijñâna-Vâdins 46
The Sâṃkhya view of A-Vidyâ 47
A-Viydâ *cannot be both real and unreal* 47-48
Experience of Prârabdha Karma offers one more objection to A-Vidyâ being the direct cause of Bondage 48
Principles governing the enumeration of Predicables stated ... 48-50
Real character of Prakṛiti incidentally described 50
Bondage is not caused by Vâsanâ 51-56
Bondage is not momentary: Theory of Transiency of Things controverted, and the Theory of Permanency of Things established by the fact of Recognition, by Scripture, etc., and by means of the Relation of Cause and Effect 56-62
The cause of Bondage is real and not ideal: Vijñâna Vâda or Bauddha Idealism criticised 62-64
Vijñâna-Vâda *logically leads to* Śûnya-Vâda, or the Theory that the World is a Void 64-66
Scriptural texts about non-existence of external things—meaning of "non-existence"—explained 65-66
Origin of Vijñâna-Vâdin Nâstikas, or Idealist Heretics ... 66
Theory of the Void criticised 66-71
Doubtful texts of the Śruti and Smṛiti explained 69-70

	Pages.
Bondage is not the result of movement	71-74
Doubtful Śrutis explained	73-74
Bondage is not caused by Adṛiṣṭam	75-76
Conjunction of Prakṛiti *with* Puruṣa *takes place through* A-Viveka- *or Non-Discrimination*	77-82
It is all the doing of Prakṛiti	78
Objections answered	79
Nature of A-Viveka explained and its identity with A-Vidyâ shown	79
A-Viveka is not a form of Non-Existence: Nature of A-Viveka further discussed: Agreement between the Yoga and the Sâṃkhya shown	80
How A-Viveka brings about Conjunction: Doctrines of the Yoga, the Nyâya and the Îśvara-Gitâ compared	80-82
A-Viveka *is eradicable by* Viveka *alone*	82-86
Theory of Darkness discussed	82-83
Doctrines of the Yoga and the Vedânta compared	84-85
Discrimination between Puruṣa *and* Prakṛiti *includes all discrimination*	86-88
"Abhimâna" in Puruṣa of birth, etc., explained	88
The Bondage of Puruṣa *is merely verbal*	88-91
Immutability of Puruṣa and Reflectional Theories of Bondage and Release defended	89-90
Bondage is not removeable by mere Learning or Reasoning, but by Spiritual Intuition of the truth about Puruṣa *and* Prakṛiti	91-92
Existence of Prakṛiti, etc., defended:	
Inference also is an instrument of right knowledge ...	92-93
Kârikâ on Sources of Human Knowledge quoted	93
The Twentyfive Tattvas *or Principles enumerated: The order of their evolution and their inter-relation as cause and effect shown*: Prakṛiti *defined*	93-98
Sattva, etc., are substances: Why they are called Guṇas. Not in the Vaiśeṣika sense of the word	94-95
Nature of Prakṛiti and her relation to the Guṇas explained ...	94
Two meanings of the word 'Prakṛiti': one technical and the other general, explained	94
The enumeration of the Tattvas is definite and exhaustive ...	96
Enumeration of Predicables in different Systems of Thought justified on the principle laid down in the Bhâgavatam ...	96-97

PAGES.

The Sâṃkhya enumeration has the support of the Upaniṣats Garbha, Praśna, and Maitreya 97-98
Scriptural declaration of one reality, without a second, explained 98
Difference between Theistic and Non-Theistic Theories pointed out 98
Proof of the existence of the Tan-mâtras 99-101
Nature of Tan-mâtras explained: Viṣṇu-Purâṇam cited in support 99
Process of inference of Tan-mâtras exhibited 100
Viṣṇu-Purâṇam on the nature of Prakṛiti quoted 100
How the Tan-mâtras are evolved: a doubtful Sloka of the Viṣṇu-Purâṇam on this point explained 101
Proof of Ahaṃkâra 102-103
Nature of Ahaṃkâra explained 102
Process of inference of Ahaṃkâra exhibited 102
Chhândogya Upaniṣat VI. ii. 3 quoted in support 102
Objections answered: Yoga-Sûtram II. 22 quoted ... 103
Proof of the Antaḥ-karaṇa Buddhi 103-105
The process of inference of Buddhi exhibited ... 104
A corroborative argument stated 104
Bṛihat-Âraṇyaka and Chhândogya Upaniṣats quoted in support 104
Threefold uses of the Antaḥ-karaṇa explained and justified by reference to the Liṅga-Purâṇam, the Vedânta-Sûtram and the Yoga-Vâśiṣṭha-Râmâyaṇam 104-105
Proof of Prakṛiti 106-108
The process of inference of Prakṛiti exhibited 106
A favourable argument stated 106
Authority of the Veda and Smṛiti referred to 106
An objection answered 106-107
Pleasure cognised by Buddhi and Pleasure inherent in Buddhi, distinguished 107
The order of evolution defended against that of the Logicians: The futility of mere reasoning, unsupported by Scripture, shown 107-108
Proof of Puruṣa 108-111
The process of inference of Puruṣa exhibited ... 109
Yoga-Sûtram IV. 24 explained and distinguished 109
Favourable arguments stated 110

PAGES.

Viṣṇu-Purâṇam I. iv. 51 and I. ii. 33 compared 110
Prakṛiti, *the Root Cause, is root-less* 111
The point argued: *Prakṛiti is merely the name given to the original starting point of evolution* 111-112
The Nyâya, *the* Sâṃkhya, *and the* Vedânta *doctrines compared*... 112-115
Scriptural texts about "production" of Prakṛiti and Puruṣa explained: "production" is in a derivative sense ... 112-114
Prakṛiti and A-Vidyâ distinguished: doubtful scriptures explained 114-115
Only the most competent can realise the truth taught: three classes of Adhikârins *described* 115-116
From Prakṛiti, *the first evolute is* Mahat, *also called* Buddhi and Manas 116-117
The next is Ahaṃkâra 117
The rest spring from Ahaṃkâra 117
But by the chain of causation the primary causality of Prakṛiti *remains unimpaired* 118
Why Prakṛiti, *and not* Puruṣa, *is the material cause* ... 118-120
Argument in favour of Puruṣa's never undergoing transformation, succinctly stated 119
Prakṛiti *is all pervading* 120-121
"All pervading"-ness explained 121
The Veda *supports the theory that* Prakṛiti *is the cause of all things and is all-pervading* 121-122
Ex nihilo nihil fit 122
The world is not unreal 122-124
Doubtful Chhândogya text VI. i. 4 explained 123
Unreality of the World refuted by the Vedânta-Sutram II. ii. 28-29 124
Bṛihat-Araṇyaka-Upaniṣat II. iii. 6 does not negate the reality of the World: Cf. the Vedânta-Sûtram III. ii. 22 124
Why nothing can come out of nothing 124-125
Karma, A-Vidyâ, *etc., cannot be the material cause of the world*... 125-126
Ritual observances cannot become the cause of Release ... 126-127
Sâṃkhya-Pravachana-Sûtram I. 2 and 6 further explained ... 126-127
The result of Karma is not permanent: Chhândogya-Upaniṣat VII. i. 6 quoted in support 127
Doubtful Śruti, Kâlâgni-Rudra-Upaniṣat 2, *e.g., explained* ... 128
Freedom from Saṃsâra *is not the result of* Karma 128-129

	PAGES.
The result of Niṣkâma Karma *also is equally transitory* ...	129-131
Kaivalya-Upaniṣat I. 2 quoted in support	130
Release producible by knowledge is not perishable	131-132
Pramâ *or Right Cognition and* Pramâṇa *or Instrument of Right Cognition, defined*: Pramâṇa is threefold	132-136
Right Knowledge resides in Puruṣa	133
The process of knowing rightly described	134
Object of Cognition discussed	135-136
Three kinds of Pramâṇa *sufficient*	137-138
Perception defined	138-139
Perception by Yogins	140-142
Contact of Buddhi with Objects is the cause of perception ...	141
Perception is not necessarily dependent upon external Senses ...	142
Îśvara *is not an object of perception*	142-143
In what sense there can be perpetual cognition of Îśvara ...	143
Why the existence of Îśvara *is above proof*	143-144
Texts which declare Îśvara, *explained*	144-145
The influence of Puruṣa *upon* Prakṛiti *is through proximity* ...	145-146
Chhândogya-Upaniṣat VI. ii. 3 explained	145
Kûrma-Purâṇam on Unconscious Creation quoted	145
The influence of Jîvas *also is through proximity*	147
Jîva defined	147
Vedic declarations vindicated	147-148
Actual agency belongs to the Antaḥ-karaṇa	148-152
How Puruṣa illuminates the Antaḥ-karaṇa	149
How Buddhi and Self are mutually reflected in each other ...	149
Reflection of Consciousness in Buddhi makes Self-Consciousness possible	150
Reflection of Buddhi in Consciousness makes cognition of objects possible	150
Theory of Mutual Reflection of Buddhi and Consciousness established by Vyâsa in the Yoga-Bhâṣyam	150
Opposite theories criticised	151-152
Definition of Inference	152-153
Division of Inference	152
Word or Verbal Testimony defined	153
Necessity of Pramâṇa *in the* Sâṃkhya Śâstra	153-154
Proof of Prakṛiti *and* Puruṣa *is by means of* Sâmânyato Dṛiṣṭa *Inference*	154-156

	PAGES.
"Pûrva-vat," "Śeṣa-vat" and "Sâmânyato Dṛiṣṭa" Inference described	155
Process of inference of Prakṛiti and Puruṣa exhibited ...	155-156
The end of Bhoga *is in Consciousness*	156-157
Two meanings of the word "Bhoga" distinguished ...	157
He who does not act, may still enjoy the fruit	157-158
The notion that Puruṣa *is the Experiencer is due to* A-Viveka ...	158-159
The fruit of Knowledge is absence of Pleasure and Pain ...	160
Mere non-perception does not prove non-existence	160-162
Kârikâ VII, on causes of non-perception, quoted	161
Non-apprehension of Prakṛiti *and* Puruṣa *by the Senses is due to their extreme fineness*	162
Proof of the subtlety of Prakṛiti, etc.	163
An objection answered	163-165
Proofs of the Theory of Existent Effects	165-171
A Vaiśeṣika theory refuted...	168
Cause and Effect are identical: The Gîtâ and the Upaniṣats Bṛihat-Âraṇyaka, Chhândogya, and Maitri quoted in support: Kârikâ IX referred to	170-171
A doubt raised as to how the existent can be said to be produced ...	171-172
The doubt removed: "Production" is only manifestation ...	172-173
"Manifestation" described...	172-173
"Destruction" is only dissolution into the cause	173-175
Re-manifestation of the same thing after dissolution, refuted ...	174
Existence of things past and gone and of things not-yet-come-to-pass, proved by perception of the Yogin	174
Theory of Manifestation defended	174-175
"Existence" and "Non-Existence" explained	175
The Theory of Manifestation does not entail non-finality ...	175-176
When non-finality is no fault	176
Creation by Will	176
The theory of the Manifestation of the existent, further defended	177-178
The rival Theory of the Production of the Non-Existent criticised	177
The two reconciled	178
Effect defined: Properties common to all effects	178-180
Different meanings of the word "Linga" mentioned ...	179
Proof of the existence of the effect as separate from the cause ...	180-182
Properties common to Prakṛiti *and her products*	182-183
The Sûtra supplemented by Kârikâ XI	182

PAGES.

Kârikâ X on difference of properties between Prakṛiti and her products quoted 183
Unity and infinity of Prakṛiti explained and supported by Viṣṇu-Purâṇam II. vii. 25-26 183
Points of dissimilarity among the Guṇas 183-185
The text supplemented by a quotation from Pañchaśikha ... 184
The Guṇas are substances 184
They are infinite 185
Similarity and dissimilarity among the Guṇas ... 185-187
Kârikâ XIII compared 186
Sâṃkhya and Vâiśeṣika doctrines compared 187
Proof that Mahat, *etc*, *are effects* 187-191
Buddhi, etc., are nourished with food: Chhândogya-Upaniṣat VI. vii. 6 and Yoga-Sûtram IV. 2 quoted in support ... 189
Kârikâ XV. compared 190
Ground of inference of cause from effect stated 191-192
The process of inference exhibited 192
The manifested is the mark of inference of the unmanifested ... 192-193
The existence of Prakṛiti *cannot be ignored* 193
The existence of Puruṣa *requires no proof* 193-195
Intention of Sûtra I. 66 explained 195
Puruṣa *is something different from* Prakṛiti *and her products* ... 195
Reasons for the above 195-199
Nature of Puruṣa *is Light or Illumination* ... 200-201
This view is supported by the Veda and Smṛiti 200
The opposite Vaiṣeśika theory discredited 200
Consciousness is not an attribute, but the essence, of Puruṣa ... 201-203
That the Self is devoid of attributes, proved 202
Description of the Sva-rupa of the Self, quoted from the Yoga-Vâśiṣṭha-Râmâyaṇam 203
The Sruti *is higher evidence than Perception* 203-205
Puruṣa's freedom from attributes proved by the Upaniṣats Bṛihat-Âraṇyaka IV. iii. 15 and Śvetâśvatara VI. 11 and by the Vedânta-Sâra 203-204
Contradictory Śrutis: their value: Rule of interpretation of Vedic texts 204
Puruṣa *is merely the Witness* 205-207
Svapna or Dream and Suṣupti or Deep Sleep described ... 206
Proof of Plurality of Puruṣas 207-208

	Pages.
The Vedânta *doctrine of Unity criticised*	208-216
The Vedânta interpretation of certain Vedic texts discarded ...	212
The doctrine of Âropa of the pseudo-Vedântins discredited ...	215
The Vedânta-Sûtram has nowhere declared the unity of the Self	215
The Vedânta-Sûtram I. i. 21-22 and II. iii. 41 establish difference	215
The Vedânta doctrines of Avachchheda and Pratibimba must be rejected, and the Sâṃkhya doctrine of Multiplicity accepted: Rule as to solution of doubts in philosophical and other matters stated	216
The Sâṃkhya *Theory is not in conflict with the* Śruti *and* Smṛiti	216-221
Upaniṣats Chhândogya VI. ii. 1, Kaṭha IV. x. 11, Brahma-Bindu 11 and 12, Aitareya I. i. 1, explained	216-217
The Sâṃkhya Theory supported by the Vedânta-Sûtram III. ii. 33, Kaṭha Upanisat IV. 15 and Muṇḍaka-Upaniṣat III. i. 3 and also by Smṛiti	219
Denotation of "That" in "Thou art That"	219
Unity is the popular conception which the Śruti, Smṛiti, etc., have taken the trouble to chasten by declarations of Plurality	220
What is condemned by the Taittiriya-Upaniṣat II. 7 is not plurality of individual Selves essentially alike one another ...	220
The Vedic declarations of Avachchheda or separation and of Pratibimba or reflection, explained with the help of Kaṭha-Upanisat V. 10	220-221
Plurality of Puruṣas *further established*	221-222
Those who have eyes to see, can see the oneness of form among the Selves	222-223
Non-Duality is disproved by recorded cases of Release ...	223-224
The Neo-Vedântins are verily a sect of the Bauddhas ...	224
Release of Vâmadeva *is absolute*	224-225
As it has been, so will it be	225-226
Puruṣas *are ever uniform*	226-227
Character of being witness is compatible with uniformity ...	227-228
Puruṣa is witness (Sâkṣî) of Buddhi alone, and the seer (Draṣṭâ) of all the rest	228
Puruṣa *is for ever released* ...	228-229
Puruṣa *is indifferent*	229

PAGES.
Seeming agency of Puruṣa *is due to influence of Buddhi* ... 229-230
Kârikâ XXII on the same subject, compared 230
The title "Sâṃkhya-Pravachana-Sûtram" explained ... 230

BOOK II: OF THE EVOLUTIONS OF PRAKRITI.

The Purpose of Creation 231-234
Kinds of Vairâgya or Dispassion stated and explained ... 232
Pain not-yet-come is of twentyone varieties 232
A-Vidyâ is destructible by means of Vidyâ 233
The Higher and the Lower Self: their proof 233-234
The Cause of Successive Creation 234-235
Who are Adhikârins or fit for Release 234
Vairâgya *cannot grow in a single Creation* ... 235-236
The Rule of Individuals 236
Proof of the Theory of Adhyâsa *or fictitious attribution* (*e.g., of Bondage, Release, etc.*) *in regard to* Puruṣa 237-238
Doubtful Śruti, Taittiriya-Upaniṣat II. 1. explained ... 237
Reality of the creative agency of Prakṛiti *proved* 238-239
Knowledge and Ignorance are the sole determinants of Release and Bondage 239-240
How the activity of Prakṛiti ceases automatically in the case of a Puruṣa possessing discriminative knowledge 240
The Theory of Adhyâsa *further argued* 240-241
The instrumental cause of Creation is Râga *or Passion* ... 241-242
The order of Creation 242-244
Taittiriya-Upaniṣat II. 1, which mentions a different order of evolution, considered in the light of Mundaka-Upaniṣat II. i. 3, Praśna-Upanisat VI. 4, and the Vedânta-Sûtram II. iii. 14 243-244
The origination of Mahat, *etc., is not for their own sake* ... 244-245
Theory of Space and Time: they are forms of Âkaśa ... 245-246
Space and Time, unlimited and limited 246
Definition of Buddhi 246-247
Different uses of the word "Mahat" explained 247
Relation of individual Buddhis to the Mahat Tattva . 247
Products of Mâhat 247-248
How contrary products arise from the same Tattva Mahat ... 248-249
Every Puruṣa is an Īśvara 248
Definition of Ahaṃkâra 249-250
Products of Ahaṃkâra 250-251

PAGES.

How the Senses and Objects were produced in the primary creation 250
Origin of Manas 251-252
Production of the external Indriyas and the Tan-Mâtras ... 251
The Devas of the Indriyas 252
The Indriyas *are eleven in number* 252-253
The Indriyas *are not formed out of the* Bhûtas *or Elements* ... 253-254
Doubtful Śrutis *explained* 254-255
The Indriyas *are not eternal* 255-256
The Indriyas *are not the same as their physiological counterparts* 256
There is not one, but many Indriyas 256-257
Conception must not be allowed to stand against Positive Evidence 257
Definition of Manas 257-258
Diverse functions of Manas *explained* 258-259
The Objects of the Indriyas 259
Puruṣa *is different from the* Indriya 259-261
The Internal Indriyas *distinguished* 261-262
Their resemblance 262-263
Prâṇa or Life-Breath is not Air: why it is called Air ... 263
The modifications of the Indriyas *are simultaneous as well as successive* 264-265
Cognition called Âlochana described 265
Aniruddha's interpretation of Sutram II. 32 criticised . 265
Number and character of the Modifications 266-267
The Sva-rûpa *of* Puruṣa *indicated* 267-268
Above illustrated 268
What moves the Indriyas *to operate* 268-269
Above illustrated 269
The number of the Instruments 270
Why the Indriyas *are called Instruments* 270-271
Pre-eminence of Buddhi *illustrated* 271-272
Why Buddhi *is the principal* 272-273
Recollection is not spontaneous to Puruṣa 273-274
Relativity of the condition of being principal and secondary ... 274
Why one particular Buddhi *and not another acts for the benefit of one particular* Puruṣa, *and not of another* ... 274-276
In what sense Karma is said to belong to Puruṣa 275
Aniruddha's *dictum* that Karma is of Puruṣa reflected in Buddhi, criticised 275-276

PAGES.

The Topic of the pre-eminence of Buddhi concluded ... 276-277
Number of the components of the Linga-Deha 277

BOOK III : OF DISPASSION.

Origin of the Gross Elements 278
Origin of the Body 279
Origin of Saṃsâra 279-280
Limit of Saṃsâra 280-281
Puruṣa *is ever free from Experience* 281-282
The Gross and the Subtle Body distinguished 282-283
Experience may take place during transmigration also ... 283
The Subtle, and not the Gross, Body causes experience to Puruṣa... 283-284
Constitution of the Subtle Body 284-286
The Subtle Body distinguished as being the container and the contained 284
The constituents of the Subtle Body are seventeen, and not eighteen in number 285
Aniruddha's interpretation of the Sûtram III. 9 criticised ... 285
How from one single Subtle Body manifold individuals arise ... 286-287
Why the Gross Organism is called a Body 287-288
" Body " means the House of Experience 287
Body is threefold : Linga-Deha, Adhiṣṭhâna-Deha, and Sthûla-Deha 288
Proof of Adhiṣṭhâna *or Vehicular Body* ... 288-290
An objection answered 290-291
The size of the Linga-Śarîra *is atomic* 291-292
Another proof of the finiteness of the Linga-Śarira 293
Cause of migration of the Linga Śarîra 293-294
Origin of the Gross Body 294
Contrary opinions stated and explained 294-295
Consciousness is not a natural product of the organisation of the Body 295-296
An objection answered 297-298
Why the Linga-Śarîra *takes a Gross Body : the cause of Release* ... 298-299
Cause of Bondage 299
Knowledge is the sole and independent cause of Release ... 299-300
Śvetâśvatara-Upaniṣat III. 8, quoted in support 300
Doubtful Śruti, Îśa-Upaniṣat XI. explained 300
Futility of the co-operation of knowledge and Action illustrated ... 301-302

PAGES.
Our conception of the Object of Worship is faulty 302
Wherein it is faulty 303-304
Fruit of Worship ... 304
Sources of Knowledge:
Dhyâna *is cessation of Râga* 304-305
Dhyâna includes Dhâraṇâ and Samâdhi also 305
How consummation of Dhyâna *is reached* 305-306
"Saṃprajñâta" and "A-Saṃprajñâta" Yoga explained ... 305-306
Practices conducive to Dhyâna 306-307
Dhâraṇâ *described* 307-308
"Dhâraṇâ" here means Prâṇâyâma 307
Âsana *described* 308
Sva-Karma *described* 309
Other means of Dhyâna 309-310
Nature of Viparyaya *or Mistake described* 310-312
A-Sakti *or Incapacity which is the cause of Mistake, is of twenty-eight sorts* 311-312
Tuṣṭi *or Complacency is ninefold* 312
Siddhi *or Perfection is eightfold* 312
Minor sub-divisions of Mistake: sixty-two in number . 312-314
Minor sub-divisions of Incapacity 314-315
Divisions of Complacency explained 315-319
Divisions of Perfection explained 319-321
The other so-called Perfections are not real . 322-323
Vyaṣti *or Specific Creation described* 323-324
Bhautika Sarga *or Elemental Creation also is for the sake of* Puruṣa 324-325
The Higher, the Lower, and the Middle World described ... 325-326
Cause of the above differences in Creation 326
The Higher Worlds cannot be the Supreme Good 326-327
There is pain in the Higher Worlds also . . 327
Dissolution into Prakṛiti *is not the Supreme Good* 327-329
Re-birth after absorption into Prakṛiti *accounted for* ... 329-330
Prakṛiti's independence how maintained 329
Proof of re-appearance, after absorption into Prakṛiti ... 330-331
The Sâṃkhya conception of Âdi Puruṣa and Îśvara ... 330
In what sense the Sâṃkhya *denies* Îśvara 331-332
Creation by Prakṛiti *is for the release of* Puruṣa 333-334
Prakṛiti's interest is bound up with that of Puruṣa ... 334

PAGES.
Prakṛiti *acts spontaneously for the benefit of* Puruṣa ... 334-335
Spontaneous activity further illustrated 335
Activity of Prakṛiti *is natural* 336
Spontaneity of Prakṛiti *is necessary* 336-337
Cessation of her activity is also spontaneous ... 337
Âtyantika Pralaya, or Final Dissolution described ... 337
Release of one does not involve release of all 338-339
Doubtful Śruti, Śvetâśvatara-Upaniṣat I. 10, explained ... 338
Release consists in what 339
How Prakṛiti *affects one* Puruṣa *and does not affect another* ... 339-341
The "Error of snake in respect to a rope" explained ... 341
The above dual character of Prakṛiti *supported* 341-342
Prakṛiti's *selection, how determined* 342-343
How Prakṛiti *ceases to act: the analogy of the fair dancer* ... 343-344
Relation of Bondage and Release to Puruṣa 345
Bondage and Release really are of Prakṛiti ... 345-346
How Prakṛiti *binds and releases herself* 346-347
A-Viveka *or Non-Discrimination itself is not Bondage* ... 347-348
How development of Viveka *or Discrimination is possible* ... 348-352
An exception to the rule laid down 352
Pure Viveka *alone is the cause of Release* 352-354
A-Samprajñâta Yoga is the means of perfect development of Viveka 353
The case of Jîvan-Mukta *considered* 354
Proofs of Release-in-life 354-356
Definition of Jîvan-Mukta quoted from the Nâradîya Smṛiti ... 356
The Jîvan-Muktas *only can be spiritual guides* 356
Worldly existence after Release explained 356-357
How retention of Body even after Release is rendered unvoidable... 357-359
Viveka *is the only means of Release* 359-360

BOOK IV: OF FABLES.

Instruction is necessary: Story of the abandoned Prince ... 361-362
Instruction, to be effective, need not be directly imparted: Story of the Piśâcha 362-363
Inculcation also is necessary: Story of Śvetaketu 363
The instructor need not necessarily be a spiritual guide: Story of the Father and the Son 363-364
All worldly pleasure is alloyed with pain: Story of the Hawk ... 364-365

	PAGES.
Things avoidable must be avoided: Story of the Snake and the Slough	365
Penance necessary for prohibited acts done: Story of the Amputated Hand	365-366
Thoughts uncongenial to Release, to be avoided: Story of Bharata	366-367
Company is to be avoided: Story of the Girl and her Bracelets	367
Hope is to be abandoned: Story of Piṅgalâ	368-369
The innate pleasure of the Chitta	368-369
Exertion is needless: Example of the Snake	369
In study, discrimination is necessary: Example of the Bee ...	369-370
Concentration of mind necessary: Story of the Arrow-maker ...	370-371
Rules are not to be transgressed: Experience in life ...	371-373
Brahmachârin defined	372
Who are the Pâṣaṇḍas	372
Forgetfulness of Rules is also harmful: Story of the She-Frog	373-374
Instruction is to be supplemented by Reflection: Story of Indra and Virochana	374-375
Time also is a factor in the attainment of Release	375-376
There is no rule as to the limit of Time required: Story of Vâmadeva	376-377
Inferior means also are useful in their own way: Example of the performers of sacrifices	377-378
Although they fail to secure permanent release	378-380
Vairâgya *is the only means of Knowledge: Story of the Swan and Milk*	380
Benefit of excellent company: Story of Alarka and Dattâtreya	380-381
Association with worldly-minded people is to be shunned: Story of the Parrot	381
Bondage results from connection with the Guṇa*: Story of the Parrot*	382
Passion is not appeased by enjoyment: Story of Saubhari ...	382-383
But through seeing the faults of Prakṛiti	383-384
Faults disqualify even for instruction: Story of Aja ...	384
Example of the dirty mirror	384-385
Knowledge necessarily is not perfect Knowledge: Example of the lotus	385-386
Release is above Lordliness	386-387

Book V: Of the Demolition of Counter-Theories.

	Pages.
Performance of Maṅgala *is necessary*	388
Îśvara *as the Creator of the World is not proved*	389-390
The facts are satisfactorily explained by Karma	389
Îśvara *as the Moral Governor of the World is not proved* ...	390-394
There is no proof of an eternal Îśvara	394-395
Inference of Îśvara *is impossible*	395-396
There is no Śabda *in regard to* Îśvara *as Creator*	396-397
Doubtful Chhândogya-Upaniṣat VI. ii. 3 explained ...	397
A-Vidyâ *does not belong to* Puruṣa	398-400
Saṃsâra *is not without beginning*	399
The nature of A-Vidyâ *discussed*	400-402
In any case, A-Vidyâ *cannot be without beginning*	403
The causality of Dharma *in Creation*	404
Proofs of Dharma	404-405
Perception is not the sole proof of existence	405
Proof of A-Dharma	405-406
Arthâpatti *is not the proof of* Dharma	406-407
Dharma, *etc., are attributes of the* Antaḥ-Karaṇa	407
The existence of the Guṇas, *etc., has nowhere been absolutely denied: Doubtful scriptures explained*	407-409
Reality of Objective Existence is established by proof ...	409-411
Vyâpti *or Logical Pervasion cannot be grasped from a single instance*	411-412
Vyâpti *defined*	412-413
Vyâpti *is not a separate Tattva*	413-414
The View of the Âchâryas *on* Vyâpti	414-415
The View of Pañchaśikha	415
Vyâpti *is not a power inherent in the essence of the thing* ...	415-419
Relation of Word and Object	419-420
Proofs of the Relation of Word and Object ...	420-421
Word does not refer to acts only	421-422
Probative force of Vidhis, Arthavâdas and Mantras considered...	421
Words Kârya-para and A-Kârya-para, Sâdhya-para and Siddha-para	422
Words convey the same in scriptural as in secular literature ...	423
An objection stated	423-424
Answer: The Vedic *objects are not absolutely supra-sensuous* ...	425-426
How there can be intuition of supra-sensuous objects ...	426

	PAGES.
Power to denote objects is inherent in Vedic *words*	426-427
Proof of the power of Vedic *words to denote objects* .	427
The Veda *is not eternal*	428
The Veda *is not the work of a person*	428-429
But still it is not eternal	430-431
Meaning of the term "Pauruṣeya"	431-432
The Veda *itself is proof of its own authority*	432-433
Reality of Objective World further established	434
Object of cognition in cases of illusion not absolutely non-existent	434
Neither is the Objective World absolutely real	434-435
The World cannot be something else than real and unreal ...	435-437
Nor is the World a reflection of what it is not	437-438
The World is both existent and non-existent	439-440
The Theory of Sphoṭa *refuted*	441-442
Varṇas *or Letters are not eternal*	442
An objection answered	442-443
Non-Duality of the Self refuted	444-445
Unity of the Self and the Non-Self contradicted by Perception ...	445-446
Śrutis *on Non-Duality explained*	446-447
On the Theory of Non-Duality there can be no material cause of the world	447-449
The Sâṃkhya and the Vedânta compared ...	448-449
Pseudo-Vedântins condemned	449
The Self is not Ananda *or Bliss*	449-452
Conflicting Śrutis compared: Rule of Interpretation: Place of Reasoning	452
The Śruti *on* Ânanda *is metaphorical*	452-453
The purpose of such metaphorical Śrutis ...	453-454
The Theory that Manas *is all-pervading, refuted*	454
Argument in support of the above	455
Manas *is not partless*	455-456
Objects eternal and non-eternal, distinguished	456
Eternality of Prakṛiti *and* Puruṣa *defended*	456-457
Doubtful Śruti, Svetâśvatara-Upaniṣat IV. 10, explained ...	457
Release is not manifestation of Ânanda...	457-458
Release is not the elimination of particular attributes ...	458-459
Neither is it the attainment of particular Worlds	459-460
It is not the cessation of connection with objects	460

	Pages.
Total extinction of the Self is not Release	460-461
The Void is not Release	461
It is not the possession of excellent enjoyables	462
It is not the absorption of the Jîva *into* Brahman	462-463
It is not the acquisition of supernatural powers	463
It is not the attainment of supreme power	463-464
The Indriyas *are not the products of the Elements*	464
Release is not attained through the knowledge of the Six Predicables of the Vaiśeṣikas	465-466
Neither through the knowledge of the Sixteen Predicables of the Naiyâyikas	466-468
The Ultimate Atoms of the Vaiśeṣikas *cannot be eternal* ...	469-470
The Sruti is against them	469
Manu-Saṃhitâ I. 27, quoted and explained	469
The Atoms are not partless	470
The Tan-mâtras are the parts of the Atoms	470
The Vaiśeṣika *Theory of Visual Perception criticised* ...	471
Magnitude is not fourfold, as maintained by the Vaiśeṣikas ...	471-472
The Vaiśeṣika *Theory of Eternal Genus criticised*	472-473
Genus exists	473-474
Genus is not a negative conception	474-475
Similarity is not a separate Tattva	475
Neither is it an inherent power of the thing	476
It is not the relation of Names and Things .	476-477
Because their relation is non-eternal	477
It cannot be from eternity	477-478
The Samavâya *or Combination of the* Vaiśeṣikas *does not exist* ...	478-479
Because there is no proof of it	479-480
Aniruddha's interpretation criticised	480
Motion is perceptible also	481-482
The Body is not composed of five Elements ...	482-483
The Body is composed of one Element only	483
Body is not necessarily gross	483-485
Meaning of Âtivâhika Body ...	484
Meaning of Body	484
Proof of Âtivâhika Body	484
How the Senses illuminate objects	485-487
In what sense the Senses are the revealers of objects ...	487
The Eye is not formed of Light	487-488
Proof of the Vṛitti *or modification of the Senses*	488

	PAGES.
Nature of the modification of the Senses described	488-489
The modification may be a quality as well as a substance ...	490-491
Ahaṃkâra *is everywhere the uniform cause of the Senses* ...	491
A doubtful Śruti *explained*	491-492
Varieties of the Gross Body...	492-493
Earth is the only material of the Gross Body	493-494
Prâṇa *is not the originant of the Body*	494-495
Prâṇa is a modification of the Indriyas... .	495
The Building of the Body is due to the Self	495-496
The superintendence of the Self is relative and not absolute ...	496-497
Puruṣas *are ever free*	497-499
Uses of the word Brahman in the Sâṃkhya and the Vedânta ...	498
Release distinguished from Deep Sleep and Trance ...	499-500
The reality of Release demonstrated	500-501
Vâsanâ *is powerless during Deep Sleep*	501-503
Release in life defended	503-504
Theory of Saṃskâra	504
The Vegetable Kingdom also is a Field of Experience ...	504-506
The evidence of the Śruti, Chhândogya-Upaniṣat VI. xi. 1 ...	505
The evidence of the Smṛiti	506
The vegetables are not moral agents	506-507
Three principal kinds of Body: Karma-Deha, Upabhoga-Deha, and Ubhaya-Deha	507-508
A fourth kind of Body	508
Eternality of individual Buddhi *refuted*	509-510
Yogic *Perfections defended*	510
Consciousness cannot be a product of the Elements	511-512
BOOK VI : OF THE RECAPITULATION OF TEACHINGS.	
The Self exists	513
It is different from the Body and the rest	514-517
How Puruṣa's *aim is fulfilled*	517
Pain is more intense than Pleasure	517-518
Pleasure is rare	518-519
All pleasure is alloyed with pain	519
All is pain : Yoga-Sûtram II. 15 quoted	519
The aim of Puruṣa *is twofold : pleasure and absence of pain* ...	520
A doubt raised and solved	520-522
A-Viveka *is from eternity*	522-523
But it is not eternal	523
The cause of the annihilation of A-Viveka	523-524

	Pages.
Proof that Viveka *is the only destroyer of* A-Viveka	524-525
A-Viveka *is the sole cause of Bondage*	525
Bondage does not over again befall the released one	525-526
Defects in the opposite view, pointed out	526-527
Nature of Release	527-528
Conflict with the Veda *avoided*	528-529
Adhikârins *are of three classes*	529
Utility of other means of Knowledge than Hearing	530
Misconception about Yogic *Posture removed*	530
Dhyâna *defined*	531
Defence of Yoga	531-532
A-Viveka *is the cause of Uparâga in* Puruṣa	532
The Uparâga *is not real, but is a mere conceit*	532-533
Means of the suppression of Uparâga	533-535
Teaching of the Ancients on the point	535-536
For practice of Yoga, there is no need of any particular locality	536
Prakṛiti *is the material of the World*	536-537
Puruṣa *cannot be the material of the World*	537
The Śruti *is against the opposite view*	537-539
The Vaiśeṣikas condemned	538
Doubtful Muṇḍaka Upaniṣat II. i. 5 explained	538-539
A misconception removed	539
Proof that Prakṛiti *is all-pervading*	539-540
Motion of Prakṛiti *is not in conflict with her being the Primal Cause*	540-541
Prakṛiti *is sui generis*	541
The Guṇas *are not the attributes, but the very form of* Prakṛiti...	542-543
Purpose of Prakṛiti's *creation*	543
Reason for diversity of creation	544
How the self-same Prakṛiti *creates as well as destroys*	544-545
Activity of Prakṛiti *is no bar to Release*	545
Creation for one Puruṣa *does not affect another*	545-546
Multiplicity of Puruṣas *is proved by the* Veda	546-547
Upâdhi *cannot explain the situation*	547-548
Even A-Vidyâ *is a contradiction to the* Vedântin's Non-Duality ...	548
Other faults in the Theory of Non-Duality	548-549
The Self cannot prove itself	549-550
Light is not a property of the Self	550-553
Doubtful Śrutis explained	553
Reality of the World established	554-556

	Pages.
Causes of unreality	554
The Universe described	554-555
Doubtful Śrutis, Chhândogya-Upaniṣat VI. i. 4 and Brahma Bindu Upaniṣat 10, explained	556
The Universe is ever existent, never created	556-557
Agency belongs to Ahaṃkâra	557
When Experience ceases	557-558
How re-birth takes place after attainment of Higher Worlds ...	558-559
Higher instruction in the Higher Worlds availeth not ...	559
A doubtful Śruti *explained*	559-560
How going is possible for the Self which is omnipresent ...	560-562
When and why the Self is called the Jîva-Âtmâ	561
Why Ânanda is attributed to the Self	562
Existence of the Body is dependent upon the Self	562-563
Formation of the Body is not possible through Adriṣtam ...	563-565
Jîva *distinguished from* Puruṣa, *i.e.*, Parama-Âtmâ... ...	565-567
Ahaṃkâra, *and not* Îśvara, *is the cause*	567-568
Brahmâ, Viṣṇu, and Rudra are Îśvaras in a practical sense only	568
There is no intelligent cause of Ahaṃkâra	568-569
Other functions of the supposed Îśvara *accounted for* ...	569-570
The Mahat Tattva is the Upâdhi of Viṣṇu	570
Causal Brahman in the Sâṃkhya Śâstra	570
In any case, the relation of Prakṛiti and Puruṣa *is from eternity*	570-571
The view of Pañchaśikha	571-572
The view of Sanandana	572-573
Whatever may be its form, the dissolution of the tie between Prakṛiti *and* Puruṣa *is the Supreme Good*	573-575
The contention of the Vedântin that the founder of the Sâṃkhya is not Kapila, the Avatâra of Viṣṇu, but Kapila the Avatâra of Agni, refuted...	574
One Kapila is mentioned in all the Śâstras	574
Conflicting text of the Mahâbhâratam explained ...	4-575

Appendix I.—(Index of Aphorisms).
Appendix II.—(Index of words).
Appendix III.—(Index of authorities quoted).
Appendix IV.—(A catalogue of some of the important works on the Sâmkhyha).
Appendix V.—(Tattva—Samâsa or Kâpila Sutram).
Appendix VI.—(Sâmkhya-Kârikâ of Iśvar Kṛiṣṇa).
Appendix VII.—(Panchaśikhâ Sutram).

APPENDIX I.

INDEX OF APHORISMS.

PAGE.

सत्तामात्राच्चेत्, सर्वैश्वर्यम् ...V, 9. 394

सत्त्वरजस्तमसां साम्यावस्था प्रकृतिः, प्रकृतेर्महान्महतोऽहंकारोऽहंकारात्पञ्चतन्मात्राणि उभयमिन्द्रियं तन्मात्रेभ्यः स्थूलभूतानि पुरुष इति पञ्चविंशतिर्गणः...I, 61 93

सत्त्वादीनामतद्धर्मत्वं तद्रूपत्वात् ...VI, 39 542

सदसत्ख्यातिर्बाधाबाधात् ...V, 56 439

सप्त दशैकं लिङ्गम्...III, 9 284

समन्वयात्...I, 131 188

समाधिसुषुप्तिमोक्षेषु ब्रह्मरूपता...V, 116 . 497

समानः प्रकृतेर्द्वयोः...I, 69 112

समानकर्मयोगे बुद्धेः प्राधान्यं लोकवल्लोकवत्...II, 47 276

समानं जरामरणादिजं दुःखम्...III, 53 327

संप्रति परिमुक्तो द्वाभ्याम्...III, 6 281

संबन्धाभावान्नानुमानम्...V, 2 395

संभवेन्न स्वतः...II, 44 273

सर्वत्र कार्यदर्शनाद्विभुत्वम्...VI, 36 539

सर्वत्र सर्वदा सर्वासंभवात्...I, 116 169

सर्वासंभवात् संभवेऽपिसत्तासंभवाद्धेयः प्रमाणकुशलैः...I, 4 21

सर्वेषु पृथिव्युपादानमसाधारण्यात्तद्व्यपदेशः पूर्ववत्...V, 112 493

सहि सर्ववित्सर्वकर्ता...III, 56 330

साक्षात् सम्बन्धात् साक्षित्वम्...I, 161 227

सात्त्विकमेकादशकं प्रवर्त्तते वैकृतादहंकारात् ...II, 18 251

सामान्यकरणवृत्तिः प्राणाद्या वायवः पञ्च...II, 31 262

सामान्यतो दृष्टादुभयसिद्धिः...I, 103 154

सामान्येन विवादाभावाद्धर्मवन्न तत्साधनम् ...I, 138 193

साम्यवैषम्याभ्यां कार्यद्वयम्...VI, 42 548

सिद्धरूपबोद्धृत्वाद्वाक्यार्थोपदेशः...I, 198 . 147

सिद्धिरष्टधा...III, 40 ... • 312

सुखलाभाभावादपुरुषार्थत्वमिति चेन्न द्वैविध्यात्...VI, 9 520

सुषुप्त्याद्यसाक्षित्वम् ...I, 148 205

सौक्ष्म्यादनुपलब्धिः...I, 109 162

स्थिरकार्यासिद्धेः क्षणिकत्वम्...I, 34 . 56

स्थिरसुखमासनम्...III, 33 308

स्थिरसुखमासनमिति न नियमः...VI, 24 . 530

स्थूलात्पञ्चतन्मात्रस्य ...I, 62 99

स्मृतेश्च...V, 122 . . 506

PAGE.

स्मृत्यानुमानाच्च...II, 43 273
स्वकर्म स्वाश्रमविहितकर्मानुष्ठानम्...III, 35 309
स्वप्नजागराभ्यामिव मायिकामायिकाभ्यां नोभयोर्मुक्तिः पुरुषस्य...III, 26 ... 301
स्वभावस्यानपायित्वादननुष्ठानलक्षणमप्रामाण्यम्...I, 8 28
स्वभावाच्चेष्टितमनभिसंधानाद् भृत्यवत् ...III, 61 . 336
स्वोपकारादधिष्ठानं लोकवत्...V, 3 390
हेतुमदनित्यमव्यापि सक्रियमनेकमाश्रितं लिङ्गम्...I, 124 178

APPENDIX II.

INDEX OF WORDS.

Word Index—Samkhya Pravachana Sutram.

PAGE.

अ

अकर्तुः i. 15 ... 156
अक्रमशः ii. 32 ... 264
अकार्य्ये i. 85 ... 129
अकार्यत्वे iii. 55 ... 329
अक्लिष्टाः ii. 33 ... 266
अंकुरः v. 48... ... 430
अंकुरवत् i. 122, v. 15, vi. 67 ... 175, 399, 570
अंकुरादिवत् v. 48 ... 430
अंकुरे vi. 61... ... 563
अग्नि iv. 22 378
अचाक्षुषाणाम् i. 60 ... 92
अचेतन i. 126 ... 182
अचेतनत्वे iii. 59 ... 334
अजः v. 98 477
अजवत् iv. 29 ... 384
अंजस्येन ii. 8 ... 240
अण्डज v. 111 ... 492
अणिमा v. 82 ... 463
अणिमादि योगः v. 82 ... 463
अणु iii. 14, v. 87 291, 469
अणुवत् i. 74, vi. 35, vi. 37 ... 118, 539, 540
अणु नित्यता v. 87 ... 469
अतद्धर्मत्वं vi. 39 ... 542
अतद्धर्मत्वात् i. 52 ... 75
अतद् रूपम् i. 155 ... 221
अत्यन्त i. 1, i. 4, i. 59, vi. 5 ... 12, 17, 21, 225
अत्यन्तपुरुषार्थाः i. 1 ... 12

PAGE.

अत्यन्त बाधः v. 26 ... 407
अत्यन्ता संभवात् i. 4 ... 21
अत्र vi. 15 524
अतिदूरादेः i. 108 ... 160
अतिशय i. 91, iv. 24 140, 380
अतिप्रसक्तेः i. 16 ... 34
अतीन्द्रिय ii. 23 .. 256
अतीन्द्रियत्वात् v. 41 ... 423
अथ i. 1 2
अदुष्ट i. 79, vi. 52 122, 554
अदुष्ट कारण जन्यत्वात् i. 79, vi. 52 ... 122, 554
अदोषः i. 123 ... 177
अद्य i. 158, vi. 37 ... 224, 540
अद्यकारणताहानिः vi. 37 ... 540
अदृष्ट i. 30, ii. 36, vi. 61, vi. 65 ... 54, 269, 563, 568
अदृष्ट द्वारा vi. 61 ... 563
अदृष्ट वशात् i. 30 ... 53
अदृष्टया i. 156 ... 222
अदृष्टेः iii. 20, v. 129, 295, 511
अदृष्टै v. 50 ... 431
अदृष्टोल्लासात् ii. 36 ... 269
अदृष्टोद्भूतिवत् vi. 65 ... 568
अद्वैत i. 154 ... 216
अद्वैतं i. 157, v. 61 223, 444
अद्वैत श्रुतिविरोधः i. 154 216
अध्यस्त iv. 21 ... 377
अध्यस्त रूपोपासनात् iv. 21 377
अध्यवसायः ii. 13 ... 246
अध्यास ii. 5 ... 237

PAGE.

अध्यासः i. 152 ... 212
अध्यासिद्धिः ii. 5 ... 237
अधारत्वात् ii. 42 ... 272
अधिकार vi. 22 ... 529
अधिकारि iii. 76 ... 352
अधिकारि त्रैविध्यात् i. 70, vi. 22 ... 115, 529
अधिकारि प्रभेदात् iii. 76 .. 352
अधिष्ठान iii. 11 ... 287
अधिष्ठानं iii. 3 ... 390
अधिष्ठानात् i. 142, v. 114 197, 495
अधिष्ठाने ii. 23 ... 256
अधिष्ठातृत्वं i. 96, i. 99 145, 148
अधिष्ठितिः v. 115 ... 496
अधिष्ठिते v. 2 ... 389
अधीना vi. 64 ... 567
अनपायित्वात् i. 8 ... 28
अनभिसंधानात् iii. 61 ... 336
अनर्थक्य v. 34 ... 416
अनर्थं ख्यापनं v. 119 ... 501
अनादि i. 27, ii. 3 51, 235
अनादिः vi. 12, vi. 67 521, 570
अनादितः iii. 62 ... 336
अनादि वासनायाः ii. 3 ... 235
अनादौ i. 158 ... 224
अनारंभे iv. 12 ... 369
अनावृत्ति i. 83, vi. 17 128, 525
अनावृत्ति श्रुतिः i. 83 ... 128
अनावृत्ति श्रुतेः vi. 17 ... 525
अनित्यं i. 124, v. 72 178, 456
अनित्यत्वात् v. 97 ... 477
अनित्यत्वे v. 91 ... 472
अनियतं iii. 25 ... 299
अनियतंकारणत्वात् iii. 25... 299
अनियतत्वे i. 26 ... 49

PAGE.

अनिर्वचनीयस्य v. 54 ... 435
अनुचिन्तनं iv. 8 ... 366
अनुच्छित्तिः vi. 13 ... 523
अनुदर्शनात् i. 2 . 19
अनुद्भवाभ्यां i. 11 ... 30
अनुपदेशः i. 9 . 28
अनुपपत्तेः v. 35 . 417
अनुपभोगे vi. 40 . 543
अनुभूयते i. 22 ... 20
अनुमानम् i. 100, i. 135, v. 11, v. 100, 152, 191, 395, 479
अनुमानात् ii. 43 ... 273
अनुमानेन i. 60 ... 92
अनुमेयत्वं v. 101 ... 481
अनुवृत्तिः vi. 35 . 539
अनुवृत्त्या iii. 77 . 352
अनुपलम्भः i. 156 ... 222
अनुश्रविकात् i. 82 ... 126
अनुशायिनः v. 125 ... 508
अनुष्ठान i. 8 . 28
अनुष्ठानं iii. 35 . 309
अनुष्ठान लक्षणं i. 8 ... 28
अनेकम् i. 124 . 178
अन्त ii. 28 . 259
अन्तः करण v. 25 ... 407
अन्तः करणस्य i. 64, i. 99 103, 148
अन्तः करणधर्मत्वं v. 25 ... 407
अन्तर v. 22, vi. 16, vi. 53 405, 525, 556
अन्तरं ii. 19, v. 94, v. 107 252, 475, 488
अन्तराय vi. 20 ... 527
अन्तराय ध्वस्तेः vi. 20 ... 527
अन्ध i. 156, iii. 81 222, 356
अन्धादृष्ट्या i. 156 ... 222

PAGE.

अन्धपरंपरा iii. 81 ... 356
अन्नमयत्व iii. 15 ... 293
अन्नाद्यवत् i. 105 ... 157
अन्य i. 17, i. 57, i. 153, iii. 66, iv. 2, v. 64, v. 93, v. 109, vi. 44 . 35, 86, 213, 339, 367, 446, 474, 491, 545
अन्यः i. 127 ... 183
अन्यं i. 127 ... 183
अन्यत् v. 72, vi. 66 456, 569
अन्यतर i. 93 ... 143
अन्यतर योगः i. 75 ... 118
अन्यतरा भावात् i. 93 ... 143
अन्यत्वात् i. 129, ... 187
अन्यत्वे i. 134, v. 16 190, 400
अन्यत्र v. 117 ... 499
अन्यथा i. 26, v. 55, v. 100, v. 114, vi. 12, vi. 13, vi. 18 .49, 437, 479, 495, 521, 523, 526
अन्यथा ख्याति v. 55 ... 437
अन्यथासिद्धेः v. 100 ... 479
अन्यधर्मत्वे i. 17, i. 153 35, 213
अन्यधर्मत्वात् i. 16 ... 34
अन्यनिवृत्तिरूपत्वं v. 93 ... 474
अन्यपरत्वं v. 64 ... 446
अन्ययोगे ii. 8 ... 240
अन्यसृष्ट्युपरागे iii. 66 ... 339
अन्यार्थोपदेशे iv. 2 ... 362
अन्याविवेकस्य i. 57 ... 86
अन्येषां vi. 32 ... 536
अन्योन्य v. 14 ... 398
अन्योन्याश्रयत्वं v. 14 ... 398
अन्योपादानता v. 109 ... 491
अन्योपसर्पणे vi. 44 ... 545
अन्वय vi. 15, vi. 63 524 565

PAGE.

अन्वयव्यतिरेकात् vi. 15, vi. 63, 524, 565
अन्वेषणा i. 122 ... 175
अपवर्गः iii. 65 .. 339
अपरे iii. 19 .. 295
अपरोक्ष v. 101 . 481
अपरोक्षप्रतीतेः v. 101 ... 481
अपलपनीयाः v. 128 ... 510
अपलापः i. 112, i. 137, i. 147, v. 20. 164, 193, 203, 404
अपवादमात्रं i. 45 ... 67
अपसदस्य vi. 34 . 537
अपसर्पणात् v. 105 ... 487
अपसिद्धान्त i. 50 . 72
आपाये i. 39 ... 60
अपि i. 2, i. 4, i. 5, i. 9, i. 13, i. 18, i. 20, i. 26, i. 27, i. 28, i. 40, i. 46, i. 52, i. 55, i. 59, i. 68, i. 74, i. 82, i. 85, i. 87, i. 94, i. 97, i. 105, i. 108, i. 112, i. 150, i. 153, i. 158, ii. 8, ii. 24, ii. 36, iii. 27, iii. 28, iii. 51, iii. 55, iii. 58, iii. 59, iii. 66, iii. 68, iii. 69, iii. 70, iii. 77, iv. 2, iv. 10, iv. 12, iv. 13, iv. 16, iv. 17, iv. 22, iv. 30, iv. 31, iv. 32, v. 7, v. 12, v. 18, v. 23, v. 49, v. 50, v. 62, v. 79, v. 80, v. 82, v 83, v. 86, v. 91, v. 96, v. 100, v. 103, v. 109, v. 118, v. 119, v. 121, v. 125, v. 126, v. 128, v. 129,

PAGE.

vi. 3, vi. 7, vi. 8, vi. 11, vi. 15, vi. 17, vi. 21, vi. 26, vi. 27, vi. 33, vi. 35, vi. 37, vi. 40, vi. 44, vi. 47, vi. 48, vi. 56, vi. 59, vi. 67...19, 21, 22, 28, 32, 37, 43, 49, 51, 51, 60, 70, 75, 77, 91, 111, 118, 126, 129, 132, 144, 147, 157, 160, 164, 208, 213, 224, 240, 256, 269, 302, 303, 326, 329, 333, 334, 339, 342, 343, 344, 352, 362, 367, 369, 369, 373, 374, 378, 384, 385, 386, 392, 396, 402, 405, 430, 431, 445, 461, 462, 463, 463, 466, 472, 476, 479, 483, 491, 500, 501, 504, 508, 509, 510, 511, 515, 518, 519, 521, 525, 525, 528, 531, 532, 537, 539, 540, 543, 545, 548, 548, 550, 560, 570

अपुरुषत्वं vi. 9 ... 520

अपुरुषार्थत्वं i. 47, i. 82, vi. 18 ... 70, 126, 526

अपुरुषार्थत्वात् v. 78 ... 460

अपुरुषेयत्वात् v. 41, v. 48 423, 430

अप्राप्त v. 104 ... 485

अप्रतीतेः i. 24, v. 58 48, 442

अप्राप्त प्रकाशत्वं v. 104 ... 485

अप्रामाण्यम् i. 8 ... 28

अप्राप्तेः v. 104 ... 485

अप्रीतिः i. 127 ... 183

अबाधात् i. 35, i. 79, v. 56 57, 122, 439

अबाधे v. 17 ... 401

अबुद्धानां i. 45 ... 67

PAGE.

अभ्यन्तराभ्यां i. 63 ... 102

अभागिनः v. 73 . 456

अभावः iii. 21 ... 296

अभावात् i. 43, i. 67, i. 80, i. 93, i. 138, i. 158, v. 10, v. 11, v. 46, v. 54, v. 99, vi. 9, vi. 33, vi. 44, vi. 48, vi. 52, vi. 64 ... ... 64, 111, 124, 143, 193, 224, 394, 395, 428, 435, 478, 520, 537, 545, 548, 554, 567

अभावे i. 43, i. 80 64, 124

अभिचेष्टा ii. 46 ... 274

अभिमानः ii. 16, vi. 28, 249, 532

अभिव्यक्ति i. 120 ... 172

अभिव्यक्तिः v. 59, v. 74, v. 95 ... 442, 457, 475

अभिव्यक्ति निबन्धनौ i. 120 172

अभिव्यक्तेः v. 51 ... 432

अभिलाषः vi. 6 ... 517

अभिषेकात् i. 84 ... 128

अभुक्तयोः v. 47 . 429

अभेदतः i. 125 ... 180

अभोक्तृत्वात् iii. 58 ... 333

अभ्यन्तरयोः i. 28 ... 51

अभ्यास vi. 29 ... 533

अभ्यासात् iii. 36, iii. 75 309, 348

अमूलं i. 67 111

अयं i. 15, i. 46 33, 70

अयोगात् i. 20, i. 31, i. 39, i. 81, i. 145...43, 54, 60, 125, 200

अयोग्यत्वात् v. 47 ... 429

अयोग्येषु v. 44 ... 427

PAGE.

अयोदाहवत् ii. 8 ... 246
अयौक्तिकस्य i. 26 ... 49
अर्जितत्वात् ii. 46 ... 274
अर्थः i. 1 12
अर्थ iv. 2, v. 106, v. 107 362, 488, 488
अर्थत्वं i. 3 20
अर्थयोः v. 37 ... 419
अर्थात् v. 24 ... 406
अलापः v. 92 ... 473
अवकाशात् v. 22 ... 405
अवगमः i. 106 ... 158
अवयव v. 27 ... 409
अवश्यं v. 82 ... 463
अवश्यम्भावित्वात् v. 82 ... 463
अवसानः i. 104 ... 156
अवसाना vi. 55 ... 557
अवस्तुजः i. 78 ... 122
अवस्तुजां i. 20 ... 43
अवस्तुत्वं i. 79 ... 122
अवस्थातः i. 14 ... 33
अवस्थात् ii. 27 ... 258
अवान्तर iii. 41 ... 312
अवान्तर भेदाः iii. 41 ... 312
अवान्तरभेदात् ii 38 ... 270
अवाह्य i. 90 ... 140
अवाह्य प्रत्यक्षत्वात् i. 90 ... 140
अविवेकः iii. 68, vi. 12, vi. 16 ... 342, 512, 525
अविवेक vi. 68 ... 571
अविवेकस्य i. 57, iii. 74 86, 347
अविवेकनिमित्त vi. 68 ... 571
अविवेकानां v. 64 ... 446
अविवेकात् i. 55, i. 57, i. 106, iii. 71, vi. 11, vi. 27 ... 77, 86, 158, 345, 521, 532
अविद्या v. 13, v. 65 ... 398, 447
अविद्यातः i. 20 ... 43
अविद्याशक्तियोगः v. 13 ... 398
अविरोधः vi. 21 ... 528
अविरोधात् vi. 48 ... 548
अविशेषः i. 6 ... 23
अविशेष vi. 19, vi. 26...526, 531
अविशेषात् i. 85, iii. 1...129, 218
अविशेषाणां iii. 4 ... 286
अविशेषापत्तिः vi 19 ... 526
अविषयः i. 108 . 160
अवृत्ति i. 82 . 126
अवृत्तियोगात् i. 82 ... 126
अव्यक्तं i. 136 . 192
अव्यभिचारात् ii. 41 ... 272
अव्यवहार्यै i. 120 . 172
अव्यापि i. 124 ... 178
अशक्य i. 9 28
अशक्तिः iii. 38 . 311
अशक्योपदेशः i. 11 ... 30
अशक्योपदेश विधिः i. 9 ... 28
अशेष ii. 42 272
अशेष संस्काराधारत्वात् ii. 42 272
अष्टधा iii. 40 ... 312
अष्टाविंशतिधा i. 13, iii. 38 14, 311
असकृत् iv. 3 ... 363
असत् i. 114, v. 56 167, 439
असतः v. 52 ... 434
असत्करत्वं i. 94 . 144
असदुत्पादः i. 114 ... 167
असन्निकृष्टार्थ i. 87 ... 132
असन्निकृष्टार्थ परिच्छित्तिः i. 87 132

PAGE.

असंगः i. 15... ... 33
असंगत्व vi. 10 ... 520
असंगत्वादिश्रुतेः vi. 10 ... 520
असंभवात् i. 49, i. 116, vi. 16, vi. 53, vi. 61, vi. 62, 72, 169, 525, 556, 563, 564
अस्फोटयोः vi. 28 ... 532
असंबद्धस्य vi. 61 ... 563
अस्मत् v. 109 ... 491
अस्मात् i. 13 ... 32
अस्मदादिवत् v. 109 ... 491
अस्ति i. 33, v. 99, vi. 1... 55, 478, 513
अस्तित्व vi. 1 ... 513
अस्य i. 27, vi. 14 51, 523
असाधारण्यात् v. 112 ... 493
असाधुना iv. 8 ... 366
असाधुनानुचिन्तनं iv. 8 ... 366
असिद्धिः i. 88, i. 111 ... 137, 163
असिद्धेः i. 34, i. 92, v. 127 56, 142, 509
असैा vi. 2 514
अहंकारः i. 61, i. 72, ii. 16, vi. 54, vi. 62, vi. 64 ... 93, 117, 249, 557, 564, 567
अहंकारात् i. 61, ii. 18... 93, 251
अहंकार कर्त्रधीना vi. 64 ... 567
अहंकारस्य i. 63 ... 102
अहंकारित्व v. 84 ... 464
अहंकारित्वश्रुतेः v. 84 ... 464
अहंकार धर्मा vi. 62 ... 564
अहिनिर्ल्वयनीश्रावत् iv. 6 365
आकार i. 89, v. 77 138, 460
आकारोपराक्लिछत्तिः v. 77... 460
आकाशवत् i. 51 ... 73
आकाशस्य i. 15 ... 208

PAGE.

आकाशादिभ्यः ii. 12 ... 245
आख्याने i. 107 ... 160
आचरणं v. 1 .. 388
आचारात् v. 1 .. 388
आचार्यः v. 31 ... 414
आचार्याः vi. 30 ... 535
आशुस्यात् i. 125, iii. 72 ... 180, 345
आत्मकः v. 57 .. 441
आत्मकं ii. 26 ... 257
आत्मनः i. 95, ii. 29, v. 61, vi. 10, vi. 33 ... 144, 256, 444, 520, 537
आत्मना v. 62 ... 445
आत्मलाभः vi. 34 ... 537
आत्मवत् vi. 13 ... 523
आत्मा v. 65, vi. 1 447, 513
आत्मानं iii. 73 ... 346
आत्मार्थं ii. 11 ... 244
आत्मार्थत्वात् ii. 11 ... 244
आत्यन्तिकम् iii. 27 ... 302
आतिवाहिकस्य v. 103 ... 483
आदि i. 26, i. 54, i. 126, i. 128, i. 139, i. 141, i. 149, ii. 10, ii. 28, iii. 21, iii. 43, iii. 46, v. 49, v. 77, v. 78, v. 80, v. 82, v. 83, v. 126, vi. 2, vi. 10, vi. 56 ... 49, 75, 182, 185, 195, 196, 207, 242, 259, 296, 315, 323, 430, 460, 460, 462, 463, 463, 509, 514, 520, 558
आदिः i. 157 ... 223
आदिदोषात् v. 77, v. 78 ... 460, 460

PAGE.

आदिना i. 33 ... 55
आदिनं iii. 53 ... 327
आदिभिः i. 60, vi. 29 ... 92, 533
आदियोगः v. 82 ... 463
आदिवत् i. 25, v. 109, vi. 61 ... 48, 491, 563
आदिषु v. 86 ... 466
आदीनां v. 25, v. 121 ... 407, 504
आदेः i. 129 ... 187
आद्यं i. 71 ... 116
आद्य i. 148, vi. 32 ... 205, 536
आद्यहेतुता i. 74 ... 118
आद्यैः i. 127 ... 183
आद्योपादानात् vi. 32 ... 536
आधिक्य i. 88 ... 157
आधिक्यं vi. 38 ... 541
आधेय v. 32, v. 36 ... 415, 417
आधेयशक्तियोगः v. 32 ... 415
आधेयशक्ति सिद्धौ v. 31 .. 417
आध्यात्मिक iii 43 ... 315
आध्यात्मिकादिभेदात् iii. 43 315
आनन्द v. 74 ... 457
आनन्दचित् v. 66 ... 449
आनन्दाभिव्यक्तिः v. 74 ... 457
आनर्थक्यं iv. 15 ... 371
आपत्तिः vi. 19 ... 526
आपत्तेः i. 113 ... 165
आप्त i. 101 ... 153
आपेक्षिकः ii. 45 ... 274
आप्तोपदेशः i. 101 ... 153
आब्रह्मस्तम्बपर्यन्तं iii. 47 ... 324
आभासमात्रं iv. 30 ... 384

PAGE.

आयतनं v. 114 . 495
आयतनत्वं v. 121 . 504
आर्जितत्वात् vi. 55 ... 557
आरोपात् i. 153 ... 213
आरंभः ii. 11, iii. 1 ... 244, 278
आरंभकस्य ii. 21, v. 113... 254, 494
आलाप ii. 21 ... 254
आविवेकात् iii. 4, iii. 47 ... 280, 324
आवृत्तिः iii. 52, iv. 3, iv. 22, vi. 56 ... 326, 363, 378, 558
आश्रम iii 35 ... 309
आश्रय v. 126, v. 127 ... 509,
आश्रयत्वं v. 14 .. 398
आश्रयविशेषे v. 128 ... 500
आश्रयसिद्धे v. 127 ... 509
आश्रये iii. 11 . 287
आश्रितं i. 124 . 178
आसन ii. 32 .. 306
आसनं iii. 34, vi. 24 ... 308, 530
आहंकारित्वं ii. 20 ... 253
आहंकारित्व श्रुतेः ii. 20, iii. 64 ... 253, 338

इ

इतर iii. 64, v. 82 ... 338, 463
इतरत् iii. 7 282
इतरथा iii. 81 .. 356
इतर येागवत् v. 82 ... 463
इतरवत् iii. 64 ... 338
इतर लाभे iv. 22 ... 378
इतरस्य iii. 5, iii. 8, iii. 27 280, 283, 302

PAGE.

इतरस्याः iii. 42 ... 314
इतरात् iii. 45, iii. 84...322, 359
इति i. 15, i. 54, i. 61, i. 68, i. 111, i. 132, i. 142, i. 163, iii. 18, iii. 19, iii. 75, v. 1, v. 31, v. 32, v. 80, v. 103, v. 107, v. 111, vi. 7, vi. 8, vi. 9, vi. 24, vi. 30, vi. 69...33, 75, 93, 111, 163, 189, 197, 229, 294, 295, 348, 388, 414, 414, 462, 483, 488, 492, 518, 518, 520, 530, 535, 572
इदानीं i. 159 ... 225
इन्द्र v. 83 463
इन्द्रादि पद योगः v. 83 ... 463
इन्द्रिय ii. 19, ii. 32, v. 113 252, 264, 494
इन्द्रियं i. 61, ii. 23 93, 256
इन्द्रियत्वात् v. 69 ... 454
इन्द्रियवृत्तिः ii. 32 ... 264
इन्द्रियशक्तितः v. 113 ... 494
इन्द्रियस्य i. 108, iv. 18...160, 375
इन्द्रियेषु ii. 39 ... 270
इन्द्रियैः ii. 19 ... 252
इन्द्रियाणां ii. 29, v. 84, v. 104 259, 464, 485
इव i. 28, i. 60, i. 150, i. 159, iii. 26, iv. 21, v. 59, v. 118, vi. 28...51, 92, 208, 225, 301, 377, 442, 500, 532
इषुकारवत् iv. 14 ... 370

ई

ईदृश iii. 57... ... 331

PAGE.

ईश्वर i. 92, iii. 57, v. 2, vi. 64 ... 142, 331, 389, 569
ईश्वर कर्त्रधीना vi. 64 ... 567
ईश्वर सिद्धिः iii. 57 ... 331
ईश्वराधिष्ठिते v. 2 ... 389
ईश्वरासिद्धेः i. 92 ... 142

उ

उकारे iii. 68 .. 342
उक्तत्वं i. 162 ... 228
उच्छित्तिः i. 56, v. 75, v. 77, v. 78, vi. 70 ... 82, 458, 460, 460, 573
उच्छित्तेः v. 82 ... 463
उच्छेदः i. 159 .. 225
उज्ज्वलितत्वात् i. 99 ... 148
उत्कर्ष i. 5 22
उत्कर्षात् i. 5 22
उत्तर i. 39 60
उत्तरं vi. 48... . 548
उत्तरायोगात् i. 39 ... 60
उत्तरेषां i. 73, vi. 73 ... 117, 530
उत्तरोत्तरयोः iii 52 .. 326
उत्थानात् iii. 54 ... 327
उत्पत्ति i. 77, ii. 22 ... 121, 155
उत्पत्तिः vi. 53 ... 556
उत्पत्तिवत् i. 123 ... 177
उत्पत्तेः iii. 8 . 283
उत्पादः i. 114 . 167
उद्भव i. 11 30
उद्भवं v 31 414
उद्भवः ii. 36, iii. 22 ... 269, 297
उद्भिज v. 111 ... 492
उद्भूतिवत् vi. 65 ... 568
उद्भूतत्वात् i. 97 . 147
उन्मत्त i. 26 . 49

PAGE.

उपकारका i. 31 ... 54
उपकार्य i. 31 ... 54
उपकार्योपकारकभावः i. 31 54
उपचयात् iii. 29 ... 304
उपजायते v. 50 ... 431
उपदानाभ्यां i. 108 ... 160
उपदिष्ट i. 9 ... 28
उपदेश i. 7, i. 9. 26, 28
उपदेशः i. 98, i. 101, i. 102, iv. 2, iv. 17, iv. 29 ... 147, 153, 153, 362, 374, 384
उपदेशश्रवणे iv. 17 ... 374
उपदिश्य iii. 99 ... 354
उपदेशात् iv. 1, iv. 3, vi. 57 361, 363, 559
उपदेशबीजप्ररोहः iv. 29 ... 384
उपद्रष्टृत्वात् iii. 79 ... 354
उपभोग i. 105, v. 124...157, 507
उपभोगात् iii. 5 ... 280
उपभोगः iii. 77, vi. 44...352, 545
उपरज्य i. 28 ... 51
उपरंजकभावः i. 28 ... 51
उपरज्योपरंजकभावः i. 28 ... 51
उपराग i. 27 ... 51
उपरागः ii. 34, vi 26, vi. 27, vi. 28...267, 531, 532, 532
उपरागात् i. 29, i. 164, ii. 15 ... 53, 229, 248
उपरागे iii. 66 ... 339
उपरागनिरोधात् vi. 26 ... 531
उपरोग v. 77 ... 460
उपलब्धिः i. 109 ... 162
उपलब्धेः i. 110, v. 94, v. 95 163, 475, 475
उपशान्त ii. 34 ... 267
उपशान्तोपरागः ii. 34 ... 267

PAGE.

उपसर्पणं iii. 70 ... 344
उपसर्पणानि iv. 19 ... 375
उपसर्पणे vi. 44 ... 545
उपहतिः iii. 30 .. 304
उपहते iv. 25 ... 381
उपादान i. 115, v. 65, v. 102 ... 168, 447, 482
उपादानं i. 76, iv. 23, v. 112 ... 120, 380, 493
उपादानत्व i. 81 ... 125
उपादानत्वयोगात् i. 81 ... 125
उपादानायोगात् v. 102 ... 482
उपादानता v. 109, vi. 32 491, 536
उपादाननियमात् i. 115 ... 168
उपादेयः iv. 23 ... 380
उपाधि i. 57 ... 73
उपाधिः i. 151, vi. 46...210, 547
उपाधिभेदे i. 150 ... 208
उपाधियोगात् i. 51, vi. 59 73, 560
उपासकानां iv. 21 ... 377
उपासनात् iv. 21 . 377
उपासने iv. 13 . 369
उपासा i. 95 . 144
उपास्य iv. 32 . 386
उपास्यसिद्धिवत् iv. 32 ... 386
उभय i. 40, i. 46, i. 102, i. 103, i. 129, i. 160, ii. 26, v. 91, v. 124 ... 60, 70, 153, 154, 187, 226, 257, 477, 507
उभयं i. 61, i. 107, v. 65 93, 160, 447
उभय था i. 47, i. 94, v. 39, vi. 26 ... 70, 144, 421, 531

PAGE.

उभयत्र v. 23, v. 100... 405, 479
उभयपक्ष समानक्षेमत्वात् i. 46 70
उभयरूपः i. 160 ... 226
उभयसिद्धिः i. 102, i. 103 153, 154
उभयात्मकं ii. 26 ... 257
उभयानित्यत्वात् v. 97 ... 477
उभयान्यत्वात् i. 129 ... 187
उभयोः i. 6, ii. 28, iii. 36, iv. 4, iv. 28, v. 24, v. 29, vi. 19 ... ... 23, 259, 301, 363, 383, 406, 412, 526
उभाभ्यां v. 63 .. 446
उरगः iii. 66 ... 339
उल्लासात् ii. 36 ... 269
उल्लेखि i. 89 ... 138
उष्मज v. 111 ... 492
उष्मजाण्डज जरायुजोद्भिज्ज-सांकल्पिकसांसिद्धिकं v. 111 492
उष्ट्र vi. 40 543
उष्ट्र कुंकुमवहनवत् iii. 58, vi. 40 333, 543

ऊ

ऊर्ध्वं iii. 48 ... 325
ऊहादिभिः iii. 44 ... 319

ऋ

ऋते i. 19, i. 59, iii. 71, iv. 17, v. 6...37, 91, 345, 374, 391

ए

एक i. 31 ... 54

PAGE.

एकः v. 120 . 503
एकं iii. 9 . 284
एक कालायेागात् i. 31 ... 54
एक तर i. 112 . 164
एकत्र i. 68 .. 111
एकत्वं ii. 21 .. 256
एकतर दृष्ट्या i. 112 ... 164
एकतरस्य i. 75, iii. 65, v. 29 ... 118, 339, 412
एकतर सिद्धेः i. 112 ... 164
एकत्वात् i. 153 ... 213
एकत्वेन i. 152 .. 212
एकदेश i. 29 ... 53
एकदेश लब्धोपरागात् i. 29 53
एक भैातिकं iii. 19 ... 295
एकरूपेण iii. 73 ... 346
एकस्य i. 150, iii. 8, v. 66 208, 283, 449
एकतरस्य i 87 ... 132
एकात्मा i. 33 . 55
एकान्ततः iii. 71 ... 345
एकान्तात् v. 115 ... 496
एकादश ii. 17 ... 250
एकादशं ii. 18, ii. 19 251, 252
एके iii. 18 294
एते vi. 62 564
एव iii. 66, iv. 10, v. 63, v. 101, vi. 16 ... 339, 367, 446, 481, 525
एवं i. 152, i. 158, iii. 28, iii. 42, v. 18, v. 23, v. 79, v. 86, vi. 26 ... 212, 224, 303, 314, 402, 403, 461, 466, 531
एषां ii. 11 244

PAGE.

औ

औदासीन्यं i. 163, iii. 65... 229; 339
औषधादि v. 128 ... 510
औषधि v. 121 ... 504

क

कण्टक ii. 7 239
कण्टक मोक्षवत् ii. 7 ... 239
कः vi. 7 518
करण ii. 31, ii. 36 259, 269
करणं ii. 38 270
करणत्वात् v. 69 ... 454
करणात् i. 117 ... 169
करणोद्भवः ii. 36 ... 269
करणत्वं ii. 29 ... 259
कर्त्ता iii. 56, vi. 54 ... 330, 557
कर्तुः i. 106, v. 46 ... 158, 428
कर्तृ vi. 49, vi. 64 ... 549, 567
कर्तृत्वं i 164 ... 229
कर्म ii. 19, ii. 46, ii. 47, iii. 10, iii. 35, iii. 51, iii. 67, v. 124, vi. 41, vi. 49, vi. 55, vi. 67... 259, 274, 276, 286, 309, 326, 341, 507, 544, 549, 557, 570
कर्तृकर्म विरोधः vi. 49 ... 549
कर्म देहोपभोगदेहोभयदेहाः v. 124, ... 507
कर्म निमित्तः vi. 67 ... 570
कर्म निमित्तयोगात् iii. 67 ... 341
कर्मविशेषात् iii. 10 ... 286
कर्मवैचित्र्यात् iii. 51, vi. 41 320, 544
कर्मणः i. 81 ... 185
कर्मणा i. 16, i. 52, v. 2 ... 34, 73, 389

PAGE.

कर्मवत् i. 32, iii. 60 55, 335
कर्माकृष्टेः iii. 62 ... 336
कर्माधिकारित्वं v. 123 ... 506
कर्मेन्द्रिय बुद्धीन्द्रियैः ii. 19, 252
कल्पना ii. 25, v. 30 257, 413
कल्पनाविरोध ii. 25 ... 257
कामचारित्वं iv. 25 ... 381
काम्ये i. 85 129
कारण i. 19, i. 38, i. 78, i. 121, i. 135, vi. 14, vi. 52 ... 59, 72, 110, 173, 191, 523, 554
कारणं v. 65 ... 447
कारणता vi. 37 ... 540
कारणत्वात् iii. 25, v. 6 ... 299, 391
कारणभावात् i. 118 ... 170
कारणलयः i. 121 ... 173
कारणलयात् iii. 54 ... 327
कारणस्य i. 155 . 221
कारणात् i. 56 . 82
कारणानुमानं i. 135 ... 191
कार्य i. 34, i. 38, i. 71, i. 110, ii. 14, ii. 17, v. 20, vi. 36, vi. 64 ... 56, 59, 116, 163, 247, 250, 404, 539, 567
'कार्यकारणभावः i. 38 ... 59
कार्यत्वं i. 73, i. 129, iii. 8, v. 45, v. 87, vi. 32 ... 117, 187, 283, 428, 469, 536
कार्यत्वश्रुतेः v. 45, vi. 32... 428, 536
कार्यत्वस्य v. 12 ... 396
कार्यतः i. 137, ii. 6 193, 238.
कार्यतां v. 58 ... 442
कार्यत्वात् v. 88 . 470

PAGE.

कार्यताप्रतीतेः v. 58 ... 442
कार्यदर्शनात् i. 110, vi. 36...163, 539
कार्यद्वयं vi. 42 ... 544
कार्यसिद्धिः vi. 64 ... 567
कार्यात् i. 135 ... 191
कार्ये v. 39 421
कार्येषु i. 97 147
काल i. 12, i. 31, iv. 20, vi. 59 ... 31, 54, 376, 560
कालनियमः iv. 20 ... 376
कालयोगतः i. 12 .. 31
कालादेः iii. 60 ... 335
कालौ ii. 12 ... 245
किंचित् v. 125 ... 508
किन्तु vi. 28... ... 532
क्रिया v. 120 ... 503
क्रियानिर्वर्तकः v. 120 ... 503
क्रियायाः v. 101 ... 481
क्रियाविशेषात् ii. 45 ... 274
कुठारवत् ii. 39 ... 270
कुतः i. 80 ... 124
कुत्र vi. 7 ... 518
कुतर्क vi. 34... ... 537
कुतर्कोपसदस्य vi. 34 ... 537
कुतस्तरां i. 80 ... 124
कुमारी iv. 9... ... 367
कुमारीशंखवत् iv. 9 ... 367
कुल iii. 70 344
कुलवधूवत् iii. 70 ... 344
कुसुमवत् ii. 35 ... 268
कुशलैः i. 4 21
कृत iv. 15, v. 50, vi. 5 ...371, 431, 517
कृतबुद्धिः v. 50 ... 431
कृत्यता vi. 5 ... 517

PAGE.

कृतकृत्यता iii. 54, iii. 84, iv. 17, iv. 32, vi. 5 327, 359, 374, 386, 517
कृतनियमलंघनात् iv. 15 ... 371
कृत्वा iv. 19 ... 375
कृति iii. 14 291
कृतिश्रुतेः iii. 14 . 291
कैवल्यार्थं i. 14 . 199
कोशकारवत् iii. 73 ... 291
क्रमशः ii. 32 ... 264
क्रमेण ii. 10 ... 242
क्लिष्ट ii. 33 ... 266
क्लिष्टा क्लिष्टाः ii. 33 ... 266
क्लेशः vi. 6 . 517

क्ष

क्षणिकत्वं i. 34 . 56
क्षणिकत्वात् v. 77 ... 460
क्षीरवत् iv. 23 ... 380
क्षुत् i. 3 20
क्षेमवत् i. 46 70

ख

ख्यातिः v. 55, v. 66 ... 437, 439
ख्यानं v. 52 ... 434

ग

गणः i. 61 ... 93
गति i. 48, i. 51, v. 70, v. 76, vi. 37, vi. 59 ... 71, 73, 455, 459, 540, 560
गतियोगे vi. 37 ... 540
गतिविशेषात् i. 48 ... 71
गतिश्रुतिः i 51 ... 73
गतिश्रुतेः v. 70, vi. 59 455, 560

PAGE.

गर्भ iii. 51 ... 326
गर्भदासवत् iii. 51 ... 326
गर्भाधान i. 33 ... 55
गुण i. 125, ii. 27, ii. 39, ii. 45, iv. 26, v. 75...180, 258, 270, 274, 382, 458
गुणपरिणामभेदात् ii. 27 ... 258
गुणप्रधानभावः ii. 45 ... 274
गुणयोगात् iv. 26 ... 382
गुणसामान्यादेः i. 125 ... 180
गुणानां i. 127, i. 128...183, 185
गुणादीनां v. 26 ... 407
गुणाभ्यां v. 107 ... 488
गुरु iv. 13 369
गुल्म v. 121... ... 504
गौणः v. 67 452
ग्रहणात् v. 28 ... 411

घ

घटवत् v. 71 ... 455
घटस्य v. 59 ... 442
घटादिभिः i. 150 ... 208
घटादिवत् i. 50, i. 129...72, 187

च

च i. 6, i. 16, i. 22, i. 36, i. 37, i. 54, i. 63, i. 77, i. 79, i. 107, i. 113, i. 118, i. 128, i. 132, i. 142, i. 144, i. 163, ii. 5, ii. 22, ii. 32, ii. 35, ii 43, iii. 4, iii. 12, iii. 15, iii. 21, iii. 36, iii. 67, iii. 78, iii. 80, v. 1, v. 26, v. 35, v. 80, v. 85, v. 111, v. 122, v. 127, v. 129, vi. 48, vi. 59 ... 23, 34, 45, 58, 58, 75, 102, 121, 122, 160, 165, 170, 185, 189, 197, 199, 229, 237, 255, 264, 268, 273, 280, 288, 293, 296, 309, 341, 354, 355, 388, 407, 417, 462, 465, 492, 506, 509, 511, 548, 560
चक्रभ्रमणवत् iii. 82 ... 356
चन्द्र vi. 56 558
चन्द्रादिलोके vi. 56 ... 558
चरमः i. 72 117
चक्षुः v. 105 . 487
चक्षमताम् i. 156 . 222
चारितार्थ्यात् iii. 69 ... 343
चातुर्भौतिकं iii. 18 ... 294
चातुर्विध्य v. 90 ... 471
चित् i. 104, vi. 50, vi. 55...156, 550, 557
चित्त i. 58, vi. 31 ... 88, 536
चित्तप्रसादात् vi. 31 ... 536
चित्सान्निध्यात् i. 164 ... 229
चित्तस्थितेः i. 58 . 88
चिदवसानः i. 104 . 156
चिदवसाना vi. 55 ... 557
चिद्रूपः vi. 50 ... 550
चिद्धर्मा i 146 . 201
चित्रवत् iii. 12 ... 288
चेत् i. 10, i. 18, i. 23, i. 30, i. 111, i. 119, iii. 22, v. 8, v. 9, v. 24, v. 60, vi. 9, vi. 26, vi. 46, vi. 61 ... 29, 37, 45, 54, 163, 171, 297, 392, 394, 406, 443, 520, 531, 547, 563.

	PAGE.
चेतनोद्देशात् ii. 7 ..	239
चेतसि iv. 29 ...	384
चेष्टनात् i. 3 ...	20
चेष्टा iii. 51 ...	326
चेष्टितं iii. 59, iii. 61 ...	334, 336
चैतन्यं iii. 20, v. 129 ...	295, 511

छ

छर्दिविधारणाभ्यां iii. 33 ...	307
छायावत् iii. 12 ...	288
छिन्नहस्तवत् iv. 7 ...	365

ज

जगत् v. 65, vi. 52 ...	447, 554
जगतः v. 18	402
जगत्सत्यत्वं vi. 52 ...	554
जगदुपादानकारणं v. 65 ...	447
जड़ i. 145 ...	200
जड़ं vi. 50 ...	550
जड़प्रकाशयोगात् i. 145 ...	200
जड़व्यावृत्तः vi. 50 ...	550
जन्म i. 149, iv. 22 ...	207, 378
जन्मश्रुतेः iv. 22 ...	378
जन्मादिव्यवस्थातः i. 149 ...	207
जन्यत्वात् i. 79, vi. 52 ...	122, 554
जनकत्वात् v. 44 ...	427
जप vi. 28	532
जपास्फटिकयोः vi. 28 ...	532
जरा iii. 53 ...	327
जरामरणादिजं iii. 53 ...	327

	PAGE.
जरायुज v. 111 ..	492
जल i. 84, vi. 61 ..	128, 563
जलादिवत् vi. 61 ...	563
जलाभिषेकवत् i. 84 ...	128
जागराभ्यां iii. 26 ...	301
जाड्य i. 85	128
जाड्यविमोकः i. 84 ..	128
जातिपरत्वात् i. 154 ...	216
जायमानयोः i. 38 ...	59
जीवत्वं vi. 63 ...	565
जीवन्मुक्तः iii. 78 .	354
जीवानां i. 97 ...	147
ज्ञानं i. 100	152
ज्ञात्वा i 22 ...	20

त

तज्जयस्य iv. 31 .	385
ततः i. 65	106

तत् i. 2, i. 3, i. 4, i. 19, i. 40, i. 43, i. 49, i. 55, i. 56, i. 57, i. 62, i. 71, i. 73, i. 74, i. 77, i. 80, i. 82, i. 87, i. 88, i. 89, i. 93, i. 96, i. 99, i. 102, i. 106, i. 109, i. 110, i. 111, i. 125, i. 133, i. 135, i. 137, i. 147, i. 153, ii. 2, ii. 3, ii. 6, ii. 8, ii. 14, ii. 17, ii. 22, ii. 34, ii. 46, iii. 3, iii. 8, iii. 11, iii. 14, iii. 22, iii. 31, iii. 55, iii. 64, iii. 79, iii. 83, iv. 16, iv. 31, v. 2, v. 6, v. 7, v. 10, v. 14 v. 19, v. 21, v. 44, v. 46, v. 49, v. 50,

PAGE.

v. 54, v. 61, v. 71, v. 85, v. 87, v. 90, v. 92, v. 95, v. 105, v. 108, v. 110, v. 112, v. 113, v. 117, vi. 8, vi. 11, vi. 29, vi. 39, vi. 46, vi. 49, vi. 51, vi. 55, vi. 58, vi. 61, vi. 62, vi. 70... 19, 20, 21, 37, 60, 64, 72, 77, 82, 86, 99, 116, 117, 118, 121, 124, 126, 132, 137, 138, 143, 145, 148, 153, 158, 162, 163, 163, 180, 190, 191, 197, 203, 213, 234, 235, 238, 240, 247, 250, 255, 267, 274, 279, 283, 287, 291, 297, 305, 329, 338, 354, 357, 373, 385, 389, 391, 392, 394, 398, 403, 404, 427, 428, 430, 431, 435, 444, 455, 465, 469, 471, 473, 475, 487, 490, 491, 493, 494, 499, 519, 521, 533, 542, 547, 549, 553, 557, 558, 563, 564, 573

तत्क्रतुः v. 146 ... 428

तत्कर्मार्जितत्वात् ii. 46, vi. 55 ... ... 274, 557

तत्कार्यः ii. 14, ii. 17 ... 247, 250

तत्कार्यतः i. 137 ... 193

तत्कार्यत्व i. 73, iii. 8 ... 117, 283

तत्कार्यत्वश्रुतेः v. 87 ... 489

तत्कृते iii. 47 ... 324

तत्र i. 33, i. 83, iii. 51, v. 64, vi. 21 ... 55, 128, 326, 446, 528

तत्वं i. 44, i. 107, iii. 75, iv. 1, v. 94, v. 107 ... 66, 160, 348, 361, 475, 488

तत्वस्य iii. 66 ... 339

तत्वाख्याने i. 107 ... 160

तत्वान्तरं v. 30, v. 94, v. 107, ... 413, 475, 488

तत्वाभ्यासात् iii. 75 ... 348

तत्वोपदेशात् iv. 1 ... 361

तत्पौरुषेयं v. 50 . 431

तत्प्रत्यक्षबाधात् i. 147 ... 203

तत्प्रतीकार चेष्टनात् i. 3 ... 20

तत्साधकं i. 87 ... 132

तत्सान्निधानात् i. 96 ... 145

तत्सम्भे i. 4 21

तत्साहित्यात् i. 135 ... 191

तत्सिद्धिः i. 2, i. 80, i. 82, i. 93, i. 125, i. 153, ii. 3, ii. 8, iii. 31, iii. 32, iii. 79, iii. 83, v. 6, v. 10, v. 21, v. 44, vi. 11, vi 29... 19, 124, 126, 143, 180, 213, 235, 240, 305, 306, 354, 357, 391, 394, 404, 427, 521, 533

तत्सिद्धेः i. 106, i. 137, ii. 2, ii. 6, v. 2, v. 105, v. 113, vi. 51 ... 158, 193, 234, 238, 389, 487, 494, 553

तत्सिद्धौ i. 88, v. 14, vi. 46, vi. 49, vi. 58 ... 137, 398, 547, 549, 558

तथा i. 112, ii. 42, iii. 7, iv. 10, vi. 6 ... 164, 272, 282, 367, 517

तद्धतिः v. 117 ... 499

तद्धाने i. 57, i. 133 ... 86, 190

PAGE.

तदधिष्ठानाश्रये iii. 11 ... 287
तद्बोधात् v. 85 ... 465
तदभावात् i. 43, v. 54 ... 64, 435
तदभावे i. 40, i. 43 ...40, 64
तद्भेदप्रतीतेः v. 61 ... 444
तद्योगः i. 19, i. 55 ...37, 77
तदयोगात् i. 40 ... 60
तद्योगात् v. 71, v. 90, v. 108, ... 455, 471, 490
तद्योगादृते i. 19 ... 37
तद्योगे v. 7, v. 14, v. 46... 392, 398, 430
तद्योगेन i. 80 ... 124
तदर्थं ii. 46 ... 274
तदर्थस्य v. 41 ... 423
तद्रूपता iv. 31 ... 385
तद्रूपत्वात् vi. 39 ... 542
तद्रूपत्वे v. 19 ... 403
तदलापः v. 92 ... 473
तद्वत् iv. 19, iv. 24, v. 75, v. 83 ... ... 375, 380, 458, 463
तद्वादः iii. 11 ... 287
तद्वादात् iii. 11 ... 287
तद्व्यपदेशः v. 110, v. 112, ... 491, 493
तद्द्वारा i. 74 ... 118
तद्वान् i. 151 ... 210
तद्विस्मरणे iv. 16 ... 373
तद्बीजात् iii. 3 ... 279
तद्दृते iii. 12 ... 288
तदसंभवात् i. 49, vi. 61, vi. 62 ... ... 72, 563, 564
तदसिद्धिः i. 111 ... 163

PAGE.

तदाकारोल्लेखि i. 89 ... 138
तदुत्पत्तिश्रुतिः ii. 22 ... 255
तदुत्पत्तिश्रुतेः i. 77 ... 121
तदुच्छित्तिः i. 56 ... 82
तदुज्ज्वलितत्वात् i. 99 ... 149
तदुपदेशः i. 102 ... 153
तदुपलब्धिः i. 109 ... 162
तदुपलब्धेः i. 110, v. 95 163, 475
तन्मात्रस्य ii. 62 ... 99
तन्मात्राणि i. 61 ... 93
तन्निवृत्तौ ii. 34 ... 267
तमः iii. 49 . 325
तमसां i. 61... ... 93
तमोविशाला iii. 49 ... 325
तयोः i. 134, iv. 18 ... 190, 375
तरङ्गवत् iii. 13 ... 290
तर्हि i. 43 64
तस्याः i. 14, i. 18 ... 33, 37
तस्मात् iii. 2, v. 62... 279, 473
तादृक् i. 24 ... 48
तादृक् पदार्थप्रतीतेः i. 24 ... 48
तु i. 58, i. 126, i. 151, iii. 38, v. 118, v. 120... 88, 182, 210, 311, 500, 503
तुच्छत्वम् i. 134 ... 190
तुष्टिः iii. 39, iii. 43 ... 312, 313
तृण v. 121 504
तेज v. 105 487
तेजोऽपसर्पणात् v. 105 ... 487
तेन i. 64, v. 63 ... 103, 446
तेषां v. 49 430
तैः i. 63 102
तैजसं v. 105 . 487

PAGE.

त्रयस्य v. 118 ... 500
त्रयाणां ii. 30, v. 124 ... 261, 507
त्रयोदशविधं ii. 38 ... 270
त्रिगुण i. 126, i. 141 182, 196
त्रिगुणात् i 136 ... 192
त्रिगुणाचेतनत्वादि i. 126 ... 182
त्रिगुणादि विपर्ययात् i. 141 196
त्रिधा v. 124 ... 507
त्रिभिः v. 38, v. 41 ... 420, 423
त्रिविध i. 1, i. 113 ... 12, 165
त्रिविधं i. 87 ... 132
त्रिविध दुःखात्यन्तनिवृत्तिः i. 1 12
त्रिविधविरोधापत्तेः i. 113... 165
त्रैविध्यात् vi. 22 ... 529
त्यागात् iii. 75 ... 348

द

दर्शनात् i. 110, ii. 22, iv. 28, v 1, v. 39, v. 53, vi. 36... 163, 255, 383, 388, 421, 434, 539
दर्पणवत् iv. 30 ... 384
दार्ढ्यार्थं vi. 23 ... 530
दासवत् iii. 51 ... 326
दिक् ii. 12 245
दिक्कालौ ii. 12 ... 245
दिङ्मूढवत् i. 59 ... 91
दीपेन v. 59 ... 42
दुःख i. 1, i. 84, iii. 53, iii. 84, v. 67, vi. 5, vi. 8... 12, 128, 327, 359, 452, 517, 519
दुःख निवृत्तेः v. 67 ... 452
दुःखपक्षे vi. 8 ... 519
दुःखबलं vi. 8 ... 519

PAGE.

दुःखात् i. 84, vi. 6 ... 128, 517
दुःखी iv. 5 ... 364
दृष्टः iii. 74, iv. 18, v. 49... 347, 375, 430
दृष्टत्वात् iv. 4, v. 118...363, 500
दृष्टबाधोप्रसक्ति v. 49 ... 430
दृष्टस्य ii. 25 .. 257
दृष्टहानि iii. 74 ... 347
दृष्टात् i. 2, i. 103 ... 19, 154
दृष्टान्त i. 37 ... 58
दृष्टान्तासिद्धेः i. 37 ... 58
दृष्टेः iii. 60 ... 335
दृष्ट्या i. 112, i. 155 ... 164, 221
देवता ii. 21 ... 254
देवतालयश्रुतिः ii. 21 ... 254
देश i. 13, i. 28, v. 80, v. 109, vi. 59 ... 32, 51, 462, 491, 560
देशभेद v. 109 ... 491
देशयोगतः i. 13 . 32
देशव्यवधानात् i. 28 ... 51
देशादिलाभः v. 80 ... 462
देहे i. 14, iii. 17, v. 113, v. 124, vi 2 ... 33, 294, 494, 507 ,514
देहधर्मत्वात् i. 14 ... 33
देहमात्रतः v. 123 ... 506
देहाः v. 124 .. 507
देहादिव्यतिरिक्तः vi. 2 ... 514
देहारंभकस्य v. 113 ... 494
देहे iii. 11 ... 287
दैव iii. 46 ... 323
दैवादिप्रभेदा iii. 46 ... 323
दोषः i. 90, i. 91, iv. 28, v. 119, vi. 12 ... 140, 140, 383, 501, 521

PAGE.

दोषदर्शनात् iv. 28 ... 383
दोषद्वयप्रसक्तेः vi. 12 ... 521
दोषबोधे iii. 70 ... 344
दोषयोगे v. 119 ... 501
दोषात् iii. 64, v. 78, v. 77 ... 338, 460, 460
द्रव्य v. 108 ... 490
द्रव्यनियमः v. 108 ... 490
द्रष्टृत्वादि ii. 29 ... 259
द्वय vi. 12 ... 521
द्वयोः i. 29, i. 31, i. 69, i. 75, i. 87, i. 126, ii. 40, iii 65, v. 66, v. 117, v. 118 ... ... 53, 54, 112, 118, 132, 182, 271, 339, 449, 449, 500
द्वाभ्यां iii. 6, iv. 10, v. 90, vi. 47, vi. 48 ... 281, 367, 471, 548, 548
द्वारा i. 74, v. 115, vi. 61... 118, 496, 563
द्वैतं vi. 46 547
द्वैविध्यात् vi. 9 ... 520
द्वा v. 118 500

ध

धर्म i. 152, v. 20, v. 25, v. 29 ... ... 212, 404, 407, 412
धर्मत्वं v. 25, v. 42 ... 407, 425
धर्मत्वात् i. 14, i. 44 ... 33, 66
धर्मत्वे i. 17, i. 153 ... 35, 213
धर्मवत् i. 138 ... 193
धर्मा vi. 62 ... 564
धर्मादि ii. 14 ... 247
धर्माध्यासः i. 152 ... 212

PAGE.

धर्मापलापः v. 20 ... 404
धर्मिग्राहक v. 98, vi. 4... 477, 516
धर्मिग्राहकबाधात् v. 98 ... 477
धर्मैः i. 128 185
धारणा ii. 32, vi. 29 ... 306, 533
धारणासनस्वकर्मणा ii. 32... 306
धूम i. 60 92
धूमादिभिः i. 60 .. 92
धेनुवत् ii. 37 .. 269
ध्रुव iii. 82 . 356
ध्रुवशरीरः iii. 82 ... 356
ध्यानम् iii. 30, vi. 25, vi. 29 ... ... 364, 531, 533
ध्यानधारणाभ्यासवैराग्यादिभिः vi. 29 533
ध्वस्तेः vi. 20 ... 527
ध्वान्तवत् i. 56, vi. 14... 82, 523
ध्वंसमात्र i. 86 ... 131

न

न i. 2, i. 7, i. 9, i. 11, i. 12, i. 13, i. 14, i. 16, i. 18, i. 19, i. 20, i. 24, i. 25, i. 26, i. 28, i. 29, i. 31, i. 33, i. 35, i. 38, i. 40, i. 41, i. 42, i. 48, i. 52, i. 55, i. 58, i. 59, i. 70, i. 76, i. 78, i. 79, i. 81, i. 82, i. 84, i. 86, i. 88, i. 90, i. 93, i. 107, i. 112, i. 114, i. 119, i. 120, i. 137, i. 138, i. 146, i. 147, i. 151, i. 152, i. 153, i. 154, i. 156, i. 157, i. 159, ii. 3, ii. 8, ii. 11,

PAGE.

ii. 20, ii. 21, ii. 24, ii. 25, ii. 44, iii. 7, iii. 8, iii. 12, iii. 13, iii. 20, iii. 25, iii. 26, iii. 27, iii. 45, iii. 54, iii 66, iii. 70, iii. 71, iii. 74, iii. 75, iii. 76, iii. 84, iv. 14, iv. 17, iv. 20, iv. 25, iv. 29, iv. 30, iv. 31, iv. 32, v. 2, v. 6, v. 7, v. 10, v. 11, v. 13, v. 15, v. 22, v. 26, v. 28, v. 30, v. 33, v. 39, v. 41, v. 42, v. 45, v. 46, v. 48, v. 52, v. 53, v. 54, v. 55, v. 57, v. 58, v. 61, v. 63, v. 65, v. 69, v. 73, v. 74, v. 75, v. 76, v. 77, v. 78, v. 80, v. 81, v. 82, v. 83, v. 84, v. 87, v. 88, v. 89, v. 90, v. 92, v. 93, v. 94, v. 96, v. 97, v. 98, v. 99, v. 100, v. 101, v. 102, v. 103, v. 104, v. 105, v. 108, v. 109, v. 111, v. 113, v. 115, v. 118, v. 119, v. 120, v. 121, v. 123, v. 125, v. 126, v. 128, v. 129, vi. 1, vi. 4, vi. 6, vi. 9, vi. 13, vi. 16, vi. 20, vi. 24, vi. 26, vi. 28, vi. 31, vi. 33, vi. 34, vi. 37, vi. 38, vi. 43, vi. 44, vi. 48, vi. 50, vi. 54, vi. 57, vi. 64 ... 19, 26, 28, 30, 31, 32, 33, 34, 37, 37, 43, 48, 48, 49, 51, 53, 54, 55, 57, 59, 60, 61, 62, 71, 115, 120, 122, 122, 125, 126, 128, 131, 137, 140, 143, 160, 164, 167, 171, 172, 193, 193, 201, 203, 210, 212, 213, 216, 222, 223, 225, 235, 240, 244, 253, 254, 256, 257, 273, 282, 283, 288, 290, 295, 299, 301, 303, 322, 327, 339, 344, 345, 347, 348, 352, 359, 370, 374, 376, 381, 384, 384, 385, 386, 389, 391, 392, 394, 395, 398, 399, 405, 407, 411, 413, 415, 421, 423, 425, 426, 428, 430, 434, 434, 435, 437, 441, 442, 444, 446, 447, 454, 456, 457, 458, 462, 462, 463, 463, 464, 459, 460, 460, 469, 470, 471, 471, 473, 474, 475, 476, 477, 477, 478, 479, 481, 482, 483, 485, 487, 490, 491, 492, 494, 496, 500, 501, 503, 504, 506, 508, 509, 510, 511, 513, 516, 517, 520, 522, 525, 527, 530, 531, 532, 536, 537, 537, 540, 541, 545, 545, 548, 553, 557, 559, 567

नयः i. 9 11

नर्तकीवत् iii. 69 ... 343

नवधा i. 14, iii. 39 ... 14, 312

नानादि विषयोपरागनिमित्तकः i. 77 ... 51

नानायेागे i. 150 ... 208

नानात्वं ii. 27 . 258

नाना v. 62 445

नाशः i. 120 .. 173

नाशत्वं vi. 14 ... 523

नास्तित्वसाधना भावात् vi. 1 513

निज i. 86, v. 31, v. 36, v.

PAGE.

43, v. 95 ... ... 131, 414, 417, 426, 475
निजशक्तियोगः v. 36 ... 417
निजशक्ति v. 43 ... 426
निजशक्त्यभिव्यक्तेः v. 51 ... 432
निजशक्त्यभिव्यक्तिः v. 95 ... 475
निज मुक्तस्य i. 86 ... 131
नित्य i. 19, i. 162 ... 37, 228
नित्यः vi. 13 ... 523
नित्यत्वं v. 45, v. 48, v. 58, v. 126 ... ... 428, 430, 442, 509
नित्यत्वे vi. 33 ... 537
नित्यता v. 87, v. 91 ... 469, 477
नित्य मुक्तः v. 7 ... 392
नित्यमुक्तत्वम् i. 162 ... 228
नित्य शुद्ध बुद्ध मुक्त स्वभावस्य i. 19 37
नित्यस्य i. 12 ... 31
निबन्धनात् i. 18, v. 89 ... 37, 471
निबन्धनौ i. 120 ... 172
निभागत्व v. 73 ... 456
निभागत्वं v. 71 ... 455
निमित्त iii. 67, v. 110, vi. 44, vi 56 ... 341, 491, 545, 558
निमित्तः vi. 67, vi. 68 ... 570, 571
निमित्तं iii. 68 ... 342
निमित्तकः i 27, vi. 69 ... 51, 572
निमित्तत्वं iii. 74 ... 347
निमित्ताभावात् vi. 44 ... 545
निमित्तस्य v. 119 ... 501

PAGE.

निमित्तव्यपदेशात् v. 110 ... 491
निमित्तसद्भावात् vi. 56 ... 558
नियत i. 56, v. 29 ... 82, 412
नियत कारणात् i. 56 ... 82
नियत धर्मसाहित्यं v. 29 ... 412
नियमः i. 41, i. 70, ii. 7, iii. 76, iv. 15, iv. 20, v. 22, v. 33, v. 39, v. 85, v. 89, v. 103, v. 108, v. 109, v. 111, v. 131, vi. 22, vi. 24, vi. 31, vi. 38 ... 61, 115, 239, 352, 371, 376, 405, 415, 421, 465, 471, 483, 490, 491, 492, 504, 529, 530, 536, 541
नियमात् i. 115 ... 168
नियोगात् iii. 52 ... 326
निर्गुण i. 54 . 75
निर्गुणत्वं vi. 10 ... 520
निर्गुणत्वात् i. 146, vi. 62... 201, 564
निर्गुणादिश्रुतिविरोधः i. 54 75
निर्धर्मत्वात् v. 74 ... 457
निर्भागत्वं v. 88 .. 470
निर्भागत्वश्रुतेः v. 73 ... 456
निर्माणं v. 114 ... 495
निर्वर्तकः v. 120 ... 503
निर्विषयं vi. 25 ... 531
निराशः iv. 11 ... 368
निरोधः iii. 33 ... 307
निरोधात् iii. 31, vi. 26 ... 305, 531
निवृत्तिः i. 1, iii. 63, iii. 69, v. 93 ... ... 12, 337, 343, 474
निवृत्त्यां vi. 5 ... 517

PAGE.

निवृत्ते i. 2 19
निवृत्तेः v. 67 ... 452
निवृत्तौ ii. 34, iii. 89 ... 267, 359
निःक्षियन्ते vi. 8 ... 519
निःशेष iii. 84 ... 359
निःशेषदुःखनिवृत्तौ iii. 84 ... 359
निष्क्रियस्य i. 49, v. 76... 72, 459
निष्पत्तिः v. 2 ... 389
निःसंगस्य v. 13 ... 398
निःसंगत्वात् v. 65 ... 447
निःसंगे vi. 27 ... 532
नृश्रृंगवत् i. 114, v. 52 ... 167, 434
नेति iii. 75 ... 348
नेदिष्ठस्य v. 101 ... 481
नैरपेक्ष्ये iii. 68 ... 342
नैष्फल्यम् v. 17 ... 401
न्याय i. 36 ... 58
न्यायात् v. 36 ... 417

प

पंकजवत् iv. 31 ... 385
पक्ष i. 46 70
पक्षे vi. 8 519
पंच i. 61, ii. 31, ii. 62, iii. 37, iv. 22, v. 27... 93, 262, 99, 310, 378, 409
पंचतन्मात्रं ii. 17 ... 250
पंचतय्यः ii. 33 ... 266
पंचविंशतिः i. 61 ... 93
पंचशिखः v. 32, vi. 68 ... 415, 571
पंचाग्नियोगतः iv. 22 ... 378
पंचावयवयोगात् v. 27 ... 409
पटवत् i. 10 ... 29
पद v. 83 463

PAGE.

पदवत् iv. 13 ... 369
पदार्थ i. 24, i. 25, v. 85 ... 48, 48, 465
परगृहे iv. 12 ... 369
परं i. 86 131
परः vi. 20 527
परत्वं v. 64 ... 446
परधर्मत्वे vi. 11 . 521
परंपरा iii. 81 . 356
परामर्शात् iv. 17 .. 374
परार्थं iii. 58 ... 333
परार्थत्वात् i. 66, i. 140. 108, 195
परिछिन्नं i. 76 ... 120
परिछित्तिः i. 87 .. 132
परिणाम ii. 27 ... 258
परिणामात् i. 130 .. 188
परिदृष्ट iii. 22 ... 297
परिनिष्ठा i. 68 ... 111
परिमाणं iii. 14, v. 90 ... 291, 471
परिमाणचातुर्विध्यं v. 90 ... 471
परि मुक्तः iii. 6 ... 281
परिवर्तमानस्य i. 152 ... 212
परोक्षात् i. 59 . 91
परोक्षाद्दृते i. 59 . 91
पल्लवादिषु v. 35 . 417
पशुवत् iii. 72 . 345
पाके iii. 63 337
पांचभौतिकः iii. 17 ... 294
पाँचभौतिकं v. 102 ... 482
पाटलि पुत्रस्य i. 28 ... 51
पारतंत्र्यम् i. 18 ... 37
पारम्पर्यतः i. 122 ... 75
पारंपर्ये i. 68, i. 75, vi. 35... 111, 118, 539
पारंपर्येण iv. 21, vi. 58, 377, 559

PAGE.

पारवश्यात् iii. 55 ... 329
पारिभाषिकः v. 5 ... 391
पिंगलावत् iv. 11 ... 368
पितापुत्रवत् iv. 11 ... 363
पिशाचवत् iv. 2 ... 362
पुत्र i. 32 55
पुत्रकर्मवत् i. 32 ... 55
पुत्रवत् vi. 4 ... 516
पुनः v. 33, vi. 17, vi 46... 415, 525, 547
पुनर्बन्धयोग vi. 17 ... 525
पुनर्वादप्रसक्तेः v. 33 ... 415
पुमर्थं vi. 40 ... 543
पुमान् i. 139 ... 195
पुरुषः i. 1, i. 3, i. 15, i. 61, i. 133, i. 149, vi. 45, vi. 54 ... 12, 20, 33, 93, 190, 207, 546, 557
पुरुष बहुत्वम् i. 149, vi. 45... 207, 546
पुरुषयोः v. 72 ... 456
पुरुषस्य i. 66, ii. 5, iii. 26, iii. 71, v. 46, vi. 6 ... 108, 237, 301, 345, 428, 517
पुरुषार्थं ii. 36, iii. 16... 269, 293
पुरुषार्थः vi. 70 ... 573
पुरुषार्थत्वम् i. 3 . 20
पूति v. 114 495
पूतिभावप्रसंगात् v. 114 ... 495
पूर्व i. 39, i. 41, iii. 8, v. 59, vi. 48 ... 60, 61, 283, 442, 548
पूर्ववत् iii. 41, v. 112, v. 121, vi. 57 ... 312, 493, 504, 559
पूर्वभाव मात्रे i. 41 ... 61
पूर्वभावित्वे i. 75 ... 118

PAGE.

पूर्वसिद्धसत्वस्य v. 59 ... 442
पूर्वापाये i. 39 ... 60
पूर्वोत्पत्तेः iii. 8 .. 283
पृथिवी v. 112 ... 493
पृथिव्युपादानं v. 112 ... 493
पौरुषेयं v. 50 . 431
पौरुषेयत्वं v. 46 ... 428
प्रकार vi. 16, vi. 53 ... 525, 556
प्रकारान्त संभवात् vi. 16, vi. 53 ... 525, 556
प्रकाश i. 145, v. 106 ... 200, 488
प्रकाशतः vi. 49 ... 549
प्रकाशत्वं v. 104 ... 485
प्रकाशयति vi. 50 .. 550
प्रकृतत्वं v. 84 ... 464
प्रकृति i. 18, i. 61, i. 133, ii. 5, iii. 68, v. 20, v. 72 ... 37, 93, 190, 237, 342, 404, 456
प्रकृतिकार्यवैचित्र्यात् v. 20 ... 404
प्रकृतिबन्धात् i. 18 ... 37
प्रकृतिपुरुषयोः v. 72 456
प्रकृतिवत् iii. 29 ... 304
प्रकृतिवास्तवे ii. 5 237
प्रकृत्युपकारे iii. 68 ... 342
प्रकृतेः i. 61, i. 65, i. 69, iii. 72, vi. 32, vi. 67 ... 93, 106, 112, 345, 536, 570
प्रतिक्रियं v. 120 ... 503
प्रणति iv. 19 ... 375
प्रणतिब्रह्मचर्योपसर्पणानि iv. 19 375
प्रतिनियत v. 6, vi. 14 ... 391, 523
प्रतिनियत कारणनाश्यत्वं vi. 14 523
प्रतिनियत कारणत्वात् v. 6 ... 391

PAGE.

प्रति नियमः vi. 15 ... 524
प्रतिबद्ध i. 100 ... 152
प्रतिबन्धदृशः i. 100 ... 152
प्रतीकार i. 3 ... 20
प्रतीकारवत् i. 3 ... 20
प्रतीति v. 40, v 44 423, 427
प्रतीतिभ्यां v. 57 ... 441
प्रतीत्य v. 57 ... 441
प्रतीत्य प्रतीतिभ्यां v. 57 ... 441
प्रतीतेः i. 42, v. 61, v. 93, v. 101 ... 62, 444, 474, 481
प्रत्यक्षं i. 89, i. 147, v. 62, v. 89, v. 94, v. 100 ... 138, 203, 445, 471, 475, 479
प्रत्यक्षत्वात् i. 90 ... 140
प्रत्यक्ष नियमः v. 89 ... 471
प्रत्यक्ष बाधात् v. 62 ... 445
प्रत्यक्षोपलब्धेः v. 94 ... 475
प्रत्यभिज्ञ i. 35 ... 57
प्रत्यभिज्ञानं v. 91 ... 471
प्रत्येक iii. 20, iii 22, v. 129 295, 297, 511
प्रत्येकं ii. 4 236
प्रत्येक परिदृष्ट iii. 22 ... 297
प्रत्येकादृष्टेः v. 129 ... 511
प्रधान i. 57, i. 125, ii. 40, ii. 45, iii. 51, iii. 58, iii. 73, v. 8, v. 12, v. 119, vi. 35 ... 86, 180, 271, 274, 326, 333, 346, 392, 396, 501, 539
प्रधानकार्यत्वस्य v. 12 ... 396
प्रधानचेष्टा iii. 51 ... 326
प्रधान व्यपदेशात् i. 125 ... 180
प्रधान शक्तियोगात् v. 8 ... 392
प्रधानस्य ii. 1, iii. 59, iii. 63, iii. 70, vi. 38, vi. 40, vi. 43 ... 231, 334, 344, 337, 541, 543, 545
प्रधानसृष्टिः iii. 58 ... 333
प्रधानानुवृत्तिः vi. 35 ... 539
प्रधानाविवेकात् i. 57 ... 86
प्रपंच iii. 21 ... 296
प्रपंचमरणाद्यभावः iii. 21 296
प्रबुद्ध iii. 66 ... 339
प्रबुद्धरज्जुतत्वस्य iii. 66 ... 339
प्रभेदा iii. 46 ... 323
प्रभेदात् iii. 76 . 352
प्रमा i. 87 ... 132
प्रमाण i. 4, ii. 25, v. 10, v. 22, v. 99, vi. 47, vi. 64. 21, 257, 394, 405, 478, 548, 567
प्रमाणकुशलैः i. 4 ... 21
प्रमाणदृष्टस्य ii. 25 ... 257
प्रमाण विरोधः vi. 47 ... 548
प्रमाणात् i. 102 ... 153
प्रमाणान्तरावकाशात् v. 222, 405
प्रमाणाभावात् v. 10, v. 99, vi. 64 394, 478, 567
प्रमाणं i. 87, ... 132
प्ररोहः iv. 29 : 384
प्रवर्तते ii. 18 ... 251
प्रवर्तनं iii. 4 . 280
प्रवृत्तस्य iii. 69 ... 343
प्रवृत्तेः i. 144 ... 199
प्रशंसा i. 95, v. 68 144, 453
प्रसक्तिः v. 49 ... 470
प्रसक्तेः v. 33, v. 34, v. 120, vi. 12 ... ... 415, 416, 503, 521
प्रसंगः v. 16 ... 400
प्रसंगात् v. 114 ... 495

PAGE.

प्रसादात् vi. 31 ... 336
प्रसिद्ध vi. 38 ... 541
प्रसिद्धाधिक्यं vi. 38 ... 541
प्राणत्वं v. 113 ... 494
प्राणाद्याः ii. 31 ... 262
प्रात्याहिक i. 3 ... 20
प्रात्याहिकक्षुत्प्रतीकारवत् i. 3 20
प्राधान्यं ii. 47 ... 276
प्राप्त i. 83, v. 106 128, 488
प्राप्तविवेकस्य i. 83 ... 128
प्राप्तार्थप्रकाशलिंगात् v. 106 ... 488
प्राप्तेः v. 104 ... 485
प्रामाण्यं v. 51 ... 432
प्रायशः iii. 7 ... 282
प्रीति i. 127 183
प्रीत्याप्रीतिविषादाद्यैः i. 127 183

फ

फल i. 105, i. 106, v. 1, v. 2 ... ... 157, 158, 388, 389
फलदर्शनात् v. 1 ... 388
फलनिष्पत्तिः v. 2 ... 389
फलावगमः i. 106 ... 158
फलोपभोगः i. 105 ... 157

ब

बधूवत् iii. 70 ... 344
बद्धः iv. 26 ... 382
बद्धयोः i. 93 ... 143
बद्धस्य i. 7 ... 26
बन्धः i. 20, i. 155, iii. 24, iii. 71, vi. 16, vi. 17 ... 43, 221, 299, 345, 525, 525
बन्धध्वंसमात्रं i. 86 ... 131

PAGE.

बन्धमोक्षौ iii. 71 . 345
बन्धाति iii. 73 . 346
बन्धाय iv. 8 . 366
बन्धायोगात् i. 20 ... 43
बलं vi. 8 519
बलवत्वात् ii. 3 . 235
बहुकल्पना v. 120 ... 503
बहुकालात् iv. 19 ... 375
बहुत्वम् i. 149, vi. 45... 207, 546
बहुभृत्यवत् ii. 4 ... 236
बहुशास्त्र iv. 13 ... 369
बहूनां v. 102 ... 482
बाध v. 16, v. 53 ... 400, 434
बाधक vi. 52 ... 554
बाधकत्वम् v. 119 ... 501
बाधकाभावात् vi. 52 ... 554
बाधत्वे v. 18 . 402
बाधदर्शनात् v. 53 ... 434
बाधा v. 49, v. 56 430, 439
बाधात् i. 147, v. 62, v. 98, vi. 4 ... ... 203, 445, 477, 516
बाधाबोधात् v. 56 ... 439
बाध्यते i. 59 ... 91
बाधिता iii. 77 . 352
बाधितानुवृत्त्या iii. 77 ... 352
बाल i. 26 49
बालोन्मत्तादिसमत्वम् i. 26... 49
बिशालः v. 16 ... 400
बीज iv. 29, v. 15, vi. 67... 384 399, 570
बीजवत् i. 10 ... 29
बीजांकुरवत् v. 15, vi. 67... 399, 570
बुद्ध्यादि v. 126 . 509
बुद्ध i. 19 37

PAGE.

बुद्धिः ii. 13, ii. 19, v. 50, v. 121, v. 126 ... 246, 252, 431, 504, 509
बुद्धेः ii. 47 ... 276
बोधः i. 60 92
बोधात् iii. 63, v. 85, vi. 43, 337, 465, 545
ब्रह्म v. 16, v. 116 400, 497
ब्रह्मचर्ये iv. 19 ... 375
ब्रह्मबाधप्रसंगः v. 16 ... 400
ब्रह्मरूपता v. 116 ... 497

भ

भरतवत् iv. 8 ... 366
भविष्यत् i. 158 ... 224
भाग v. 73, v. 107 456, 488
भागगुणाभ्यां v. 107 ... 488
भागलाभः v. 73 ... 456
भागस्य v. 81 ... 462
भागयोगः v. 81 ... 462
भावः i. 31, i. 38, i. 44, i. 119, ii. 45, v. 37, v. 93, v. 114 ... 54, 59, 66, 171, 274, 419, 474, 495
भावना iii. 29 ... 304
भावनोपचयात् iii. 29 ... 304
भावप्रतीतेः v. 93 ... 474
भावमात्रे i. 41 ... 61
भावयोगः i. 119 ... 171
भावात् i. 118, i. 143, vi. 1 170, 198, 513
भावित्वात् v. 82 ... 463
भावे i. 40, i. 80, i. 119 60, 124, 171
भिद्यते i. 151 ... 210
भुक्तिः vi. 55 ... 557

PAGE.

भूत v. 84, v. 129 464, 511
भूतचैतन्यं v. 129 ... 511
भूतप्रकृतत्वं v. 84 ... 464
भूतानि i. 61 . 93
भूतियोगे iv. 32 . 386
भृत्य v. 115 496
भृत्यद्वारा v. 115 . 496
भृत्यवत् iii. 61 . 336
भृत्यवर्गेषु ii. 40 . 271
भेकीवत् iii. 16 ... 373
भेद ii. 24, v. 61 256, 444
भेदसिद्धौ ii. 24 ... 256
भेदाः iii. 41, v. 120 ... 312, 503
भेदात् ii. 27, iii. 43, v. 66 ... 258, 315, 449
भेदे v. 109 491
भोक्तृ i. 143, v. 121 ... 198, 504
भोक्तुः v. 114 ... 495
भोक्तृभोगायतनत्वं v. 121... 504
भोक्तृभावात् i. 143 ... 198
भोगः i. 104, v. 114, v. 121, vi. 59 ... 156, 495, 504, 560
भोगदेशकाललाभः vi. 59 ... 560
भोगात् iii. 8, iv. 27 ... 283, 382
भोगायतननिर्माणं v. 114 ... 495
भौतिकानि ii. 20 ... 253
भ्रान्तानां ii. 23 ... 256

म

मन्त्रवत् iii. 54 .. 327
मणिः ii. 35 268
मणिवत् i. 96 . 145
मदशक्तिवत् iii. 22 ... 297
मध्य iii. 77 352

PAGE.

मध्यविवेकतः iii. 77 ... 352
मध्ये iii. 50 325
मनः i. 71, ii. 26, ii. 40, vi. 25 ... ... 116, 257, 271, 531
मनसः v. 69... ... 454
मन्दानां v. 68 ... 453
मरण iii. 21, iii. 53 296, 327
मल ii. 28 259
मलिन iv. 29, iv. 30 ... 384
मलिन चेतसि iv. 29 ... 384
मलिनदर्पणवत् iv. 30 ... 384
महतः i. 61, vi. 66 93, 569
महत् i. 129, ii. 10, ii. 15 187, 242, 248
महदाख्यम् i. 71 ... 116
महदादिक्रमेण ii. 10 ... 242
महदादेः i. 129 ... 187
महान् i. 61 93
मातृपितृजं iii. 7 ... 282
मात्रस्य i. 62 ... 99
मात्राणि i. 61 ... 93
मात्रेभ्यः i. 61 ... 93
मान v. 98, vi. 4 471, 516
मायिकामायिकाभ्यां iii. 26 301
मुक्त i. 19, i. 93, i. 95, i. 157, v. 47, vi. 44... 37, 143, 144, 223, 429, 545
मुक्तबद्धयोः i. 93 ... 143
मुक्तस्य i. 86, vi. 17 131, 525
मुक्तात्मनः i. 95 ... 144
मुक्तामुक्तयेः v. 47 ... 429
मुक्तिः iii. 23, iii. 26, v. 74, v. 85, vi. 20... 298, 301, 457, 465, 527
मुक्तोपभोगः vi. 44 ... 545

PAGE.

मुनिवत् iv. 27 ... 382
मूर्तत्वात् i. 50 . 72
मूर्तत्वे iii. 13 . 290
मूल i. 67 . 111
मूलतः iii. 49 ... 325
मूलाभावात् i. 67 ... 111
मूलिकार्थो i. 16 . 17
मूले i. 67 . 111
मोक्षः i. 7 . 26
मोक्षवत् ii. 7 ... 239
मोक्षस्य i. 5 ... 22
मोक्षसाधनोपदेशविधिः i. 7 26
मोक्षार्थं ii. 1 ... 231
मोक्षेषु v. 116 .. 497
मोक्षौ iii. 71... .. 345
मंगल v. 1 388
मंगलाचरणं v. 1 . 388

य

यः i. 33 . 55
यज्ञ iv. 21 ... 377
यज्ञादेः v. 42 ... 425
यज्ञोपासकानां iv. 21 ... 377
यत् i. 87, i, 89, vi. 70 132, 138, 573
यथा vi. 6 517
यस्मिन् v. 50 ... 431
यावत् i. 158 ... 224
युक्तितः i. 59 ... 91
युगपत् i. 38 ... 59
युगपज्जायमानयोः i. 38 ... 59
योगः i. 55, i. 119, ii. 9, iii. 55, v. 13, v. 32, v. 36, v. 81 v. 86, v. 128, vi. 17 ... 77, 171, 241, 329, 398, 415, 417, 463, 463, 510, 525

PAGE.

योगतः i. 12, i. 13, iv. 22 31, 32, 378
योगवत् v. 82 ... 463
योगसिद्धयः v. 128 ... 510
योग्य v. 44 427
योग्यत्व vi. 33 ... 537
योग्यत्वाभावात् vi. 33 ... 537
योग्यायोग्येषु v. 44 ... 427
योगात् i. 19, i. 40, i. 51, i. 82, ii. 39, iii. 13, iii. 67, iv. 24, iv. 26, v. 8, v. 27, v. 71, v. 90, v. 102, v. 108, v. 91 ... 37, 60, 73, 126, 270, 290, 341, 380, 382, 382, 409, 455, 471, 482, 490, 492
योगिनां i. 90 ... 140
योगे ii. 47, iv. 9 v. 7, v. 14, v. 49, v. 119, vi. 37 ... 276, 367, 392, 398, 430, 501, 540
योगेन i. 80 124

र

रजः i. 61, iii. 50 93, 325
रज्जु iii. 66 339
रजोविशाला iii. 50 ... 325
रस ii 28 259
राग ii. 9, iii. 30, iv. 25, iv. 27 241, 304, 381, 382
रागविरागयोः ii. 9 ... 241
रागशान्तिः iv. 27 ... 382
रागात् v. 6 391
रागाहते v. 6 ... 391
रागादिभिः iv. 9 ... 367
रागिणां vi. 51 ... 553

PAGE.

रागोपहतिः iii. 30 .. 304
रागोपहते iv. 25 .. 381
राजपुत्रवत् iv. 1 ... 361
राज्ञः iii. 16 293
रूप i. 98, i. 160, ii. 28, iv. 21, v. 16, vi. 50 ... 147, 226, 259, 377, 471, 550
रूपता iv. 31, v. 116 385, 499
रूपत्वात् vi. 39 ... 542
रूपत्वं v. 93 ... 474
रूपत्वे v. 19, v. 66 403, 449
रूपनिबन्धात् v. 89 ... 471
रूपादिरसमलान्तः ii. 28 ... 259
रूपैः iii. 73 ... 346

ल

लक्षणं i. 8 . 28
लघ्वादिधर्मैः i. 128 ... 185
लघु i. 128 ... 185
लता v. 121 ... 504
लब्ध i. 29, i. 91, iv. 24 ... 53, 141, 380
लब्धातिशययोगात् v. 24 ... 380
लय i. 121, vi. 30 173, 535
लयविक्षेपयोः vi. 30 ... 535
लाभः v. 73, v. 80, vi. 9, vi. 34, vi. 59 456, 462, 520, 537, 560
लिंगं i. 124, iii. 9, vi. 69... 178, 284, 572
लिंगशरीर vi. 69 ... 572
लिंगात् i. 136, v. 61, v. 106 192, 444, 488
लिंगादिभिः v. 21 ... 404
लिंगानां iii. 16 ... 293
लीन i. 91 140

PAGE.

लीनवस्तुलब्धातिशयसंबन्धात् i. 91 140
लेशतः iii. 83 ... 537
लोकवत् ii. 40, ii. 46, ii. 47, iv. 15, v. 3, vi. 43 ... 271, 274, 276, 371, 390, 545
लोकस्य vi. 57 ... 559
लोके v. 40, vi. 56 423, 558
लोहवत् i. 99 ... 148
लंघनात् iv. 15 ... 371

व

वत्साय ii. 37 ... 269
वनस्पति v. 121 . 504
वह्निवत् v. 126 . 509
वन्हेः i. 60 ... 92
वयं i. 25 ... 48
वशात् i. 30 ... 54
वस्तु i. 44, i. 58, i. 91, v. 30 ... 66, 122, 140, 413
वस्तुकल्पनाप्रसक्तेः v. 30 ... 413
वस्तुत्वे i. 21... ... 45
वस्तुधर्मत्वात् i. 44 ... 66
बहुकल्पनाप्रसक्तेः v. 120 .. 503
बहुभिः iv. 9... ... 367
बहुशास्त्रगुरूपासने iv. 13 ... 369
वा i. 87, i. 91, i. 95, i. 97, i. 106, i. 123, i. 125, i. 133, ii. 1, ii. 4, ii. 60, iii. 62, iii. 65, iv. 7, iv. 24, v. 5, v. 29, v. 69, v. 95, v. 100, v. 104, vi. 68, vi. 70... 132, 140, 144, 147, 158, 177, 180, 190, 231, 236, 335, 336, 339, 365, 380, 391, 412, 454, 475, 479, 485, 571, 573.

PAGE.

वाक्यार्थे i. 98 ... 147
वाक्यार्थोपदेशः i. 98 ... 147
वाङ्मात्रं i. 58 ... 88
वाचकं v. 37... .. 419
वाच्य v. 37 .. 419
वाच्यवाचकभावः v. 37 ... 419
वाद v. 33 . 415
वादिनः i. 25 . . 48
वादि विप्रतिपत्तेः i. 111 ... 163
वामदेव i. 157 ... 223
वामदेववत् iv. 20 ... 376
वामदेवादि i. 157 ... 223
वायवः ii. 31 ... 262
वाह्य i. 28, i. 42, i. 63, v. 121 51, 62, 102, 504
वाह्यप्रतीतेः i. 42 ... 62
वाह्य बुद्धिकल्पना v. 121 ... 504
वाह्या भ्यन्तरयेाः i. 28 ... 51
वाह्याभ्यन्तराभ्यां i. 63 ... 102
वासनया v. 119 . 501
वासनाया ii. 3 ... 235
विकल्पै iii. 25 . 299
विक्षेपयेाः vi. 30 ... 535
विचित्रभोगानुपपत्तिः i. 17... 35
विजातीय द्वैता पत्तिः i. 22... 45
विज्ञानं i. 89 138
विज्ञानमात्रं i. 42 . 62
विदित i. 155 ... 221
विदित बन्धकारणस्य i. 155... 221
विद्यमानत्वात् v. 103 ... 483
विद्या v. 18 ... 402
विद्याबाधत्वे v. 18 ... 402
विधिः i. 7, i. 9 ...26, 28
विनश्यति i. 44 ... 66
विना iii. 45 . 322
विनाश ii. 22 . 255

PAGE.

विनाशादर्शनात् ii. 22 ... 255
विनाश्य i. 44 ... 66
विपर्ययात् i. 141, iii. 24 196, 299
विपर्ययभेदाः iii. 37 ... 310
विपरीतम् ii. 15 ... 248
विभुत्वं vi. 36 ... 539
विभुक्त ii. 1, vi. 43 231, 545
विभुक्तबोधात् vi. 43 ... 545
विभुक्तमोक्षार्थं ii. 1 .. 231
विमुक्ति v. 68, vi. 58 453, 558
विमुक्तिप्रशंसा v. 68 ... 453
विमुक्तिश्रुतिः vi. 58 ... 558
विमोकः i. 84 ... 128
विमोचयति iii. 73 ... 346
वियोगान्ताः v. 80 ... 462
विरज्यते iii. 66 ... 339
विरक्तस्य ii. 2, iv. 23 234, 380
विरागयोः ii. 9 ... 241
विरुद्ध i. 152 ... 212
विरुद्धोभयरूपा i. 23 ... 45
विरोधः i. 54, i. 113, i. 154, ii. 25, iv. 9 vi. 47, vi. 49, vi. 51 ... 75, 165, 216, 257, 367, 548, 549, 553
विरोधात् i. 36, vi. 34 58, 537
विरोचनवत् iv. 17 ... 374
विवाद i. 138 ... 193
विवादाभावात् i. 138 ... 193
विविक्त iii. 63 ... 337
विविक्तबोधात् iii. 63 ... 337
विवेक iii. 75 ... 348
विवेकतः iii. 77 ... 352
विवेकस्य i. 83 ... 128
विवेकसिद्धिः iii. 75 ... 348

PAGE.

विवेकात् iii. 84 ... 359
विवेचकाः vi. 8 ... 519
विशाला iii. 47, iii. 50 325, 325
विशिष्टस्य vi. 63 ... 565
विशेष i. 97, iii. 1, v. 75, v. 76, vi. 26 ... 147, 278, 458, 459, 531
विशेषकार्येषु i. 97 ... 147
विशेषगतिः v. 76 ... 459.
विशेषगुणोच्छित्तिः v. 75 ... 458
विशेषण v. 34 ... 416
विशेषणानर्थक्यप्रसक्तेः v. 34 416
विशेषात् i. 48, iii. 10 ... 71, 286
विशेषारंभः iii. 1 ... 278
विशेषे v. 120 ... 509
विषय i. 27, i. 108 51, 160
विषाद i. 127 ... 183
विस्मरणे iv. 16 . 375
विहित iii. 35 . 309
वीजांकुरवत् i. 122 ... 175
वीजात् iii. 3 . 79
वीरुध v. 121 . 504
वृक्ष v. 121 ... 504
वृक्षगुल्म लतौषधि वनस्पति तृणवीरुधादीनां v. 121 504
वृत्तयः ii. 33 ... 266
वृत्तिः ii. 31, ii. 32, iii. 31, v. 106, v. 109 ... 262, 264, 305, 488, 488
वृत्तितः v. 105 ... 487
वृत्तिनिरोधात् iii. 31 .. 305
वृत्तिसिद्धिः v. 106 ... 488
वेदस्य v. 41 . 423
वेदानां v. 45 . 428
वेदार्थ v. 40 . 423
वेदार्थप्रतीतेः v. 40 ... 423

PAGE.

वैकृतात् ii. 18 ... 251
वैचित्र्यात् iii. 51, v. 20, vi. 2, vi. 41 ... 326, 404, 514, 544
वैचित्र्यं vi. 41 .. 544
वैधर्म्यम् i. 127, i. 128... 183, 185
वैराग्य vi. 29 ... 533
वैराग्यात् iii. 36 ... 309
वैराग्याय vi. 51 ... 553
वैशिष्ट्ये v. 123 ... 506
वैशिष्ट्य श्रुतेः v. 123 ... 506
वैशिष्ट्यात् v. 42, v. 95...425, 475
वैशेषिक i. 25 ... 48
वैशेषिकादिवत् i. 25 ... 48
वैशम्याभ्यां vi. 42 ... 544
व्यक्तिभेदः iii. 10 ... 286
व्यतिरिक्तः i. 139, vi. 2... 195, 514
व्यतिरेकात् vi. 15, vi. 63 ... 524, 565
व्यपदेशः v. 110, v. 112 ... 491, 493
व्यपदेशात् i. 125, v. 110, vi. 3 ... 180, 491, 515
व्यभिचारात् i. 40 ... 60
व्यवच्छिद्यते v. 43 ... 420
व्यवधानात् i. 28 ... 51
व्यवस्था i. 29, v. 124 ... 53, 507
व्यवस्थातः i. 149, vi. 45...207, 546
व्यवहार i. 120 ... 172
व्यवहाराव्यवहारौ i. 120 ... 172
व्याघातात् v. 55 ... 437
व्यापकत्वं v. 69 ... 454
व्यापकत्वे vi. 59 ... 560
व्यापिनः i. 12 ... 31
व्याप्तिः v. 29 ... 412
व्यावृत्तं i. 160 ... 226
व्यावृत्त्या vi. 30 ... 535

PAGE.

व्युत्पत्त्या v. 43 ... 426
व्युत्पन्नस्य v. 40 . 423
व्योमवत् vi. 59 . 560

श

शक्य i. 117 . 169
शक्तस्य i. 117 ... 169
शक्यकरणात् i. 117 ... 169
शक्त्युद्भवानुद्भवाभ्याम् i. 11 30
शक्ति i. 11, v. 8, v. 13, v. 31, v. 32, v. 33, v. 36, v. 43, v. 51, v. 95 ... 30' 392, 398, 414, 415, 415, 417, 426, 432, 474
शक्तितः i. 132, v. 113 ... 189, 494
शक्तिभेदे ii. 24 . 256
शंखवत् iv. 10 ... 367
शब्दः i. 101, v. 37, v. 57, v. 58 ... ... 153, 419, 441, 442
शब्दनित्यत्वं v. 58 ... 442
शब्दार्थयोः v. 37 ... 419
शरीर i. 139, iii. 82, v. 102, vi. 69 ... ... 195, 356, 482, 572
शरीरस्य iii. 2 ... 279
शरिरादिव्यतिरिक्तः i. 139 ... 195
शान्तिः iv. 27 ... 382
शिला vi. 4 516
शिलापुत्रवद्धर्मिग्राहकमानबाधात् vi. 4 ... 516
शिष्ट v. 1 388
शिष्टाचारात् v. 1 . 388
शुक्र i. 10 29
शुक्रपटवत् i. 10 ... 29

PAGE.

शुकवत् iv. 25, iv. 26 ... 381, 382
शुद्ध i. 19 ... 37
शुद्धस्य iii. 29 ... 304
शून्यं i. 43, i. 44, v. 79 ... 64, 66, 461
श्येनवत् iv. 5 ... 364
श्रवणमात्रात् ii. 3 ... 235
श्रवण iv. 17 ... 374
श्रुघ्नस्थ i. 28 ... 51
श्रुघ्नस्थ पाटलिपुत्रस्थयोः i. 28 51
श्रुत्या i. 147 ... 203
श्रुति i. 36, i. 51, i. 54, i. 83, i. 154, ii. 21, iii. 86, v. 12, v. 21, vi. 34, vi. 51, vi. 58 ... 58, 73, 75, 128, 216, 254, 355, 396, 404, 537, 553, 558
श्रुतितः v. 1 ... 388
श्रुतिन्यायविरोधात् i. 36 ... 58
श्रुतिलिंगादिभिः v. 21 ... 404
श्रुतिविरोधः vi. 51 ... 553
श्रुतेः i. 5, i. 17, ii. 20, ii. 22, iii. 14, iii. 15, iv. 22, v. 15, v. 45, v. 70, v. 73, v. 84, v. 87, v. 123, vi. 10, vi. 17, vi. 32, vi. 59 ... ... 22, 121, 253, 255, 291, 293, 378, 399, 428, 455, 456, 464, 469, 506, 520, 525, 536, 560

ष

षट् i. 25, iv. 13, v. 85 ... 48, 369, 465
षट् पदवत् iv. 13 ... 369
षट् पदार्थनियमः v. 85 ... 465

PAGE.

षट् पदार्थ वादिवादिनः i. 25 48
षष्ठी vi. 3 515
षष्ठीव्यपदेशात् vi. 3 ... 513
षोडश v. 86... .. 466
षोडशादि v. 86 ... 466

स

स iii. 56 330
संकल्पिते iii. 28 .. 303
सक्रियत्वात् v. 70 ... 455
सक्रियं i. 124 . 178
सकृत् v. 28 ... 411
सकृद्ग्रहणात् v. 28 ... 411
संगापत्तिः v. 8 . 392
संग्रहः i. 26 . 49
संघात iii. 13 . 290
संघातयोगात् iii. 13 ... 290
संज्ञा v. 96 479
संज्ञामात्रं i. 68 . 111
संज्ञासंज्ञिसंबन्ध v. 96 ... 476
संज्ञि v. 96 476
सतः v. 53 434
सत् i. 89, v. 56, vi. 53 ... 138, 439, 556
सत्कार्य v. 60 ... 443
सत्कार्यसिद्धान्तः v. 60 ... 443
सत्तामात्रात् v. 9 ... 394
सत्यत्वं vi. 52 ... 554
सत्व i. 61 93
सत्वरजस्तमसां i. 61 .. 93
सत्वविशाला iii. 48 ... 325
सत्वस्य v. 59 ... 442
सत्वादीनां vi. 39 ... 542
सदसद्ख्यातिः v. 56 ... 439
सद्भावात् vi. 56 ... 558
सदुत्पत्तिः vi. 53 ... 556

PAGE.

सनन्दनाचार्यः vi. 69 ... 572
सन्निधानात् i. 96 ... 145
सप्तदश iii. 9 ... 284
सप्तभिः iii. 73 ... 346
सबीजं v. 117 ... 499
सम्प्रति iii. 6 ... 281
सम्बन्ध v. 11, v. 28, v. 37, v. 38, v. 96, v. 97, v. 98, v. 107 ... 395, 411, 419, 420, 476, 477, 477, 488
संबन्धात् i. 12, i. 91 ... 31, 140
संबन्धनित्यता v. 97 ... 477
संबन्धसिद्धिः v. 28, v. 38 ... 411, 420
संबन्धाभावात् v. 11 ... 395
संबन्धार्थं v. 107 ... 488
संभवात् i. 4 ... 21
संभवे i. 4 ... 21
संभवेत् ii. 44 ... 273
समत्वं i. 26 ... 49
समन्वयात् i. 131 ... 188
समवायः v. 99 ... 478
संबद्धं i. 89 138
संबन्धात् i. 161 ... 227
समाधि iv. 14, v. 116 ... 370, 497
समाधि सुषुप्तिमोक्षेषु v. 116, 497
समाधिहानिः iv. 14 ... 370
समान i. 46, i. 50, i. 69, ii. 42, iii. 53, v. 24, v. 36 ... 70, 72, 112, 276, 327, 406, 417
समानकर्मयोगे ii. 47 ... 276
समानत्वम् i. 55, i. 86, vi. 65 ... 77, 131, 568

PAGE.

समानधर्मापत्तौ i. 50 ... 72
समानन्यायात् v. 36 ... 417
समुच्चयः iii. 25 . 299
समुच्चयविकल्पौ iii. 25 ... 299
संयोगाः v. 80 .. 462
सर्पति v. 107 . 488
सर्पवत् iv. 12 ... 369
सर्व i. 4, i. 5, i. 12, i. 16, i. 88, i. 116, iii. 56, v. 9, v. 78, v. 104 ... 21, 22, 31, 120, 137, 169, 330, 394, 460, 485
सर्वं iii. 29, v. 72 ... 304, 456
सर्वकर्त्ता iii. 56 ... 330
सर्वत्र i. 116, i. 159, vi. 36 ... 169, 225, 539
सर्वदा i. 116 ... 169
सार्वप्रत्तेः v. 104 ... 485
सर्वसम्बन्धात् i. 12 ... 31
सर्वसिद्धेः i. 88 ... 137
सर्वासंभवात् i. 4, i. 116 ... 21, 169
सर्ववित् iii. 56 . 330
सर्वेषु v. 112 . 493
सर्वैश्वर्यम् v. 9 . 394
सर्वोच्छित्तिः v. 78 ... 460
सर्वोत्कर्षश्रुतेः i. 5 ... 22
सर्वोपादानम् i. 76 ... 120
संवित्तिः v. 27 . 409
ससंगत्वात् iii. 72 ... 345
संस्कार ii. 42, iii. 33, v. 120 ... ... 272, 357, 503
संस्कारभेदा v. 120 ... 503
संस्कारलेशतः iii. 83 ... 357

PAGE.

संस्क्रियते i. 33 ... 55
संसार v. 15 ... 399
सांसिद्धिकं v. 111 ... 492
संसृतिः iii. 3, iii. 16 ... 279, 293
संहत i. 66, i. 140 ... 108, 195
संहतपरार्थत्वात् i. 66, i. 140 ... 108, 195
सांकल्पिक v. 111 ... 492
साक्षात् i. 161 ... 227
साक्षित्वं i. 148, i. 161 ... 205, 227
सात्त्विकं ii. 18 ... 251
सादि v. 15 399
सादित्वं v. 19 ... 403
सादिसंसारश्रुतेः v. 15 ... 399
सादृश्यं v. 94 ... 475
साधकं i. 87, vi. 48 ... 132, 548
साधकतमत्व ii. 39 ... 270
साधकतमत्वगुणयोगात् ii. 39 270
साधकाभावात् vi. 48 ... 548
साधन i. 7. i. 138, v. 60 26, 193, 443
साधना vi. 1 ... 513
साध्यत्व i. 85 ... 129
साध्यत्वाविशेषात् i. 85 ... 129
साध्यत्वेन i. 82 ... 126
साधर्म्यं i. 128 ... 185
सामान्य ii. 31 ... 262
सामान्यतः i. 103 ... 154
सामान्यकरणवृत्तिः ii. 31 ... 262
सामान्यस्य v. 91 ... 471
सामान्यादेः i. 125 ... 180
सामान्येन i. 138 ... 193

PAGE.

साम्य vi. 42 ... 544
साम्यावस्था i. 61 . 93
साम्यवैषम्याभ्यां vi. 42 ... 544
सारादानं iv. 13 ... 369
सांसिद्धिकं iii. 20 ... 295
सांहत्ये, iii. 22, v. 129 ... 297, 511
सांहित्यं v. 29 . 412
साहित्यात् i. 135 ... 191
सिद्ध i. 98, v. 59, v. 60 ... 147, 442, 443
सिद्धयः v. 128 ... 510
सिद्धरूपबोधधृतत्वात् i. 98... 147
सिद्धसाधनं v. 60 ... 443
सिद्धस्य i. 95, i. 147 ... 144, 203
सिद्धा iii. 57 ... 331
सिद्धान्त i. 21, v. 60 45, 443
सिद्धान्तहानिः i. 21 ... 45
सिद्धिः i. 2, i. 78, i. 80, i. 82, i. 93, i. 102, i. 103, i. 125, i. 153, ii. 3, ii. 5, ii. 8, iii. 31, ii. 32, iii. 40, iii. 44, iii. 57, iii. 75, iii. 79, iii. 83, iv. 19, v. 6, v. 10, v. 21, v. 24, v. 28, v. 38, v. 44, v. 106, vi. 11, vi. 29, vi. 57, vi. 64...19, 122, 124, 126, 143, 153, 154, 180, 213, 235, 237, 240, 305, 306, 312, 319, 331, 348, 354, 357, 375, 391, 394, 404, 406, 411, 420, 427, 488, 521, 533, 559, ... 567
सिद्धिवत् iv. 32, v. 128 ... 386, 510

PAGE.

सिद्धेः i. 37, i. 88, i 106, i. 112, i. 137, ii. 2, ii. 6, v. 2, v. 100, v. 105, v. 113, vi. 51 ... 58, 137, 158, 164, 193, 234, 238, 389, 479, 487, 494, 553

सिद्धौ i. 88, ii. 24, v. 14, v. 36, vi. 46, vi. 49, vi. 58 ... ... 137, 256, 398, 417, 547, 549, 558

सुखं iii. 34, iv. 5, v. 27, vi. 9, vi. 24 ... 308, 364, 409, 520, 530

सुखदुःखी iv. 5 ... 364

सुखलाभाभावात् vi. 9 ... 520

सुखसंवित्तिः v. 27 ... 409

सुखात् vi. 6... ... 517

सुखी iv. 11, iv. 12, vi. 7 368, 369, 518

सुषुप्ति i. 148, v. 116 ... 205, 497

सुषुप्त्याद्यसाक्षित्वम् i. 148, 205

सूदवत् iii. 63 ... 337

सूपकारवत् iii. 16 ... 293

सृष्टिः ii. 9, iii. 47, iii. 58, iii. 63, iii. 66, vi. 40, vi. 41, vi. 43 ... 241, 324, 333, 337, 339, 543, 544, 545

सृष्टिनिवृत्तिः iii. 36 ... 337

सृष्टिवैचित्र्यात् vi. 41 ... 544

सृष्टेः ii. 11 244

सौक्ष्म्यात् i. 109 ... 162

स्थान vi. 31 ... 536

स्थाननियमः vi. 31 ... 536

स्थितेः i. 58 88

PAGE.

स्थिरः i. 33, i. 34, iii. 34, vi. 24 ... 55, 56, 308, 530

स्थिरकार्यसिद्धेः i. 34 ... 56

स्थिरता v. 91 . 492

स्थिरतायोगात् v. 91 ... 492

स्थिरसुखं vi. 24 ... 530

स्थिरसुखमासनम् iii. 34 ... 308

स्थूल i. 61, iii. 7, v. 103, 93, 282, 483

स्थूलभूतानि i. 61 ... 93

स्थूलात् i. 62 .. 99

स्फोट v. 57... .. 441

स्फोटात्मकः v. 57 ... 441

स्मृत्या ii. 43 . 273

स्मृतेः v. 122 ... 506

स्यात् vi. 13 ... 523

स्व iii. 35, vi. 67 309, 570

स्वकर्म iii. 35 ... 309

स्वकर्मणा iii. 32 ... 306

स्वतः ii. 44, iii. 58, v. 51 273, 333, 432

स्वप्न iii. 26 ... 301

स्वप्नजागराभ्यां iii. 26 ... 301

स्वभावतः i. 7 ... 26

स्वभावस्य i. 8, i. 19 ... 28, 37

स्वभावात् iii. 61 ... 336

स्वरूप v. 33 . 415

स्वरूपतः v. 42 . 425

स्वरूपशक्ति v. 33 . 415

स्ववचः v. 55 .. 437

स्ववचोव्याघातात् v. 55 ... 437

स्वस्थः ii. 34 ... 267

स्वस्वामिभावः vi. 67 ... 570

स्वामिभावः vi. 67 ... 570

स्वामी v. 115 ... 496

स्वाम्यधिष्ठितिः v. 115 ... 496

PAGE.

स्वातंत्र्यात् iii. 12 ... 288
स्वार्थं ii. 1 ... 231
स्वार्थलक्षणं ii. 30 ... 261
स्वाश्रमविहितकर्मानुष्ठानं iii. 35 309
स्वोपकारात् v. 3 ... 390

ह

हान i. 108 160
हानं i. 57 86

PAGE.

हानिः i. 21, iii. 74, iv. 14, vi. 37 ... 45, 347, 370, 540
हाने i. 57, i. 75, i. 133 ... 86, 118, 190
हानोपदानाभ्यां i. 108 ... 160
हि i. 33, iii. 56, vi. 62 ... 55, 330, 564
हेमुमत् i. 124 ... 178
हेयः i. 4, iii. 52 21, 326
हेयहानं iv. 23 ... 380
हंस iv. 23 . 380
हंसक्षीरवत् iv. 23 . 380

Index of Words in Kapila Sutram (Tatva Samasa).

	Page.
अतः 1 ...	... 2
अथ, 1, ...	... 2
अध्यात्मं 7 ...	... 9
अधिदैवं 7 ...	... 9
अधिभूतं 7 ...	... 9
अनुग्रह 17 ...	... 17
अनुभूयते 22 ...	... 20
अभिबुद्धयः 8	... 10
अविद्याः 12	... 13
अशक्तिः 13	... 14
अष्टधा 15 ...	... 15
अष्टाविंशतिधा 13	... 14
अष्टौ 2 ...	... 3
एतत् 22 ...	... 20
कथयामि 2	... 3
कर्मयोनयः 9	... 11
कर्मात्मनः 11	... 12
कृतकृत्यः 22	... 20
च 7 ...	... 9
चतुर्दशविधः 18	... 17
ज्ञात्वा 22 ...	... 20
तत्वे 1 ...	... 2
त्रिविधं 21 ...	... 19
त्रिविधः 19, 20	...18, 19
त्रिविधेन 22	... 20
तु 3 ...	... 4
तुष्टिः 14 ...	... 14

	Page.
पंच 8, 9, 10, 11, 12	...10, 11, 12, 13
त्रैगुण्यम् 5 ...	... 7
दश 16 ...	16
दुःखेन 22	20
न 22 ...	20
नवधा 14 ...	14
पंचपर्वा 12	13
पर्वा 12 ...	13
पुनः 22 ...	20
पुरुषः 4 ..	5
प्रकृतयः 2 ...	3
प्रतिसञ्चरः 6	8
प्रमाणाम् 21	19
बन्धः 19 ...	18
भूतसर्गः 18	17
वायवः 10 ...	12
मोक्षः 20 ...	19
मूलिकार्थाः 16	16
विकारः 3	4
षोडशकः 3	4
संचरः 6 ...	8
सम्यक् 22	20
समासः 1	2
सर्गः 17	17
स्यात् 22 ...	20

APPENDIX III.

INDEX OF AUTHORITIES QUOTED.

INDEX OF AUTHORITIES QUOTED.

N.B.—The numbers refer to the pages.

PAGES.

Atharva-Śiras-Upaniṣat 24
Amara-Kośa 44, 224, 262
Îśa-Upaniṣat ... 84, 300
Ṛig-Veda 555
Aitareya-Upaniṣat 217
Kaṭha-Upaniṣat 17, 41, 73, 160, 216, 219, 221, 306, 332, 408, 458, 484
Kâlâgni-Rudra-Upaniṣat 128
Kâlikâ-Purâṇam 200
Kâvyâdarśa 551
Kumâra-Sambhava 518
Kûrma-Purâṇa ... 7, 27, 69, 81, 113, 237, 238, 268, 283, 521
Kena-Upaniṣat 447
Kaivalya-Upaniṣat 25, 130
Garuḍa-Purâṇa 310, 362
Garbha-Upaniṣat 97
Gauḍapâda's Mâṇḍukya-Kârikâ 69, 89
Chhândogya-Upaniṣat ...2, 17, 23, 58, 102, 104, 122, 123, 127, 146, 171, 189, 192, 216, 217, 233, 238, 253, 293, 304, 374, 379, 397, 400, 409, 445, 447, 449, 492, 493, 505, 556, 568
Jâbâla-Upaniṣat 1
Taittirîya-Âraṇyaka 378
Taittirîya-Upaniṣat ... 220, 237, 243, 292, 452, 453
Dhâtu-Pâṭha 490, 566
Nâradîya-Purâṇa 344
Nâradîya-Smṛiti 356
Nṛisiṃha-Tâpanî-Upaniṣat 39,64
Nyâya-Bindu 139
Nyâya-Sûtram 81, 82, 286, 358, 433, 466, 467, 468
Pañchaśikhâ-Sûtram 184
Padma-Purâṇa ... 9,46
Parâśara-Upa-Purâṇa 7
Pâṇini-Sûtram ... 228
Prabodha-Chandra-Udaya ... 546

PAGES.

Praśna-Upaniṣat 97, 243
Bṛihat-Araṇyaka-Upaniṣat ... 3, 5, 20, 34, 76, 90, 104, 110, 114, 124, 133, 171, 178, 200, 203, 204, 229, 233, 234, 238, 242, 247, 254, 255, 259, 261, 292, 299, 330, 348, 349, 350, 354, 355, 376, 393, 397, 400, 402, 405, 432, 435, 449, 451, 453, 530, 547, 551, 552, 555
Brahma-Bindu-Upaniṣat ... 69, 74, 89, 216, 218, 409, 556, 562
Brahma-Sûtram ... 8, 10, 46, 84, 85, 104, 107, 124, 206, 215, 243, 263, 280, 434, 536
Bhagavat-Gîtâ ... 4, 6, 11, 41, 74, 79, 80, 88, 137, 145, 170, 376, 555, 558, 567, 575
Bhâgvata-Purâṇam 129, 251, 365, 533, 570, 574
Matsya-Purâṇam 250
Manu-Saṃhitâ ... 108, 138, 279, 287, 317, 351, 365, 469, 484
Mahâ-Nârâyaṇa-Upaniṣat 300, 378
Mahâ-Bhâratam ... 6, 7, 11, 74, 81, 114, 231, 250, 285, 368, 369, 372, 483, 484, 574
Mâṇḍukya-Kârikâ ... *Vide* Gauḍapâda's Mâṇḍukya-Kârikâ.
Mârkaṇḍeya-Purâṇa 25, 107, 252, 370
Muṇḍaka-Upaniṣat ... 219, 243, 255, 263, 322, 342, 445, 464, 538
Maitrî-Upaniṣat 58, 97, 171, 192, 254
Yoga-Bhâśyam 17, 18, 36, 120, 134, 150, 176, 305
Yoga-Vâśiṣṭham 18, 105, 134, 173, 203, 268, 290
Yoga-Sûtram ... 1, 14, 17, 22, 41, 42, 80, 81, 84, 103, 109, 120, 134, 189, 236, 266, 267, 308, 320, 329, 338, 352, 358, 519, 527, 534, 535
Râmâyanam 365
Linga-Purâṇa 64, 104
Vâyu-Purâṇa 250
Viṣṇu-Purâṇa ...5, 8, 26, 66, 99, 100, 101, 110, 113, 157, 176, 183, 187, 214, 367, 372, 382, 383, 384, 440, 466, 516, 519, 524
Vedânta-Sâra 204
Vedânta-Sûtram—*Vide* Brahma-Sûtram.
Vaiśeṣika-Sûtram 465
Sâśvata 508
Siśupâlavadha 157
Śulika-Upaniṣat 50

	Pages.
Śvetâśvatara-Upaniṣat	11, 25, 73, 74, 76, 114, 204, 208, 300, 337, 376, 396, 397, 399, 457, 514, 547, 566
Sarva-Darśana-Saṃgraha	44
Sâṃkhya-Kârikâ ...	24, 40, 78, 93, 98, 129, 161, 171, 179, 182, 183, 186, 190, 197, 199, 230, 251, 262, 264, 270, 282, 283, 289, 299, 311, 314, 318, 321, 323, 324, 326, 328, 335, 344, 345, 346, 351
Sâṃkhya-Tattva-Kaumudî	23, 265
Sâṃkhya-Sûtram ...	13, 14, 18, 79, 98, 126, 127, 134, 198, 211, 389, 498
Saura-Purâṇa	39, 50
Quotations not traced ...	3, 12, 19, 24, 26, 39, 50, 58, 69, 71, 81, 83, 84, 87, 90, 95, 98, 108, 112, 113, 115, 117, 130, 139, 142, 144, 146, 152, 159, 170, 200, 201, 205, 207, 219, 221, 223, 226, 227, 233, 246, 247, 260, 287, 288, 293, 328, 332, 355, 357, 364, 368, 370, 371, 377, 405, 407, 408, 428, 436, 438, 440, 444, 449, 452, 453, 457, 459, 462, 474, 489, 494, 499, 505, 506, 521, 526, 538, 543, 546, 552, 567.

APPENDIX IV.

CATALOGUE OF SOME OF THE IMPORTANT WORKS ON THE SÂMKHYA.

A CATALOGUE OF SOME OF THE IMPORTANT WORKS ON THE SÂMKHYA.

A List of Recognised Text-Books of the Sâṃkhya School (Taken from Fitz-Edward Hall's Collection).

1. Sâṃkhya-Pravachana-Sûtram attributed to Ṛisi Kapila.
2. Sâṃkhya-Pravachana-Sûtra-Vṛitti by Aniruddha.
3. Sâṃkhya-Pravachana-Sûtra-Vṛitti-Sârah by Mahâdeva Sarasvatî, more commonly known as Vedântin Mahâdeva.
4. Sâṃkhya-Pravachana-Bhâṣyam by Vijñâna Bhikṣu.
5. Laghu-Sâṃkhya-Sûtra-Vṛitti by Nâgoji Bhatta or Nâgeśa Bhatta, surnamed as Upâdhyâya.
6. Tattva-Samâsaḥ, attributed to Ṛisi Kapila.
7. Sâṃkhya-Taraṅgaḥ, a Commentary on No. 1, by Viśveśvaradatta Miśra, ascetically called Deva Tîrtha.
8. Sarvopakâriṇî, a Commentary on No. 6. Author is not known.
9. Sâṃkhya-Sûtra-Vivaraṇam, ditto. ditto.
10. Sâṃkhya-Krama-Dîpikâ, also called Sâṃkhyalaṅkarah and Sâṃkhya-Sûtra-Prakṣepikâ, ditto. ditto.
11. Tattva-Yâthârthya-Dîpanam, ditto, by Bhâvâ Ganeśa Dîkṣita.
12. Tattva-Samâsa-Vyâkhyâ, by Kṣemânanda.
13. Sâṃkhya-Kârikâ, also called Saptatih, by Îśvara Kṛiṣṇa.
14. Sâṃkhya-Karikâ-Bhâṣyam, by Gauḍapâda.
15. Sâṃkhya-Tattva-Kaumudî, shortly called Tattva-Kaumudî, by Vâchaspati Miśra.
16. An exposition of No. 14, by Yati Bhâratî.
17. Tattvârnavaḥ, otherwise called Tattvâmṛita-Prakṣinî, a Commentary on No. 14, by Râghavânanda Sarasvatî.
18. Tattva-Chandraḥ, ditto, by Nârâyaṇa Tîrtha Yati.
19. Kaumudî-Prabhâ, ditto, by Svapneśvara.
20. Sâṃkhya-Tattva-Vilâsaḥ, also called Sâṃkhya-Vṛitti-Prakâśaḥ and Sâṃkhyârtha-Sâṃkhyâyikâ, by Raghunâtha Tarka Vâgîśa Bhaṭṭâchârya.
21. Sâṃkhya-Chandrikâ, a Commentary on No. 12, by Nârâyaṇa Tîrtha.
22. Sâṃkhya-Sâra-Vivekaḥ, by Vijñâna Bhikṣu.
23. Sâṃkhya-Tattva-Pradîpaḥ, by Kavirâja Yati or Kavirâja Bhikṣu.
24. Sâṃkhyârtha-Tattva-Pradîpikâ, by Bhatta Keśava.
25. Sâṃkhya-Tattva-Vibhâkaraḥ, perhaps by Vansîdhara.
26. Sâṃkhya-Kaumudî, by Râmkṛiṣṇa Bhaṭṭâchârya.
27. Râja-Vârtikam, attributed to Raṇaraṅga Malla, king of Dhârâ.

APPENDIX V.

TATTVA-SAMÂSA OR KÂPILA-SÚTRAM.

APPENDIX VI.

SÂMKHYA-KÂRIKÂ OF IS'VARAKṚIṢṆA.

TABLE OF CONTENTS.

PAGES.

Kârikâ I.

The problem of Evil or Suffering ... 1
Pain is threefold... ... 1
Deliverance from Pain is Release ... 1
Pain includes *possible* pain also 2
The Sâṃkhya is the only means of deliverance ... 2
Its effect is certain and permanent 2
Ordinary remedies produce temporary results only ... 2

Kârikâ II.

Scriptural means also are defective 2
The Sâṃkhya consists in discriminative knowledge of the Subject, Puruṣa, and the Object, the Manifest and the Unmanifest ... 3

Kârikâ III.

The Subject is Puruṣa 3
He is neither an evolvent nor an evolute 4
The Unmanifest is the Root Evolvent, Prakṛiti ... 4
She is not an evolute 4
The Manifest comprises Mahat, Ahaṃkâra, and the five Tanmâtras which are evolutes as well as evolvents, and the eleven Indriyas and the five Gross Elements which are evolutes only and not evolvents 4

Kârikâ IV.

The above twenty-five Tattvas have to be known 4
Sources of knowledge are Perception, Inference, and Testimony... 4
All other means of knowledge are included in the above ... 4

Kârikâ V.

Perception defined 5
Inference is threefold ... 5
Inference defined 5
Testimony defined 5
Process of perceptual cognition described 5
Threefold inference described 5

Pages.

Kârikâ VI.

Objects are either sensible or super-sensible. 6

Super-sensible objects are proved from Inference and from Testimony 6

Kârikâ VII.

Prakṛiti and Puruṣa are not objects of Perception 7

Perception is not the sole test of reality 7

Admittedly existent things are not perceived 7

Causes which obstruct perception 7

Kârikâ VIII.

Prakṛiti, being subtile, is non-perceptible 7

Prakṛiti is proved from her products 7

Mahat, etc. are the products of Prakṛiti... 7

They both resemble and differ from Prakṛiti ... 7

Kârikâ IX.

Effect infers *some* cause, and not a particular one 8

But the existence of the Pradhâna has to be proved ... 9

The theories of effect examined 9

The existent is not produced from the non-existent... ... 9

Effects are not the Vivarta or revolutions of a single existence ... 9

The non-existent is not produced from the existent 9

The existent is produced from the existent ... 9

The effect is identical with the cause 9

Reasons for the doctrine 9

Kârikâ X.

The differences between the Manifest and the Unmanifest ... 9

Kârikâ XI.

The resemblances between them 10

The differences between them and Puruṣa 10

Their resemblances 10

A doubt as to the multiplicity of Puruṣa removed ... 11

Kârikâ XII.

The Guṇas are Sattva, Rajas, and Tamas 12

Their Svarûpa or essential form described 12

What objects they fulfil 12

What functions they mutually perform 12

How the Guṇas subserve one another 12

How they co-exist throughout the Universe ... 13

Pages.

Kârikâ XIII.
The respective properties of the Guṇas stated 13
These are contrary to one another 13
How contraries can co-operate towards a common end 13
The example of the lamp 13

Kârikâ XIV.
Proof of the properties of the Unmanifest 14
Proof of the Unmanifest 15

Kârikâs XV-XVI.
Proof of the Unmanifest continued 15
The first transformation of the Unmanifest are the Guṇas ... 16
How a single cause accounts for the diversity in Creation ... 16
The transformations of the Guṇas are homogeneous and heterogeneous 16
The example of the rain-water ... 17

Kârikâ XVII.
Proof of Puruṣa 17
Puruṣa is not an aggregate 17

Kârikâ XVIII.
Proof of the multiplicity of Puruṣa 18

Kârikâ XIX.
Proof of the Sâṃkhya conception of the nature of Puruṣa ... 18

Kârikâ XX.
The seeming agency of Puruṣa is a reflection of the real agency of the Manifest 19
The seeming intelligency of the Manifest is a reflection of the real intelligence of Puruṣa 19
Their mutual reflection takes place through conjunction ... 19

Kârikâ XXI.
The object of their conjunction is the exhibition of the Pradhâna to Puruṣa, and the isolation of Puruṣa 20
The example of the halt and the blind 20
Creation is through conjunction 20

Kârikâ XXII.
The evolutes of Prakṛiti 21
Their inter-relation 21
The order of their evolution... 21

Pages.

Kârikâ XXIII.

Buddhi defined 22
Its products are Sâttvic and Tâmasic 22
The Sâttvic ones are virtue, knowledge, dispassion, and power 22
The Tâmasic ones are the opposite ... 22
Stages of dispassion explained 22
"Power" explained 23
"Sâttvic" and "Tâmasic" explained 23

Kârikâ XXIV.

Ahaṃkâra defined 23
The creation of Ahaṃkâra is twofold: the eleven Indriyas and the five Tan-mâtras 23
Abhimâna explained 23

Kârikâ XXV.

From Ahaṃkâra, dominated by Sattva, are the Indriyas ... 24
From Ahaṃkâra, dominated by Tamas, are the Tan-mâtras ... 24
The part Rajas plays in the evolution of the products of Ahaṃkâra 24
Terms "Vaikṛita," "Bhûtâdi," and "Taijasa" explained ... 24

Kârikâ XXVI.

The Indriyas are those of Cognition and of Action ... 24
Names of the two classes of Indriyas given .. 24

Kârikâ XXVII.

Manas is the Indriya both of Cognition and of Action ... 25
The uncommon function of Manas is Saṃkalpa or Imagination 25
Cause of the variety of the Indriyas and of external objects ... 26
Process of sensuous cognition referred to 26

Kârikâ XXVIII.

What functions the Indriyas severally perform ... 26

Kârikâ XXIX.

The common and uncommon functions of the three Internal Indriyas 27
The Internal Indriyas are Buddhi, Ahaṃkâra, and Manas ... 27
The vital airs are produced from them, and not from the elemental Air 27

Pages.

Kârikâ XXX.

In perception, there is the joint operation of the three Internal Indriyas and one of the external ones... 27
Their functions may be successive as well as simultaneous ... 28
In inference, revelation, and recollection, there is the joint operation of the three Internal Indriyas only 28
Their functions may be successive as well as simultaneous ... 28
Inference, revelation, and recollection must follow perception ... 28

Kârikâ XXXI.

How the Indriyas come to act jointly and in harmony ... 28
Theory of some sort of sensuous resonance 28
The Indriyas act spontaneously 28
The purpose of Puruṣa is the final cause of their activity ... 28

Kârikâ XXXII.

The Indriyas are thirteen in number ... 29
Their general functions and the effect thereof ... 29

Kârikâ XXXIII.

There are three Internal Indriyas and ten external ones 30
The latter are object to the former 30
In what sense they are object 30
The external Indriyas operate at time present ... 30
The Internal ones at times past, present and future ... 30

Kârikâ XXXIV.

The objects of the Indriyas of cognition are both gross sound, etc., and subtile sound, etc., in the form of the Tan-mâtras ... 30
Sound is the only object of Speech 30
The other Indriyas of action have sound and all the rest as their object 30

Kârikâ XXXV.

The Internal Indriyas reach to all objects, through the external ones 31
The former are compared to a house of which the latter may be said to be the gates 31

Kârikâ XXXVI.

The example of the lamp repeated ... 31
The external Indriyas present all objects to Buddhi... 31
Puruṣa can experience objects through all, in Buddhi only ... 31

Pages.

Kârikâ XXXVII.
Buddhi discriminates the subtile difference between Prakṛiti and Puruṣa 32
Buddhi is supreme among the Indriyas 32

Kârikâ XXXVIII.
The Tan-mâtras are indiscernibles 32
The Gross Elements are their products 32
They are discernibles 32
Nature of the Tan-mâtras explained 32

Kârikâ XXXIX.
The discernibles enumerated 33
Gross and Subtile Bodies distinguished 33

Kârikâ XL.
Character of the Subtile Body described 34
The cause of its migration stated 34

Kârikâ XLI.
The Subtile Body ever seeks a Gross one 35
The doctrine of an intermediate Body called Vehicular ... 35

Kârikâ XLII.
The migration of the Subtile Body : the example of the dramatic performer 35
Its causes : the Bhâvas 36

Kârikâ XLIII.
Bhâvas are instinctive, essential, and acquired 36
These explained 37

Kârikâ XLIV.
Result of virtue 37
Result of vice 37
Result of knowledge 37
Result of ignorance or error 37
Bondage is threefold : Prâkṛitika, Vaikṛitika, and Dâkṣiṇaka ... 37
Bondage described 37

Kârikâ XLV. ... ...
Result of dispassion 38
Result of passion 38
Result of power 38
Result of weakness 38

Pages.

Kârikâ XLVI.

Pratyaya-Sarga explained 38
Its divisions are Error, Incapacity, Complacency, and Perfection 39
Their sub-divisions are fifty 39
The cause of this diversity explained 39

Kârikâ XLVII.

There are five kinds of Error 39
Twenty-eight kinds of Incapacity 39
Nine kinds of Complacency 39
Eight kinds of Perfection 39

Kârikâ XLVIII.

The sub-divisions of Error 39
A-Vidyâ has eight varieties 40
Asmitâ has eight 40
Râga has ten 40
Dveṣa has eighteen 40
Abhiniveśa has eighteen ... 40

Kârikâ XLIX.

The sub-divisions of Incapacity: ... 40
Eleven injuries of the eleven Indriyas 40
Seventeen injuries of Buddhi 40
The injuries of Buddhi denote the contrary states of Complacencies and Perfections 40

Kârikâ L.

The sub-divisions of Complacency: ... 40
Internal five 40
External five ... 40

Kârikâ LI.

The sub-divisions of Perfection 41
Error, Incapacity, and Complacency are obstacles to Perfection 41

Kârikâ LII.

Creation is twofold; from Buddhi and from the Tan-mâtras ... 42
Why a two-fold creation is necessary 42

Pages.

Kârikâ LIII.
The sub-divisions of Elemental Creation 42
Celestial beings are of eight kinds ... 42
The grovelling are of five kinds 42
The human is of one kind 43

Kârikâ LIV.
Worlds higher, lower, and intermediate characterised 43

Kârikâ LV.
There is suffering in the higher worlds also ... 43
Pain is universal 43
So long as the Subtile Body remains, there can be no escape from pain 43

Kârikâ LVI.
Prakṛiti's creation is individualistic ... 44
For the release of each respective Puruṣa 44
And utterly unselfish 44

Kârikâ LVII.
Prakṛiti's activity is spontaneous 44
Purposive activity is seen in unintelligent things 45
The example of the secretion of milk for the calf ... 45
Interposition of an Îśvara is impossible ... 45

Kârikâ LVIII.
Spontaneity of Prakṛiti further illustrated 45
To act for the release of Puruṣa is an inner necessity of the nature of Prakṛiti 46

Kârikâ LIX.
How Prakṛiti's activity ceases spontaneously ... 46
The example of a fair dancer ... 46

Kârikâ LX.
The unselfishness of Prakṛiti demonstrated ... 46

Kârikâ LXI.
How Prakṛiti does not energise over again, in regard to the released Puruṣa... 47
The example of a lady of high birth 47

Kârikâ LXII.
Bondage, transmigration, and release are really of Prakṛiti and not of Puruṣa 47

Pages.

Kârikâ LXIII.
How Prakṛiti herself binds and releases herself ... 47
Virtue, dispassion, and power, without knowledge, avail not ... 47
Kârikâ LXIV.
How discriminative knowledge can be fully developed 48
What is perfect development of knowledge ... 48
Kârikâ LXV.
Relation of Prakṛiti and Puruṣa after release ... 48
Kârikâ LXVI.
After release, there remains still conjunction of Prakṛiti and Puruṣa 49
Their conjunction, as such, is not the cause of creation 49
The purpose of creation is to free Puruṣa from bondage ... 49
Kârikâ LXVII.
Jîvan-mukti, or release in life, stated and explained 49
Perfect knowledge kills the germ of re-birth 49
The Body is sustained by Prârabdha Karma which originated it 50
Prârabdha and other kinds of Karma explained ... 50
Kârikâ LXVIII.
When a Jîvan-mukta is finally released 50
Kârikâ LXIX.
The origin of the Sâṃkhya Śâstra is from Kapila ... 51
Kârikâ LXX.
The tradition of the Sâṃkhya Śâstra: 51
Kapila taught it to Asuri, and Âsuri to Pañchaśikha 51
Pañchaśikha elaborated it in various ways ... 51
Kârikâ LXXI.
How Iśvarakṛiṣṇa got it 52
The Sâṃkhya-Kârikâ is a compendium of the original Śâstras ... 52
Kârikâ LXXII.
The Sâṃkhya-Kârikâ is also called the Saptati or Of Seventy verses 53
The Sâṃkhya-Pravachana-Sûtram is also called the Ṣaṣṭi-Tantra or Of sixty Topics 53
The Saptati compared with the Ṣaṣṭi-Tantra ... 53
The sixty topics enumerated ... 53

criminative knowledge can be fully developed

perfect development of knowledge ...

V.

of Prakriti and Puruṣa after release is ...

VI.

lease, there remains still conjunction of Prakriti

a ...

njunction, as such, is not the cause of creation

pose of creation is to free Puruṣa from bondage

VII.

ukti, or release in life, stated and explained

nowledge kills the germ of re-birth ...

y is sustained by Prârabdha Karma which origina

ha and other kinds of Karma explained ...

VIII.

Jîvan-mukta is finally released ...

X.

in of the Sâṃkhya Śâstra is from Kapila

X.

ition of the Sâṃkhya Śâstra ...

aught it to Âsuri, and Âsuri to Pañchaśikha

ikha elaborated it in various ways ...

XI.

arakriṣṇa got it

khya-Kârikâ is a compendium of the original Śâstras

THE SÂMKHYA-KÂRIKÂ.

The Sâṃkhya is the only means of the Supreme Good.

दुःखत्रयाभिघातात् जिज्ञासा तदवघातके हेतौ ।
दृष्टे सापार्था चेन्नैकान्तात्यन्ततोऽभावात् ॥ १ ॥

दुःखत्रयाभिघातात् Duḥkha-traya-abhighâtât, from the disagreeable occurrence, affection or action (abhighâta) of the threefold pain or causes of suffering. जिज्ञासा Jijñâsâ, the desire to know, enquiry. तदवघातके Tat-avaghâtake, preventive or counter-active thereof, *i.e.*, of the threefold pain. हेतौ Hetau, into the means. दृष्टे Driṣṭe, there existing visible or ordinary means. सा Sâ, it, *i.e.*, the enquiry. अपार्था Apa-arthâ, purpose-less, superfluous. चेत् Chet, if it is said. न Na, no. एकान्तात्यन्ततोऽभावात् Ekânta-atyanta-taḥ-abhâvât, because of the absence of certainty and permanency.

I. From the disagreeable occurrence of the threefold pain, (proceeds) the enquiry into the means which can prevent it; nor is the enquiry superfluous because ordinary (means) exist, for they fail to accomplish certain and permanent prevention of pain.

ANNOTATION.

1. Wise men want to demonstrate that which, by being known, would accomplish the Supreme Good. Knowledge about the subject matter of the proposed Śâstra is the means of accomplishing the Supreme Good. The present Kârikâ, therefore, introduces an enquiry into that subject.—Vâchaspati Miśra's *Tattva-Kaumudî.*

2. The subject-matter of the Sâṃkhya System comprises the well-known Twenty-five Tattvas or Principles, from the knowledge of which results the destruction of the three kinds of pain. Cf. Gauḍpâda's *Bhâṣyam.*

3. The Supreme Good is Mokṣa, or Release which consists in the permanent impossibility of the incidence of pain in any form whatever, that is, in recovering that state of the pristine purity of the Self in which the occurrence of pain is impossible, in other words, in the realisation of the Self as Self pure and simple.

4. Pains, according to the place of their origin, are divided primarily into two classes: internal and external. Internal pains, again, are either bodily or mental. These are called Âdhyâtmika or intra-organic. External pains are either Âdhibhautika or caused by created beings, namely, man, beast, bird, reptile, and the immobile, or Âdhidaivika or caused by supernatural agencies, such as Yakṣa, Râkṣasa, Vinâyaka, etc. Now, pain, such as it is, cannot be ignored, because it is experienced by every individual being.

5. Pain is not a condition of the pure Self. It resides in the Internal Instrument of Action and Cognition, that is, the inner sense, or Buddhi, and is a particular modification of that component element of it which is called Rajas. "Abhighâta" is the contact of the power of Sentiency with pain as an object of disagreeable sensation.

6. It may be objected that when such obvious remedies as medicines, desirable objects, skill in political arts and sciences, employment of gems and charms, etc., for the alleviation and removal of pain, do exist, whilst the knowledge of the Tattvas is difficult of attainment and to be acquired only by long study and traditional tuition through many generations, the investigation proposed is needless. To this, the answer is that the obvious means are neither Ekânta or absolute, nor Atyanta or final; that is, there is in them no certainty of the cessation of pain nor of the non-recurrence of pain that has ceased. Therefore, the good accomplished by them is not the Supreme Good. The means of accomplishing the Supreme Good must possess these two properties. Such a means is the knowledge of the Tattvas. The enquiry, therefore, is certainly not needless.

7. But our opponent may contend that, though the obvious means may fail, still there are means declared in the Vedas, which bring about absolute and final cessation of pain, and that, consequently, the proposed enquiry is quite superfluous. Accordingly, the next Kârikâ declares:

Scriptural, like ordinary, means are defective.

दृष्टवदानुश्रविकः सह्यविशुद्धिक्षयातिशययुक्तः ।
तद्विपरीतः श्रेयान् व्यक्ताव्यक्तज्ञविज्ञानात् ॥ २ ॥

दृष्टवत् Drista-vat, like the ordinary (means). आनुश्रविकः Ânuśravikaḥ, the revealed, Vedic, scriptural. सः Saḥ, it, *i.e.*, the Vedic means. हि Hi, for. अविशुद्धिक्षयातिशययुक्तः A-viśuddhi-kṣaya-atiśaya-yuktaḥ, attended with impurity, waste, and excess. तद्विपरीतः Tat-viparîtaḥ, the opposite thereof, *i.e.*, of ordinary and scriptural means. श्रेयान् Sreyân, preferable. व्यक्ताव्यक्तज्ञविज्ञानात् Vyakta-a-vyakta-jña-vijñânât, as it consists in discriminative knowledge of the Manifest, the Unmanifest, and the Knower.

II. Like the ordinary, is the scriptural (means ineffectual), for it is attended with impurity, waste, and excess. (The means which is) the opposite of both is preferable, as it consists in a discriminative knowledge of the Manifest, the Unmanifest, and the Knower.

ANNOTATION.

8. "Scriptural" here refers to the rituals laid down in the Vedas, and not to their Jñâna-Kâṇḍa portion, for Discriminative Knowledge also is enjoined in them.

The scriptural means are, *e.g.*, the drinking of the Soma juice, performance of sacrifices such as the Jyotiṣṭoma, the Aśvamedha, etc. They are "impure" from sacrifice of animals, etc. The result produced by them is liable to "waste," for even heaven and the gods pass away in course of time. They are also inequal in the distribution of their rewards.

9. The "opposite of both" that is, that which is absolute and final in its result, and is free from impurity, deficiency, and inequality. Such a means is the discriminative knowledge of Prakṛiti and Puruṣa.

10. "Vijñâna" means knowledge of discrimination. Knowledge of the Manifest leads to the knowledge of its cause, the Unmanifest. And knowledge of both as existing for the sake of another, leads to the knowledge of the Self. The Manifest begins with Mahat and includes Ahaṃkâra, the five Tan-mâtras, the eleven Indriyas, and the five Great Elements. The Unmanifest is the Pradhâna, *i.e.*, Prakṛiti. The Knower is Puruṣa. These are the Twenty-five Tattvas.

11. The mutual differences of the Manifest, the Unmanifest, and the Knower are declared in the next Kârikâ.

The Manifest, the Unmanifest, and the Knower distinguished.

मूलप्रकृतिरविकृतिर्महदाद्याः प्रकृतिविकृतयः सप्त ।
षोड़शकस्तु विकारः न प्रकृतिर्न विकृतिः पुरुषः ॥ ३ ॥

मूलप्रकृतिः Mûla-prakṛitiḥ, the root-evolvent. अविकृतिः A-vikṛitiḥ, non-evolute. महदाद्याः Mahat-âdyâḥ, Mahat, etc. प्रकृतिविकृतयः Prakṛiti-vikṛitayaḥ, evolvent-evolutes. सप्त Sapta, seven. षोडशकः Ṣodaśakaḥ, sixteen. तु Tü, merely. विकारः Vikâraḥ, evolute. न Na, not. प्रकृतिः Prakṛitiḥ, evolvent. न Na, not. विकृतिः Vikṛitiḥ, evolute. पुरुषः Puruṣaḥ, Puruṣa.

III. The Root Evolvent is no evolute ; Mahat, etc., are the seven evolvent-evolutes ; the sixteen are mere evolutes ; (that which is) neither evolvent nor evolute, is Puruṣa.

12. By "Prakṛiti" is meant that which procreates or evolves—the Pradhâna, that is, that in which all things are contained; and in its general significance, it denotes that which becomes the material cause of another Tattva.

13. The Root Evolvent is the state of equipoise of Sattva, Rajas, and Tamas. It has no root of its own and is the root of all things. Hence it is not a product. To imagine a root for the Root Evolvent would entail infinite regression.

14. Evolvent-Evolutes: Mahat springs from the Pradhâna and, in its turn, gives rise to Ahaṃkâra; Ahaṃkâra, in its turn, to the Tan-mâtras of Sound, Touch, Smell, Form, and Taste; and these, in their turn, respectively to the gross elements of Ether, Air, Earth, Fire, and Water.

15. It is next to be considered how the existence of the Tattvas described above can be rationally established. The causes of cognition and non-cognition are, therefore, expounded in the following four Kârikâs.

Sources of knowledge enumerated.

दृष्टमनुमानमाप्तवचनं च सर्वप्रमाणसिद्धत्वात् ।
त्रिविधं प्रमाणमिष्टं प्रमेयसिद्धिः प्रमाणाद्धि ॥ ४ ॥

दृष्टम् Dṛiṣṭam, the seen, sensuous, perception. अनुमानम् Anumânaṃ, inference. आप्तवचनं Âpta-vachanaṃ, statement of trustworthy persons. च Cha, and. सर्वप्रमाणसिद्धत्वात् Sarva-pramâna-siddha-tvât, because all proofs are established. त्रिविधं Tri-vidhaṃ, threefold. प्रमाणम् Pramâṇaṃ, proof. इष्टं Iṣṭaṃ, desired. प्रमेयसिद्धिः Prameya-siddhiḥ, establishment of the existence of the things to be proven, *viz.*, the Twenty-five Tattvas. प्रमाणात् Pramâṇât, from proof. हि Hi, verily.

IV. Perception, Inference, and Testimony (are the Proofs ; by these) all proofs being established, Proof is intended to be threefold. From Proof verily is the establishment of the Provables.

Perception, Inference, and Testimony defined.

प्रतिविषयाध्यवसायो दृष्टं त्रिविधमनुमानमाख्यातम् ।
तल्लिङ्गलिङ्गिपूर्वकमाप्तश्रुतिराप्तवचनन्तु ॥ ५ ॥

प्रतिविषयाध्यवसाय: Prati-viṣaya-adhyavasâyaḥ, ascertainment of each respective object by the senses. दृष्टं Dṛiṣṭaṃ, perception. त्रिविधम् Trividhaṃ, threefold. अनुमानम्,

Anumânam, inference. आख्यातम् Âkhyâtam, declared. तत् Tat, it. लिङ्गलिङ्गिपूर्वकम् Liṅga liṅgi-pûrvakam, preceded by the mark and by that of which, it is the mark. आप्तश्रुति: Âpta-śrutiḥ, trustworthy person and the Veda. आप्तवचनम् Âpta-vachanam, trustworthy statement, testimony. तु Tu, while.

V.   Perception is the ascertainment of each respective object (by the Senses). Inference has been declared to be threefold.   It is preceded by the mark and it is preceded by the thing of which it is the mark.   While Testimony is the statement of trustworthy persons and the Veda.

ANNOTATION.

16.   Vâchaspati Miśra interprets "Prati-viṣaya-adhyavaṣâyaḥ" as follows : Adhyavaṣâya, that is, the operation of Buddhi, in other words, cognition, based on or depending upon Prati-viṣaya, that is, that which functions in regard to, that is, comes into contact with, the several objects, in other words, the Senses.

17.   The same authority describes the process of perceptual cognition thus : On the modification of the Senses apprehending objects, when there takes place the subdual of the Tâmas of Buddhi, there is predominance of the Sattva, which is variously called Adhyavaṣâya, Vṛitti, and Jñâna.   And the favour that is hereby done to the power of intelligence, that is the fruit ; it is the consciousness of Pramâ or Right Cognition.   For the Buddhi Tattva, being derived from Prakṛiti, is unintelligent ; hence its Adhyavaṣâya also is unintelligent, like a jar, etc. Similarly, the other modifications of the Buddhi Tattva, such as pleasure, etc., also are unintelligent.   While Pûruṣa, unassociated with pleasure, etc., is intelligent.   Yet he, by the falling of the shadow of cognition, pleasure, etc., reflected by those residing in the Buddhi Tattva, becomes, as though possessed of cognition, pleasure, etc.   This is how the intelligent one is favoured.   And by the falling of the shadow of intelligence, Buddhi and also its Adhyavaṣâya, though unintelligent, appear, as though intelligent.

18.   Anumâna is inference, by means of the mark, of the thing of which it is the mark, and vice versâ.   The Methods of Inference are either of Agreement, called Vîta, or of Difference, called A-Vîta.   A-Vîta inference is called Śeṣa-vat, because it has the Śeṣa or the remainder or the residue as its subject matter.   E.g., Earth is not not-Earth, because it possesses smell.   Gauḍapâda explains Śeṣa-vat to be inference in respect of the Śeṣa or remainder of the class ; e.g., having found a drop of water taken from the sea to be salt, the saltness of the rest also is inferred.

Vîta inference is two-fold: Pûrva-vat and Sâmânyato Driṣṭa. Pûrva-vat is the inference of an individual of a genus particular instances of which have previously been seen; *e.g.*, the inference of fire from smoke, in a mountain, fire having previously been seen in the kitchen. Sâmânyato Driṣṭa is inference of a thing particular instances of which same kind have not previously been seen, but particular instances of a kind similar to which have previously been seen in analogous cases; that is, in this case, the particular is not seen but the genus is seen. *E.g.*, Karaṇa-tva or instrumentality, that is, the capability of effecting an act is, as a genus, a known thing, because it has been seen in the axe which is an instrument of cutting. But an Indriya or Power of Cognition and Action (commonly rendered as Sense Organ) does not belong to the same class as the axe, and is also not an object of perception. Now, cognition and action are acts, and as the act of cutting cannot be effected without an instrument, so the acts of cognition and action cannot be effected without some instrument. Thus is inferred the existence of the Indriyas as the Instruments of Cognition and Action.

Âpta means Âchâryas, such as Brahmâ and the rest.

Super-Sensible objects how proved.

सामान्यतस्तु दृष्टादतीन्द्रियाणां प्रतीतिरनुमानात् ।
तस्मादपि चासिद्धं परोक्षमाप्तागमात् सिद्धम् ॥ ६ ॥

सामान्यतः Sâmânyataḥ, of the generic. तु Tu, but. दृष्टात् Driṣṭât, from the seeing. अतीन्द्रियाणां Ati-indriyâṇâṃ, of things transcending the senses. प्रतीतिः Pratîtiḥ, approach, intuition, cognition. अनुमानात् Anumânât, from inference. तस्मात् Tasmât, from that. अपि Api, even. च Cha, and also, from Śeṣa-vat inference (Vâchaspati). असिद्धं A-siddhaṃ, not-established. परोक्षम् Parokṣam, super-sensuous. आप्तागमात् Âpta-âgamât, from Testimony and Revelation. सिद्धम् Siddham, proved.

VI. (Intuition of sensible things is from perception). But the intuition of super-sensible things is from Sâmânyato Driṣṭa and Seṣa-vat Inference. And, super-sensible things not established from that even, are established from Testimony and Revelation.

19. Prakriti and Puruṣa are not objects of perception and therefore they are unreal, argue our opponents; for a hare's horn or a castle in the air is not perceived, because it is unreal. It is, accordingly, next pointed out that perception cannot be the sole test of reality, because there are well-known causes from which even admittedly existent things are not perceived. These causes are declared in the next Kârikâ.

Causes of failure of external perception enumerated.

अतिदूरात् सामीप्यादिन्द्रियघातान्मनोऽनवस्थानात् ।
सौक्ष्म्याद्व्यवधानादभिभवात् समानाभिहाराच्च ॥ ७ ॥

अतिदूरात् Ati-dûrât, from extreme distance. *N.B.*—The word Ati qualifies distance as well as all the rest. सामीप्यात् Sâmîpyât, from nearness. इन्द्रियघातात् Indriya-ghâtât, from impairment of the senses. मनोऽनवस्थानात् Manaḥ-anavasthânât, from non-presence of mind. सौक्ष्म्यात् Saukṣmyât, from fineness. व्यवधानात् Vyavadhânât, from intervention. अभिभवात् Abhibhavât, from suppression by others. समानाभिहारात् Samâna-abhihârât, from intermixture with likes. च Cha, and others.

VII. (Apprehension of even existing things may not take place) through extreme remoteness, nearness, impairment of the senses, non-presence of the mind, extreme fineness, intervention, suppression by other matters, intermixture with likes, and other causes.

Why Prakṛiti is not an object of perception.

सौक्ष्म्यात्तदनुपलब्धिर्नाभावात् कार्यतस्तदुपलब्धेः ।
महदादि तच्च कार्यं प्रकृतिसरूपं विरूपं च ॥ ८ ॥

सौक्ष्म्यात् Saukṣmyât, from extreme fineness. तदनुपलब्धिः Tat-anupalabdhiḥ, non-apprehension thereof, *i.e.*, of Prakṛiti. न Na, not. अभावात् Abhâvât, from non-existence. कार्यतः Kârya-taḥ, from effects. तदुपलब्धेः Tat-upalabdheḥ, because of the apprehension thereof. महदादि Mahat-âdi, Mahat and the rest. तत् Tat, that. च Cha, and. कार्यं Kâryaṃ, effect. प्रकृतिसरूपं Prakṛiti-sarûpaṃ, similar to Prakṛiti. विरूपं Virûpaṃ, dissimilar. च Cha, and.

VIII. From extreme fineness is the non-apprehension of Prakṛiti, and not from her non-existence, because there is apprehension of her from the effect. And that effect is Mahat, etc., similar and dissimilar to Prakṛiti.

20. "Similar and dissimilar to Prakṛiti": for these resemblances and differences, see Kârikâs X and XI.

21. But from the effects, a mere cause or cause in the abstract is deduced, and not its nature, and, on this point, different conclusions have been arrived at by different thinkers. Thus, some Buddhists, say that the existent is produced from the non-existent; *e.g.*, from the non-existence, by destruction, of the seed is produced the sprout. 2. Some, the Vedântins, say that the effects are the Vivarta or revolution of one

single existent thing, and are not themselves ultimately real. 3. Some, the Vaiśeṣikas, Naiyâyikas, etc., say that from the existent, *i.e.*, the Ultimate Atoms, is produced the non-existent. 4. The elders, the Sâṃkhyas, say that from the existent is produced the existent. Of these, on the first three alternatives, the Pradhâna is not established. For the characteristic of being the Pradhâna, *i.e.*, that in which all things are contained, and of being of the nature of Sattva, Rajas and Tamas, belonging to the Cause of the World, consists in being of the nature of Sound and all other Pariṇâma or transformations, the essences of which possess the distinctions of pleasure, pain, and bewilderment. Now, if the existent is to be produced from the non-existent, how can a non-existent, nameless, form-less cause possess the nature of Sound, etc., in the form of pleasure, etc.? for there is no proof of the identity of nature between the existent and the non-existent. If, again, the diversity of Sound, etc., is the Vivarta of a single existent thing, still it would not follow that the existent is produced from the existent. For a one without a second cannot have identity of nature with the diversity; on the contrary, the apprehension of the non-diversity under the characteristic of the diversity is an error pure and simple. With those also, again, namely Kaṇâda, Gotama, and others, who say that it is from the existent that the non-existent is produced, the cause cannot be of the nature of the effect, because there is no proof of the unity of the existent and the non-existent. Hence there can be no proof of the Pradhâna on these theories. In order, therefore, to establish the existence of the Pradhâna, the next Kârikâ determines that the effect must be existent from before its "productfon."

Effects pre-exist in their causes.

असदकरणादुपादानग्रहणात् सर्वसम्भवाभावात् ।
शक्तस्य शक्यकरणात् कारणभावाच्च सत् कार्यम् ॥ ६ ॥

असदकरणात् A-sat-a-karaṇât, from the non-effectuation of the non-existent. उपादानग्रहणात् Upâdâna-grahaṇât, from the selection of material for the effect. सर्वसम्भवाभावात् Sarva-sambhava-abhâvât, from the absence of the production of every thing by every means. शक्तस्य Śaktasya, of the competent. शक्यकरणात् Śakya-karaṇât, from the effectuation of the producible. कारणभावात् Kâraṇa-bhâvât, from the nature of the cause. सत् Sat, existent. कार्यम् Kâryam, effect.

IX. The effect is ever existent, because that which is non-existent, can by no means be brought into existence; because effects take adequate material causes; because all things are not produced from all causes ; because a competent cause can effect that only for which it is competent ; and also because the effect possesses the nature of the cause.

ANNOTATION.

22. That which is non-existent, etc. : *e.g.* a hare's horn.

Effects take, etc. : Oil, for instance, can be produced from mustard seeds, but not a piece of cloth.

All things are not produced, etc. : Did effects not pre-exist in their causes, then, in mustard seeds, for example, there would be non-existence of a piece of cloth, a jar, in fact, of every other thing as well as of oil, and it would be quite as easy to produce a piece of cloth, a jar, and all the rest from them as it is to produce oil. But such is not the case.

A competent cause can effect, etc. : Competency means potentiality, the unmanifested state of the effect. A lump of clay, for instance, is potentially a jar ; in it the jar lies hidden, unmanifested ; it is manifested in the form of the jar by the operation of the potter.

The effect possesses the nature, etc. : The colour, weight, touch, etc. of a piece of cloth for instance, are the colour, weight, touch, etc., of the threads from which it is made. This could not have been so, were not cause and effect identical in essence.

The Manifest and the Unmanifest contrasted.

हेतुमदनित्यमव्यापि सक्रियमनेकमाश्रितं लिङ्गम् ।
सावयवं परतन्त्रं व्यक्तं विपरीतमव्यक्तम् ॥ १० ॥

हेतुमत् Hetu-mat, possessing or depending on a cause. अनित्यम् A-nityam, non-eternal, perishable. अव्यापि A-vyâpi, unpervading, finite. सक्रियम् Sakriyam, mobile, mutable. अनेकम् Anekam, multitudinous, manifold. आश्रितं Âśritam, supported, dependent. लिङ्गम् Lingam, mergent, mark. सावयवं Sâvayavam, made up of parts. परतन्त्रं Para-tantram, subordinate. व्यक्तं Vyaktam, the manifested. विपरीतम् Viparîtam, the reverse. अव्यक्तम् A-Vyaktam, the unmanifested.

X. The Manifest is producible, non-enternal, non-pervading, mobile, multiform, dependent, (serving as) the mark (of inference), a combination of parts, subordinate. The Unmanifest is the reverse (of this).

ANNOTATION.

23. *Sakriya*, migratory : Buddhi and the rest leave, one after another, bodies which they had taken up and enter into other bodies : this is their movement. The movement of the Body, Earth, etc., is indeed well-known.

Aneka, multitudinous : There are as many of them as there are Puruṣas ; Earth and the rest also are multiplied according to the differences of Bodies, jars, etc.

Âśrita, supported : They are supported by their respective causes.

Liṅga, mergent, mark : Buddhi and the rest are marks of the Pradhâna. Gauḍapâda explains the word to mean "subject to dissolution." At the time of the Dissolution the five Great Elements merge into the Tanmâtras, and these together with the eleven Indriyas, into Ahaṃkâra, and this, into Buddhi ; and that merges into the Pradhâna.

Paratantra, subordinate: Buddhi, for instance, when it has to produce its own effect, namely, Ahaṃkâra, has to draw upon Prakṛiti ; otherwise, being weak or exhausted, it will not be able to produce Ahaṃkâra. Similarly, by Ahaṃkâra and the rest also is awaited the inflow of Prakṛiti in the production of their own effects.

24. *Viparîta*, reverse : The Unmanifest is causeless, eternal, all pervading, motion-less, single, self-sustained, the subject of the mark or non-mergent, part-less, and supreme.

The Manifest, the Unmanifest and the Knower contrasted and compared.

त्रिगुणमविवेकि विषयः सामान्यमचेतनं प्रसवधर्मि ।
व्यक्तं तथा प्रधानं तद्विपरीतस्तथा च पुमान् ॥ ११ ॥

त्रिगुणम् Tri-guṇam, having or constituted by the three Guṇas, *viz.*, Sattva, Rajas, and Tamas. अविवेकि A-viveki, non-discriminative. विषयः Viṣayaḥ, objective. सामान्यम् Sâmânyam, common. अचेतनं A-chetanam, non-intelligent. प्रसवधर्मि Prasava-dharmi, prolific. व्यक्तं Vyaktam, the Manifest. तथा Tathâ, so. प्रधानं Pradhânam, the Pradhâna, Prakṛiti. तद्विपरीतः Tat-viparîtaḥ, the reverse of this. तथा Tathâ, so. च Cha, yet. पुमान् Pumân, Puruṣa.

XI. The Manifest is constituted by the three Guṇas, is non-discriminative, objective, common, non-intelligent, prolific. So is also the Pradhâna. Puruṣa is the reverse of them both (in these respects), and yet is similar (to the Pradhâna and also to the Manifest in those other respects mentioned in the preceding Kârikâ.)

ANNOTATION.

25. *A-viveki*: Just as the Pradhâna is not discriminated from itself, even so are not Mahat and the rest also discriminated from the Pradhâna, because of their essential identity. Or, A-viveka is to create by uniting

together, for none of them singly are capable of producing their own effects, but, on the contrary, only by uniting together.

Viṣaya: because it is the Object as distinguished from the Subject, to be apprehended and made use of by all Puruṣas alike.

26. *Tathâ cha*, and yet is similar: that is, as the Pradhâna is, in the preceding Kârikâ, declared to be without cause, etc., such is Puruṣa. Thus, "* * * The Manifest is multitudinous; the Unmanifest is single; so is Puruṣa also single.* * *" (Gauḍapâda)." "But when similarity to the Pradhâna belongs to Puruṣa in respect of non-causability, eternality, etc., and likewise multiplicity is his similarity to the Manifest, how is it said that" the reverse of them both is Puruṣa? To this, it is replied: Tathâ cha: Cha has the sense of Api, even, yet; although there is similarity in respect of non-causability, etc., yet he possesses dissimilarity in respect of not being constituted by the three Guṇas, etc. Such is the meaning" (Vâchaspati Miśra). "The S. Chandrikâ confirms the interpretation: 'The phrase *tathâ cha* implies that (soul) is analogous to the undiscrete principle in non-causability and the rest, and analogous to discrete principles in manifold enumeration.' This is, in fact, the Sâṃkhya doctrine, as subsequently laid down by the text, ver. 18, and is conformable to the Sûtra of Kapila; 'Multitude of souls is proved by variety of condition': that is, 'the virtuous are born again in heaven, the wicked are regenerated in hell; the fool wanders in error, the wise man is set free.' Either, therefore, Gauḍapâda has made a mistake, or by his *eka* is to be understood, not that soul in general is one only, but that it is single, or several, in its different migrations; or, as Mr. Colebrooke renders it (R.A.S. Trans. vol. I. p. 31) 'individual.' So in the Sûtras it is said 'that there may be various unions of one soul, according to difference of receptacle, as the etherial element may be confined in a variety of vessels.' This singleness of soul applies therefore to that particular soul which is subjected to its own varied course of birth, death, bondage, and liberation; for, as the commentator observes, 'one soul is born, not another (in a regenerated body)' The singleness of soul, therefore, as asserted by Gauḍapâda, is no doubt to be understood in this sense." (*Wilson*).

Characteristics of the Guṇas described.

प्रीत्यप्रीतिविषादात्मकाः प्रकाशप्रवृत्तिनियमार्थाः ।
अन्योन्याभिभवाश्रयजननमिथुनवृत्तयश्च गुणाः ॥ १२ ॥

प्रीत्यप्रीतिविषादात्मकाः: Prîti-aprîti-visâda-âtmakâh, of the nature of pleasure, pain and dulness. प्रकाशप्रवृत्तिनियमार्थाः: Prakâśa-pravṛitti-niyama-arthâḥ adapted to serving the purpose of, or capable of causing, illumination, activity, and, restraint. अन्योन्याभिभवाश्रयजननमिथुनवृत्तयः : Anya-anya-abhibhava-âśraya-janana-mithuna-vṛittayaḥ, having mutual domination, dependence, production, consociation, and co-existence. Vâchaspati does not consider the term Vṛitti as a distinct condition; he interprets it as Kriyâ, act, operation or function, and compounds it with each of the foregoing terms. च Cha, and. गुणाः : Guṇâḥ, the Guṇas.

XII. The Guṇas possess the nature of pleasure, pain and dulness; serve the purpose of illumination, activity, and restraint; and perform the function of mutual domination, dependence, production, and consociation.

ANNOTATION.

27. Possess the nature, etc: *Hereby* the intrinsic forms of the Guṇas Sattva, Rajas, and Tamas are declared. The force of the word Âtmâ, nature, is that it is a reply to those who think that pleasure is nothing but absence of pain, and that pain is nothing but absence of pleasure. For Âtmâ denotes being, something positive, and is a negation of non-being.

28. Serve the purpose, etc: *Hereby* the purposes served by the Guṇas respectively are declared. *Artha* means *prayojana* or purpose. Gauḍapâda interprets the term in the sense of competency, fitness, capability.

29. Perform the functions, etc: *Hereby* the various operations of the Guṇas are declared.

Dependence: Although dependence, that is, co-existence by the relation of the container and the contained is not possible, still that is the support of that, the operation of which depends upon it. Thus, Sattva, by resting on activity and restraint, subserves Rajas and Tamas with illumination; Rajas, by resting on illumination and restraint, subserves Sattva and Tamas with activity; Tamas, by resting on illumination and activity, subserves Sattva and Rajas with restraint.

Production: Production is transformation, and it is of the same form as the Guṇas; hence causability is not entailed, owing to the absence of a cause which is a different Tattva. Neither is non-eternality entailed, owing to the absence of dissolution into a different Tattva.

Consociation: That is, the Guṇas are constant companions of one another.

Co-existence is explained by Guaḍapâda thus: As a beautiful and amiable woman, who is a source of delight to every one else, is the cause of misery to the other wives of her husband, and of bewilderment to the dissolute; so does Sattva produce the functions of Rajas and Tamas. As a king, assiduous in protecting his people, and curbing the profligate, is the cause of happiness to the good, of misery and mortification to the wicked; so does Rajas produce the functions of Sattva and Tamas. Similarly, Tamas produces the functions of Sattva and Rajas, as clouds, overshadowing the heavens, cause delight upon earth, animate by their rain the active labours of the husbandman, and overwhelm absent lovers with despair. In this manner, the Guṇas perform the functions of one another.

The Co-operation of the Guṇas explained.

सत्त्वं लघु प्रकाशकमिष्टमुपष्टम्भकं चलं च रजः ।
गुरु वरणकमेव तमः प्रदीपवच्चार्थतो वृत्तिः ॥ १३ ॥

सत्त्वं Sattvaṃ, sattva. लघु Laghu, alleviating, light. प्रकाशकम् Prakâśakam, enlightening, illuminating. इष्टम् Iṣṭam, desired, considered. उपष्टम्भकं Upaṣṭambhakaṃ, urgent, exciting. चलं Chalam, versatile, restless. च Cha, and. रजः Rajaḥ, rajas. गुरु Guru, heavy. वरणकम् Varaṇakam enveloping, covering, obscuring. एव Eva, to be sure. तमः Tamaḥ, tamas. प्रदीपवत् Pradîpa-vat, like a lamp. च Cha, and. अर्थतः Artha-taḥ, for a purpose. वृत्तिः Vṛittiḥ, function, operation.

XIII. Sattva is considered to be light and illuminating, and Rajas, to be exciting and restless, and Tamas, to be indeed heavy and enveloping. Like a lamp (consisting of oil, wick, and fire), they co-operate for a (common) purpose (by union of contraries).

ANNOTATION.

30. Contraries need not necessarily oppose and counteract one another. As co-operation of contraries for a common purpose is seen in the case of a lamp, even so is it the case with the Guṇas which co-operate with one another to serve a common purpose, *viz.*, the experience and release of Puruṣa.

31. Granted, one may say, that non-discriminativeness, etc., are proved by perception in the case of Earth, etc., which are objects of perception; but how can Sattva, etc., which are not objects of perception, be said to be non-discriminative, objective, common, non-intelligent, and prolific (Kârikâ XI)? To this, the reply is given in the next Kârikâ.

Proof of the properties of the Unmanifest.

अविवेक्यादेः सिद्धिस्त्रैगुण्यात्तद्विपर्ययाभावात् ।
कारणगुणात्मकत्वात् कार्यस्य अव्यक्तमपि सिद्धम् ॥१४॥

अविवेक्यादेः A-viveki-âdeh, of non-discriminativeness, etc. सिद्धिः Siddhiḥ, proof. त्रैगुण्यात् Traiguṇyât, from their being constituted by the three Guṇas or from their manifesting the three qualities of pleasure, pain, and dulness. तद्विपर्ययाभावात् Tat-viparyaya-abhâvât, from the absence of non-discriminativeness, etc., in the reverse thereof; *i.e.*, of the Manifest and the Unmanifest, *i.e.*, Puruṣa; from the absence of the reverse of Traiguṇya in the Unmanifest; from the absence of the divergence or non concomitance or disagreement between the properties in question and the Manifest and the Unmanifest or the Unmanifest only. कारणगुणात्मकत्वात् Kâraṇa-guṇa-âtmaka-tvât, from the effect's containing the attributes of the cause. कार्यस्य Kâryasya, of the effect. अव्यक्तम् A-Vyaktam, the Unmanifest. अपि Api, also. सिद्धम् Siddham, proved, established.

XIV. The proof of non-discriminativeness, and the rest (in the Manifest and the Unmanifest) is from their being constituted by the three Guṇas and from absence of their non-concomitance. From the effect possessing the attributes of the cause is proved the Unmanifest also.

ANNOTATION.

32. According to Vâchaspati, the proof of non-discriminativeness and the rest is by the method of agreement, thus:—

Whatever possesses pleasure, pain, and dulness, is non-discriminative, etc.,

As, for instance, are the objects of the senses;

Prakṛiti, Mahat, etc., possess pleasure, pain, and dulness;

They are, therefore, non-discriminative, etc:

and also by the method of difference, thus:—

Whatever is not non-discriminative, etc., does not possess pleasure, pain and dulness,

As, for instance, is the case with Puruṣa.

But Prakṛiti, Mahat, etc., possess pleasure, pain, and dulness;

They are, therefore, not-non-discriminative, etc.

But the proof of these attributes must be subject to the proof of their alleged substratum. How then is this, namely, the Pradhâna proved? Thus: The effect characterised as Mahat, etc., possessing the form of pleasure, pain, and dulness, must have the nature or essence of pleasure, pain, and dulness inhereing in its own cause; so that its cause, possessing the nature of pleasure, pain, and dulness, that is, the Pradhâna Unmanifest, is established.

33. Gauḍapâda's interpretation is different from the above. According to him, the properties of non-discriminativeness, etc., are proved in the Manifest from their being constituted by the three Guṇas, through the absence of divergence, that is, because the properties of non-discriminativeness, etc., have never been found except in conjunction with the property of being constituted by the three Guṇas. And their existence in the Unmanifest is proved from the absence of divergence, that is, from the invariable and universal concomitance of the Manifest and the Unmanifest: just as, wherever there is the cloth, there are the yarns; similarly whoever sees the Manifest, sees the Unmanifest as well; and also from the effect possessing the nature of the cause: thus, from the effect, *viz.*, Mahat and the rest which are non-discriminative, objective, common, non-intelligent, and prolific, is proved that their cause, namely, the Unmanifest, possesses the same properties.

Proof of the Unmanifest.

भेदानां परिमाणात् समन्वयात् शक्तितः प्रवृत्तेश्च ।
कारणकार्यविभागादविभागाद् वैश्वरूपस्य ॥ १५ ॥
कारणमस्त्यव्यक्तं प्रवर्तते त्रिगुणतः समुदयाच्च ।
परिणामतः सलिलवत् प्रतिप्रतिगुणाश्रयविशेषात् ॥१६॥

भेदानां Bhedânâm, of differentiated particulars, specific objects, of the evolutes, Mahat and the rest. परिमाणात् Parimâṇât, from finiteness, measurableness. समन्वयात् Samanvayât, from homogeneity, agreement. शक्तितः Sakti-taḥ, from power. प्रवृत्तेः Pravṛitteḥ, from activity, from production. च Cha, and. कारणकार्यविभागात् Kâraṇa-kârya-bibhâgât, from differentiation of cause and effect. अविभागात् A-vibhâgât, from non-differentiation, from reunion. वैश्वरूपस्य Vaiśvarûpasya, of the formal Universe. कारणम् Kâraṇam, cause. अस्ति Asti, exists. अव्यक्तं A-Vyaktam, Unmanifest. प्रवर्तते Pravartate, energises, operates. त्रिगुणतः Tri-guṇa-taḥ, through or of the three Guṇas, Sattva, Rajas, and Tamas. समुदयात् Sam-udayât, through combination, co-operation. च Cha, and. परिणामतः Pariṇâma-taḥ, through transformation. सलिलवत् Salila-vat, like water. प्रतिप्रतिगुणाश्रयविशेषात् Prati-prati-guṇa-âśraya-viśeṣât, through differences according to the differences of the several receptacles of the Guṇas, or differences created by the Guṇas severally based on the principal Guṇa.

XV-XVI. Of the particulars (*e.g.*, Mahat and all the rest down to the earth), there exists an Unmanifest cause:

because the particulars are finite; because they are homogeneous; because production is through power; because there is differentiation of effect from cause or difference of cause and effect; and because there is reunion of the multiform effect with the cause.

It operates, in the form of the three Guṇas and by combination, undergoing transformation, (diversified) according to the differences severally of the other Guṇas depending on the principal Guṇa.

ANNOTATION.

34. Because they are homogeneous: Homogeneousness is the possession of a common form among a number of distinct individuals. The presence of a common form infers a common origin.

Because production is through power: Power inhering in the cause is nothing but the unmanifested state of the effect.

Differentiation and reunion: Discrete products of every sort of form from Mahat down to a jar, for instance, successively rise from their causes at the time of creation and disappear into them at the time of destruction and universal dissolution. The ultimate points in the process of evolution and involution are one and the same. It is the absolute unmanifested state of a single entity. It is called the Unmanifest, the Pradhâna and Prakṛiti.

35. It operates etc.: The Guṇas of which the nature is to undergo transformation, never rest, even for a moment, without transforming themselves. Their transformation may be homogeneous or heterogeneous. Homogeneous transformation takes place during Pralaya or the period of latency intervening Creation and Dissolution, when Sattva transforms as Sattva, Rajas as Rajas, and Tamas as Tamas. Such is the meaning of the phrase Tri-guṇa-taḥ, in the form of the three Guṇas severally. Heterogeneous transformation takes place during Creation and Dissolution. For this, combination of the Guṇas with one another in different proportions is necessary. Such combination is rendered possible by the diversified activity of the Guṇas in the evolution of Mahat and all the rest, of which each successive one is more and more specified than, and differentiated from, its predecessor. And this differentiation is brought about by the difference in the ratio in which the subsidiary Guṇas combine and co-operate with the principal Guṇa. Thus, as regards the eleven Indriyas

and the five Tan-mâtras, while Rajas is equally operative in the evolution of both, the former arise from Ahaṃkâra in which Sattva is predominant and Tamas is dormant; whereas the latter arise from Ahaṃkâra in which Tamas is predominant and Sattva is dormant.

Salila-vat: As simple water shed by the clouds, coming into contact with various situations, is modified as sweet, sour, bitter, pungent, or astringent, in the character of the juice of the cocoa-nut, palm, bel, karanja, amalaka, wood-apple, etc.

Proof of Puruṣa.

संघातपरार्थत्वात् त्रिगुणादिविपर्ययादधिष्ठानात् ।
पुरुषोऽस्ति भोक्तृभावात् कैवल्यार्थं प्रवृत्तेश्च ॥ १७ ॥

संघातपरार्थत्वात् Saṃghâta-para artha-tvât, since an aggregate or structure of manifold parts into one whole is for the sake of another of a different character त्रिगुणादिविपर्ययात् Tri-Guṇa-âdi-viparyayât, since there must exist an entity in which there is the reverse of the properties of being constituted by three Guṇas, and the rest mentioned in Kârikâ XI. अधिष्ठानात् Adhiṣṭhânât, since there must be superintendence over Buddhi and other products of the Guṇas. पुरुषः Puruṣaḥ Puruṣa. अस्ति Asti, exists. भोक्तृभावात् Bhoktṛi-bhâvât, since there must be an experiencer of pleasure and pain. कैवल्यार्थं Kaivalya-arthaṃ, for the sake of isolation. प्रवृत्तेः Pravṛitteḥ, since activity is. च Cha, and.

XVII. Puruṣa exists: since the aggregate must be for the sake of the non-aggregate; since there must exist an entity in which the properties of being constituted by the three Guṇas and the rest do not appear; since there must be a superintendent; since there must be an experiencer; and since activity is for the sake of abstraction.

ANNOTATION.

36. Since there must exist an entity, etc.: Hereby is prevented the inference of an aggregate by the aggregate. For all aggregates possess the three Guṇas, whereas Puruṣa is free from them, as declared in Kârikâ XI. Therefore, the entity for which the aggregate is, must be a non-aggregate. And Puruṣa is a non-aggregate.

Proof of Multiplicity of Puruṣa.

जननमरणकरणानां प्रतिनियमादयुगपत् प्रवृत्तेश्च ।
पुरुषबहुत्वं सिद्धं त्रैगुण्यविपर्ययाच्चैव ॥ १८ ॥

जननमरणकरणानां Janana-maraṇa-karaṇânâṃ, of birth, death, and the instrument of cognition and action. प्रतिनियमात् Prati-niyamât, individual allotment. अयुगपत्

A-yugapat, non-simultaneous. प्रवृत्तेः Pravritteḥ, from activity or occupation. च Cha, and. पुरुषबहुत्वं Puruṣa-bahu-tvaṃ, multiplicity of Puruṣas. सिद्धं Siddhaṃ, established. त्रैगुण्यविपर्ययात् Traiguṇya-viparyayât, from absence of the condition of the three Guṇas, from diverse modification of the three Guṇas. च Cha, and. एव Eva, verily.

XVIII. From the individual allotment of birth, death and the Instruments, from non-simultaneous activity (towards the same end), and from the diverse modification of the three Guṇas, multitude of Puruṣas is verily established.

ANNOTATION.

37. Birth consists in conjunction with body, Indriya, Manas, Ahaṃkâra, Buddhi, and experience, and death consists in their abandonment. So that they do not entail the transformation of Puruṣa. The distribution of body and the rest, which is different in each individual case, must imply a plurality of Puruṣas, as, otherwise, on the birth of one, all would be born and on the death of one, all would die.

Non-simultaneous activity towards the same end : as, *e.g.*, some are busy with virtuous, others with vicious, actions; some cultivate dispassion, others knowledge.

Diverse modification of the three Guṇas: thus, though birth is common to all, one possessing Sattva is happy, another possessing Rajas, is wretched, and a third possessing Tamas, is dull.

Proof of the Nature of Puruṣa.

तस्माच्च विपर्यासात् सिद्धं साक्षित्वमस्य पुरुषस्य ।
कैवल्यं माध्यस्थ्यं द्रष्टृत्वमकर्तृभावश्च ॥ १९ ॥

तस्मात् Tasmât, from that. च Cha, and. विपर्यासात् Viparyâsât, from contrast, divergence. सिद्धं Siddhaṃ, proved. साक्षित्वं Sâkṣi-tvaṃ, to be the witness. अस्य Asya, of this. पुरुषस्य Puruṣa-sya, of Puruṣa. कैवल्यं Kaivalyaṃ, aloneness, solitariness. माध्यस्थ्यं Mâdhyasthyaṃ, indifference, to be the bystander. द्रष्टृत्वम् Draṣṭṛi-tvaṃ, to be the spectator. अकर्तृभावः A-kartṛi-bhâvaḥ, non-agent-ship च Cha, and.

XIX. And from that contrast it is proved that this Puruṣa is witness, solitary, indifferent, spectator, and non-agent.

ANNOTATION.

38. That contrast: that is, Puruṣa is not constituted by the three Guṇas, is discriminative, is not objective but subjective, is not common, is intelligent, and is not prolific (see Kârikâ XIV).

Because he is intelligent and subjective, he is spectator and witness. A witness is one to whom objects are shown. Prakṛiti exhibits herself to Puruṣa.

From his not being constituted by the three Guṇas follow his solitariness and indifference. For solitariness consists in the absolute non-existence of the three sorts of pain, and indifference denotes absence of love for pleasure and hate for pain. But pleasure and pain are properties of the three Guṇas. And because Puruṣa is not constituted by the three Guṇas, he is absolutely free from pleasure, pain and bewilderment.

And since he is discriminative and non-prolific, he is not the agent.

But if Puruṣa is a non-agent, how does he make determination? as I will perform acts of merit, I will not perform acts of demerit: hence Puruṣa must be the agent; neither is Puruṣa the agent;--thus there is, may say our opponent, defect in both the theories. Accordingly, the seeming agency of Puruṣa is explained in the next Kârikâ.

The agency of Puruṣa is not real, but fictitious.

तस्मात्तत्संयोगादचेतनं चेतनावदिव लिङ्गम् ।
गुणकर्तृत्वे च तथा कर्तेव भवत्युदासीनः ॥ २० ॥

तस्मात् Tasmât, therefore. तत्संयोगात् Tat-saṃyogât, from conjunction therewith, *i.e.*, with the intelligent Puruṣa. अचेतनं A-chetanaṃ, the non-intelligent. चेतनावत् Chetanâ-vat, possessing intelligence. इव Iva, like, as if. लिङ्गम् Liṅgam, the effect, Mahat and the rest. गुणकर्तृत्वे Guṇa-kartṛi-tve, in the case of the agency of the Guṇas. च Cha, and. तथा Tathâ, likewise. कर्ता Kartâ, agent. इव Iva, like, as if. भवति Bhavati, becomes. उदासीनः Udâsînaḥ, indifferent, *i.e.*, Puruṣa.

XX. Therefore (the inference that intelligence and agency belong to one and the same subject is a mistake.) Through conjunction with Puruṣa, the non-intelligent Effect appears as if it were intelligent, and although agency is of the Guṇas, the indifferent (Puruṣa) appears, in the same way, as if he were the agent.

39. Liṅgam here denotes Mahat, Ahaṃkâra, Manas and the five Tan-mâtras. See Kâṛikâ XL.

40. The confusion then is due to the conjunction of Prakṛiti and Puruṣa. And conjunction means mutual approach and co-operation,

which necessarily pre-supposes some object or purpose to be achieved. That purpose can be nothing but mutual benefit, as declared in the following Kârikâ.

Object of the conjunction of Puruṣa and Prakṛiti.

पुरुषस्य दर्शनार्थं कैवल्यार्थं तथा प्रधानस्य ।
पङ्ग्वन्धवदुभयोरपि संयोगस्तत्कृतः सर्गः ॥२१॥

पुरुषस्य Puruṣa-sya, of Puruṣa. दर्शनार्थं Darśana-artham, for the sake of seeing or exhibition. कैवल्यार्थं Kaivalya-artham, for the sake of separation. तथा Tathâ, likewise. प्रधानस्य Pradhâna-sya, of the Pradhâna. पङ्ग्वन्धवत् Paṅgu-andha-vat, like that of the halt and the blind. उभयोः Ubhayoḥ, of both. अपि Api, also. संयोगः Saṃyogaḥ, conjunction. तत्कृतः Tat-kṛitaḥ, originated by that, *i.e.*, conjunction. सर्गः Sargaḥ, creation, evolution.

XXI. The conjunction of Puruṣa and the Pradhâna is, like that of the halt and the blind, for mutual benefit, that is, for the exhibition of the Pradhâna to Puruṣa and for the isolation of Puruṣa. From this conjunction proceeds Creation.

ANNOTATION.

41. The halt and the blind: "As a lame man and a blind man, deserted by their fellow-travellers, who, in making their way with difficulty through a forest, had been dispersed by robbers, happening to encounter each other, and entering into conversation so as to inspire mutual confidence, agreed to divide between them the duties of walking and of seeing; accordingly the lame man was mounted on the blind man's shoulders, and was thus carried on his journey, whilst the blind man was enabled to pursue his route by the directions of his companion. In the same manner, the faculty of seeing is in soul, not that of moving; it is like the lame man: the faculty of moving, but not of seeing, is in nature; which resembles, therefore, the blind man. Further, as a separation takes place between the lame man and the blind man, when their mutual object is accomplished, and they have reached their journey's end, so nature, having effected the liberation of soul, ceases to act; and soul, having contemplated nature, obtains abstractedness; and, consequently, their respective purposes being effected, the connexion between them is dissolved."—Gauḍapâda's Bhâṣya, translated by Wilson.

The Evolutions of Prakṛiti and the order of their evolution stated.

प्रकृतेर्महांस्ततोऽहंकारस्तस्माद्गणश्च षोडशकः ।
तस्मादपि षोडशकात् पञ्चभ्यः पञ्च भूतानि ॥ २२ ॥

प्रकृतेः Prakṛiteḥ, from Prakṛiti. महान् Mahân, Mahat. ततः Tataḥ, thence, from Mahat. अहंकारः Ahaṃkâraḥ, Ahaṃkâra. तस्मात् Tasmât, therefrom, from Ahaṃkâra. गणः Gaṇaḥ, set, group, series. च Cha, and. षोडशकः Ṣoḍaśakaḥ, sixteenfold. तस्मात् Tasmât, from that. अपि Api, again. षोडशकात् Ṣoḍaśakât, from sixteenfold. पञ्चभ्यः Pañcha-bhyaḥ, from the five. पञ्च भूतानि Pañcha bhûtâni, the five gross elements.

XXII. From Prakṛiti (evolves) Mahat; thence, Ahaṃkâra; and from this, the sixteenfold set; from five, again, among the sixteenfold, the five Elements.

ANNOTATION.

42. The sixteenfold set: that is, the eleven Indriyas and the five Tan-mâtras. From five, etc: that is, from the lower five among the sixteen, that is, the five Tan-mâtras.

Five Elements: *viz.*, Ether, Air, Fire, Water and Earth.

43. The synonyms of Prakṛiti are Pradhâna, that in which all things are contained, Brahmâ, that which expands, A-vyakta, the unmanifest, Bahu-dhânaka, that in which manifold things are contained, Mâyâ, that which measures or limits.

The synonyms of Mahat are Buddhi, that which makes things known, Âsurî, probably Chheda-bheda-âdi-âtmikâ as in the medical science, that is, that which causes separation, differentiation, etc., Mati, that by which things are understood, Khyâti, that by which things are manifested, Jñânâ, that by which knowledge is acquired, Prajñâ, that by which perfect knowledge is obtained.

The synonyms of Ahaṃkâra are Bhûta-âdi, the origin of the Bhûtas or elements, Vaikṛita, the modified, Taijasa, partaking of Tejas, *i.e.*, Rajas, Abhimâna, self-consciousness.

By Tattva is meant the Tva, *i.e.*, condition or existence of Tat, or that by which all the three worlds are pervaded. Prakṛiti, Mahat, Ahaṃkâra, Manas, the Indriyas, the Tan-mâtras and the Elements are then the physical and metaphysical existences, realities, or principles pervading all the three worlds.

Buddhi and its modifications described.

अध्यवसायो बुद्धिर्धर्मो ज्ञानं विराग ऐश्वर्यम् ।
सात्त्विकमेतद्रूपं तामसमस्माद्विपर्यस्तम् ॥ २३ ॥

अध्यवसाय: Adhyavasâyaḥ, ascertainment. बुद्धि: Buddhiḥ, Mahat, Buddhi. धर्म: Dharmaḥ, virtue, merit. ज्ञानं Jñânaṃ, knowledge. विराग: Virâgaḥ, dispassion. ऐश्वर्यम् Aiśvaryam, lordliness, power. सात्त्विकम् Sâttvikam, partaking of Sattva. एतद्रूपं Etata-rupam, its forms. तामसम् Tâmasam, partaking of Tamas. अस्मात् Asmât, from this. विपर्यस्तम् Viparyastam, the reverse.

XXIIII. Ascertainment is Buddhi. Virtue, knowledge, dispassion and power are its forms or manifestations or modifications, partaking of Sattva. Those partaking of Tamas, are the reverse of these.

ANNOTATION.

44. Ascertainment is Buddhi: this statement in apposition is intended to teach that there is no difference between the function and the fuctionary.

Ascertainment is to arrive at the certainty that this is a jar, this I will do, etc., which is above the stage of doubt, differentiation, assimilation, and deliberation.

Virtue is that which is the cause of happiness and release, and includes the fruits of sacrifices and of the practice of Yoga as taught by Patañjali.

Knowledge is the manfestation of the discrimination between Prakṛiti and Puruṣa.

Dispassion is absence of Râga or passion. It has four names: the name of Yatamâna, Vyatireka, Ekendriya and Vaśîkâra. Passion and the like, which act like dyes of different hues, reside in the Chitta or the Retentive Faculty. By them the Indriyas, the Powers of Cognition and Action, are employed on their respective objects. Now, the endevour, *i.e.*, the putting forth of energy for the purpose of boiling down and dissolving them, with the desire that the Indriyas may not go out to the objects, is designated as Yatamâna. And when the boiling is once begun, some passions will become boiled, while others will be in the course of being boiled. In that stage, the relation of before and after thus coming into existence, the ascertainment of the boiled by means of their discrimination from those that are in the course of being boiled, is designated as Vyatireka. They being thus disabled to excite the Indriyas to activity, the persistence of the boiled passions in the mind in the form of mere longing, is designated as Ekendriya The surcease of even the mere longing in regard to sensible and scriptural objects of enjoyment, even though they be near at hand, which, in its appearance, is subsequent to the first three stages, is designated as Vaśîkâra.—Vâchaspati.

Power is will-power or thought-power, whereby a Yogin becomes at will light as a leaf or heavy as a hill, whereby he can ascend to the sun on a sunbeam or can touch the moon with the tip of his finger, etc.

Partaking of Sattva : that is, when Sattva becomes predominant in Buddhi, by subduing Rajas and Tamas.

Partaking of Tamas : that is, when Tamas becomes predominant in Buddhi, by subduing Sattva and Rajas.

The reverse are vice, ignorance, passion and weakness.

Ahaṃkâra and its Modifications described.

अभिमानोऽहंकारस्तस्मात् द्विविधः प्रवर्तते सर्गः ।
एकादशकश्च गणस्तन्मात्रपञ्चकश्चैव ॥ २४ ॥

अभिमानः Abhimânaḥ, consciousness, self-assertion अहंकारः Ahaṃkâraḥ, Ahaṃkâra. तस्मात् Tasmât, from it. द्विविधः Dvi-vidhaḥ, twofold. प्रवर्तते Pravartate, proceeds सर्गः Sargaḥ, creation, evolution. एकादशकः Ekâdaśakaḥ, elevenfold. च Cha, and. गणः Gaṇaḥ, set, series. तन्मात्रपञ्चकं Tan-mâtra-pañchakam, the pentad of the Tan-mâtras. च Cha, and. एव Eva, nothing else.

XXIV. Self-assertion is Ahaṃkâra. From it proceeds a twofold evolution only : the elevenfold set and also the fivefold Tan-mâtra.

ANNOTATION.

45. The elevenfold set comprises the eleven Indriyas, *i.e.*, the five Indriyas of cognition and the five Indriyas of action and Manas.

The fivefold Tan-mâtra comprises the subtile particles or essences which are Sound, Touch, Form, Taste, and Smell. Whatever word conveys the sense of subtilty or fineness is a synonym of Tan-mâtra.

Self-assertion : All that is considered (âlochita) and reasoned (mata) refers to me, in this I am competent, all these objects of sense are for my sake only, this does not concern any one else but me, hence I am,—such abhimâna, self-assertion or consciousness by reference to oneself, from its having an uncommon or unique operation of its own, is called Ahaṃkâra, by working upon which Buddhi determines that this is to be done by me.

Transformations of Ahaṃkâra distinguished.

सात्त्विक एकादशकः प्रवर्तते वैकृतादहंकारात् ।
भूतादेस्तन्मात्रः स तामसस्तैजसादुभयम् ॥ २५ ॥

सात्त्विकः Sâttvikaḥ, partaking of Sattva, in which Sattva is dominant, pure. एकादशकः Ekâdaśakaḥ, elevenfold. प्रवर्तते Pravartate, proceeds. वैकृतात् vaikṛitât, modified by the predominance of Sattva ; an older term conveying the same sense as Sâttvika. अहंकारात् Ahaṃkârât, from Ahamkâra. भूतादेः Bhûta-âdeḥ, from the original of the elements in which Tamas is dominant ; an older term conveying the same sense as Tâmasa. तन्मात्रः Tan-mâtraḥ, the Tan-mâtras. सः Saḥ, it. तामसः Tâmasaḥ, Tâmasa, having Tamas dominant in it. तैजसात् Taijasât, from Taijasa, which is an older term having the sense of Râjasa, that in which Rajas is dominant. उभयम् Ubhayam, both, *i.e.*, the Indriyas and the Tan-mâtras.

XXV. The Sâttvika elevenfold set proceeds from the Vaikṛita Ahaṃkâra ; from the Bhûtâdi Ahaṃkâra, the Tan-mâtras ; they are Tâmasa ; from Taijasa-Ahaṃkâra, proceed both.

ANNOTATION.

46. From the Taijasa, both : Of the three Guṇas, Rajas alone is exciting and restless (see Kârikâ XIII). Rajas alone, therefore, is active while Sattva and Tamas are inert. These must then depend upon the activity of Rajas for the evolution of their products. It is in this sense that from the Taijasa proceed both, and not that a duplicate set of the Indriyas and the Tan-mâtras simultaneously issue from the Râjasa Ahaṃkâra.

Indriyas enumerated.

बुद्धीन्द्रियाणि चक्षुःश्रोत्रघ्राणरसनत्वगाख्यानि ।
वाक्पाणिपादपायूपस्थान् कर्मेन्द्रियाण्याहुः ॥ २६ ॥

बुद्धीन्द्रियाणि Bûddhi-indriyâṇi, the Indriyas or Powers of cognition. चक्षुःश्रोत्रघ्राणरसनत्वगाख्यानि Chaksuḥ-śrotra-ghrâṇa-rasana-tvak-âkhyâni, called the eyes, ears, nose, tongue, and skin. वाक्पाणिपादपायूपस्थान् Vâk-pâṇi-pâda-pâyu-upasthân, speech, hands, feet, excretory organ and organ of generation. कर्मेन्द्रियाणि Karma-indriyâṇi, the Indriyas or Powers of action. आहुः Âhuḥ, they say.

XXVI. Those called the eyes, the ears, the nose, the tongue and the skin are said to be the Indriyas of cognition, and the speech, hands, feet, the excretory organ and the organ of generation, to be the Indriyas of action.

Manas described.

उभयात्मकमत्र मनः संकल्पकमिन्द्रियञ्च साधर्म्यात् ।
गुणपरिणामविशेषान्नानात्वं बाह्यभेदाश्च ॥ २७ ॥

उभयात्मकम् Ubhaya-âtmakam, possessing the nature of both, *i.e.* Indriyas of cognition and of action. अत्र Atra, herein, in the set of Indriyas. मनः Manaḥ, Manas. संकल्पकम् Saṃkalpakam, that which forms a complete idea at last, by means of assimilation and differenitation ; reflective ; deliberative ; combinative. इन्द्रियं Indriyaṃ, indriya. च Cha, as well. साधर्म्यात् Sâdharmyât, from homogeneousness. गुणपरिणामविशेषात् Guṇa-pariṇâma-viśeṣât, from differences in the transformation of the Guṇas. नानात्वं Nânâ-tvaṃ, manifoldness ; variety ; diverseness. बाह्यभेदाः Bâhya-bhedâḥ, external diversities. च Cha, and.

XXVII. Among the Indriyas, Manas possesses the nature of both. It is deliberative, and is as well an Indriya, as it is homogeneous with the rest. The variety of the Indriyas is due to the differences in the transformation of the Guṇas, and so are the external diversities (of objects of the senses).

ANNOTATION.

47. Nature of both : The presence of Manas is necessary both in respect to cognition and in respect to action ; for, to quote from Locke, "a man whose mind is intently employed in the contemplation of some objects, takes no notice of impressions made by sounding bodies upon the organ of hearing : therefore it is evident that perception is only when the mind receives the impression." Similarly, there can be no movement of the hands, etc., without the co-operation of Manas.

48. Saṃkalpa or deliberation is the uncommon or distinctive function of Manas. By the form of deliberation, Manas is marked out, because, when a thing is first simply observed by the sense as It is something, and doubt arises as to whether it be this or whether it be that, Manas perfectly images it as It is this and not that, that is to say, discriminates the thing as a particular substance possessing specific attributes. In other words, from the materials of the senses, Manas creates percepts. These are then transferred to Ahaṃkâra, which regards them either as concerning itself or not concerning itself. Thus coloured with the personal equation, they are next taken up by Buddhi, which makes certain their true nature and determines conduct accordingly. Such, in brief, is the process of sensuous cognition propounded in the Sâṃkhya Darśana.

4

49. But Manas thus possesses a unique definition of its own, yet it does not lie altogether out of the category of the Indriyas, like Buddhi and Ahaṃkâra; for, unlike them, it is, along with the other Indriyas, produced from the same material cause, *viz.*, Ahaṃkâra modified by the predominance of Sattva. Hence, Manas also is an Indriya.

50. But how, from the same material, are diverse effects, *viz.*, eleven Indriyas of eleven sorts, produced? Further, the eleven Indriyas necessarily imply, and must depend for their existence upon, eleven different sorts of objects. How is this diversity created? when the Pradhâna, Buddhi, and Ahaṃkâra are non-intelligent, and Puruṣa is a non-agent. Is it created by Îśvara or by Svabhâva or Spontaneity? The answer is, that a certain Spontaneity is the cause of the variety of the Indriyas and their objects. Just as through Spontaneity, secretion of milk takes place for the growth of the calf, so the Guṇas become spontaneously modified by the forms of the eleven Indriyas for the benefit of Puruṣa. Similarly, through particular transformation of the Guṇas spontaneously, external objects of various kinds are produced; for whatever is the modification of the Guṇas, is their object; hence, external objects must be understood to be the products of the Guṇas.

"Vâchaspati understands the allusion to external objects to be merely illustrative; that is, the internal organs are diversified by the modification of the qualities, in the same manner that external objects are varied by the same modification".—Wilson's free translation.

Vijñâna Bhikṣu reads the passage as Bâhya-bhedât cha, and from the variety of external objects, instead of Bâhya-bhedâḥ cha, and so are the external diversities.

The Functions of the Indriyas described.

शब्दादिषु पञ्चानामालोचनमात्रमिष्यते वृत्तिः ।
वचनादानविहरणोत्सर्गानन्दाश्च पञ्चानाम् ॥ २८ ॥

शब्दादिषु Śabda-âdi-ṣu, in respect to sound and the rest, *i.e.*, form, touch, taste, and smell. पञ्चानां Pañchânâm, of the five, *i.e.*, senses of cognition. आलोचनमात्रम् Âlochana-mâtram, observation simply, the mere observation of things, the identity of which is not free from doubt. इष्यते Iṣyate, is considered. वृत्तिः Vṛittiḥ, modification, function. वचनादानविहरणोत्सर्गानन्दाः Vachana-âdâna-viharaṇa-utsarga-ânandâḥ, speech, manipulation, locomotion, excretion and generation. च Cha, and. पञ्चानाम् Pnchanâm, of the five, Indriyas of action.

XXVIII. The function of the five, in respect to sound and the rest, is considered to be observation simply. Speech, manipulation, locomotion, excretion and generation are considered to be the functions of the other five.

The common and uncommon functions of the Antaḥ-Karaṇas distinguished.

स्वालक्षण्यं वृत्तिस्त्रयस्य सैषा भवत्यसामान्या ।
सामान्यकरणवृत्तिः प्राणाद्या वायवः पञ्च ॥ २६ ॥

स्वालक्षण्यं Svâlakṣaṇyaṃ, the condition of having specific or distinctive or uncommon or characteristic definitions of their own. वृत्तिः Vṛittiḥ, function, operation. त्रयस्य Traya-sya, of the three, *viz.*, Buddhi, Ahaṃkâra, and Manas. सा Sâ, the same. एषा Eṣâ, this. भवति Bhavati, is. असामान्या A-sâmânyâ, uncommon, peculiar to each. सामान्यकरणवृत्तिः Sâmânaya-karaṇa-vṛittiḥ the common function or modification of the Instruments. प्राणाद्याः Prâṇa-âdyâḥ, Prâṇa and the rest, *viz.*, Apâna, Samâna, Udâna, and Vyâna, the five vital airs, life-breaths. वायवः Vâyavaḥ, airs. पञ्च Pañcha, five.

XXIX. Of the three (internal Instruments), their own definitions are their respective functions. These, the same, (functions) are peculiar to each. The common modification of the Instruments is the five airs beginning with Prâṇa.

ANNOTATION.

51. It is to be noted that the five vital airs are taught to be the modifications jointly of Buddhi, Ahaṃkâra, and Manas, and not of the elements, as otherwise might be imagined.

The functions of the Indriyas are successive as well as simultaneous.

युगपच्चतुष्टयस्य तु वृत्तिः क्रमशश्च तस्य निर्दिष्टा ।
दृष्टे तथाप्यदृष्टे त्रयस्य तत्पूर्विका वृत्तिः ॥ ३० ॥

युगपत् Yugapat, simultaneous, consentaneous. चतुष्टयस्य Chatuṣṭayasya, of the quartet, *viz.*, Buddhi, Ahaṃkâra, Manas, and one of the external senses. तु Tu, but. वृत्तिः Vṛittiḥ, function. क्रमशः Krama-śaḥ, successively, gradually. च Cha, and. तस्य Tasya, its, of the quartet. निर्दिष्टा Nirdiṣtâ, found. दृष्टे Driṣṭe, in the case of the seen, in regard to sensible objects, in the case of perceptual cognition. तथापि Tathâ api, so too. अदृष्टे A-driṣte, in regard to supra-sensible objects, in the case of the unseen, in the case of cognition by inference, testimony, revelation, and recollection. त्रयस्य Traya-sya, of the triad, *viz.*, Buddhi, Ahaṃkâra, and Manas. तत्पूर्विका Tat-pûrvikâ, preceded by that, the seen. वृत्तिः Vṛittiḥ, function.

XXX. Of all the four, the functions are instantaneous; their functions are found to be successive also. This is in regard to sensible objects. In regard to unseen objects, so too are the functions of the three, but preceded by that.

ANNOTATION.

52. Instantaneous: as when one suddenly comes across a tiger in a dark night, one's eyes at once observe, Manas considers, Ahaṃkâra identifies, and Buddhi determines, and the man immediately runs away for his life.

Successive: as when a man sees in dim light something moving in front of him and doubt arises as to what it might be; his Manas considers that it is nothing but a robber; his Ahaṃkâra makes him self-conscious that he is approaching towards him; and his Buddhi determines, I must move away.

So too: that is, in the case of non-perceptual cognition, the functions of Buddhi, Ahaṃkâra, and Manas may be simultaneous as well as successive.

But preceded by that: Hereby the condition of cognition by inference, revelation, and recollection is laid down, which may be stated in the phraseology of Locke as that nothing can be in the intellect which was not previously in the senses. For there can be no inference or revelation or recollection of what has never before been perceived.

How the Indriyas act in harmony with one another.

स्वां स्वां प्रतिपद्यन्ते परस्पराकूतहेतुकां वृत्तिम् ।
पुरुषार्थ एव हेतुर्न केनचित् कार्यते करणम् ॥ ३१ ॥

स्वां स्वां Svâṃ svâṃ, own, own. प्रतिपद्यन्ते Pratipadyante, reach, enter into. परस्पराकूतहेतुकां Paraspara-âkûta-hetukâṃ, of which the cause is proneness to activity arising from mutual sympathy. वृत्तिम् Vṛittim, function, modification. पुरुषार्थः Puruṣa-arthaḥ, the purpose of Puruṣa. एव Eva, alone. हेतुः Hetuḥ, cause, motive. न Na, not. केनचित् Kena chit, by any one whatever. कार्यते Kâryate, wrought, made to act. करणम् Karaṇam, instrument.

XXXI. The Instruments enter into their respective modifications to which they are incited by mutual desire. The purpose of Puruṣa is the only (cause of the activity of the Instruments). By none whatever is an Instrument made to act.

The number, functions and effects of the Indriyas described.

करणं त्रयोदशविधं तदाहरणधारणप्रकाशकरम् ।
कार्यश्च तस्य दशधाहार्यधार्यं प्रकाश्यञ्च ॥ ३२ ॥

करणं Karaṇam, instrument. त्रयोदशविधं Trayodaśa-vidhaṃ, thirteenfold. तत् Tat, it. आहरणधारणप्रकाशकरं Âharaṇa-dhâraṇa-prakâśa-karam, performer of apprehension, sustentation and manifestation. कार्यं Kâryaṃ, effect. च Cha, and. तस्य Tasya, its. दशधा Daśa-dhâ, tenfold. आहार्यं Âhâryaṃ, apprehensible. धार्यं Dhâryaṃ, sustainable. प्रकाश्यं Prakâśyaṃ, manifestable. च Cha. and.

XXXII. The Instrument is of thirteen sorts. It performs apprehension, sustentation, and manifestation. And its effect or act, *viz.*, the apprehensible, the sustainable, and the manifestable, is (each) tenfold.

ANNOTATION.

53. Apprehension is of the five instruments of action. Their effects are speech, manipulation, locomotion, excretion and generation, which being distinguished as earthly and non-earthly, become tenfold.

Sustentation is of the five vital airs, which support the Body. The thing to be sustained, *i.e.*, Body, is fivefold according as it is made of Earth, Water, Fire, Air, and Ether, and these, again, being distinguished as celestial (divya) and non-celestial, become tenfold.

Manifestation is of the five instruments of cognition. The things to be manifested are sound, touch, form, taste, and smell, and these being distinguished as celestial and non-celestial, become tenfold.

Gauḍapâda explains the Kârikâ differently. According to him, the instruments of action apprehend and sustain, those of cognition manifest. The action or effect of these instruments is tenfold, *viz.*, sound, etc., and speech, etc. Thus, what is manifested by the instruments of cognition, is acquired and maintained by those of action.

The Thirteen Indriyas described and distinguished.

अन्तःकरणं त्रिविधं दशधा बाह्यं त्रयस्य विषयाख्यम् ।
साम्प्रतकालं बाह्यं त्रिकालमाभ्यन्तरं करणम् ॥ ३३ ॥

अन्तःकरणं Antaḥ-Karaṇaṃ, the internal instrument. त्रिविधं Tri-vidhaṃ, threefold. दशधा Daśa-dhâ, tenfold. बाह्यं Bâhyaṃ, external. त्रयस्य Trayasya, of the three. विषयाख्यम् Viṣaya-âkhyam, called object. साम्प्रतकालं Sâmprata-kâlaṃ, at time present. बाह्यं Bâhyaṃ, external. त्रिकालम् Tri-kâlam, at three times, *i.e.*, time past, present and future. आभ्यन्तरं Âbhyantaraṃ, internal. करणम् Karaṇam, instrumen.

XXXIII. The internal Instrument is threefold; the external, tenfold, called the object of the three. The external instrument operates at time present; the internal at all the three times.

ANNOTATION.

54. Called the object of the three: because the external instruments of cognition and action are the channels through which the three internal instruments of Buddhi, Ahaṃkâra, and Manas come into contact with, and exercise their functions in regard to, the external objects.

Objects of the Indriyas described.

बुद्धीन्द्रियाणि तेषां पञ्च विशेषाविशेषविषयाणि ।
वाग्भवति शब्दविषया शेषाणि तु पञ्चविषयाणि ॥३४॥

बुद्धीन्द्रियाणि Buddhi-indriyâṇi, the Indriyas of cognition. तेषां Teṣâṃ, of these. पञ्च Pañcha, five. विशेषाविशेषविषयाणि Viśeṣa-aviśeṣa-viṣayâṇi, having as their objects gross sound, etc., causing pleasure, pain, and dulness, and subtile sound, etc., in the form of the Tan-mâtras. वाक् Vâk, speech. भवति Bhavati, is. शब्दविषया Śabda-viṣayâ, having sound as object. शेषाणि Śeṣâṇi, the rest, *i e.*, hands, feet, the excretory organ and the organ of generation. तु Tu, but. पञ्चविषयाणि Pañcha-viṣayâṇi, having all the five, sound, etc., as objects.

XXXIV. Among these (ten Indriyas) the five Indriyas of cognition have for their objects things gross and subtile. Speech has sound (alone) for its object. But the rest have (all) the five as their objects.

ANNOTATION.

55. But the rest have the five etc.: for, a jar, *e.g.*, which may be taken hold of by the hand, possesses sound, touch, form, taste, and smell; the foot treads upon the earth of which sound and the rest are the characteristics; the excretory organ separates that in which these five abide; and the organ of generation produces the secretion in which all these five are present.

Why Buddhi is principal among the Indriyas.

सान्तःकरणा बुद्धिः सर्वं विषयमवगाहते यस्मात् ।
तस्मात्त्रिविधं करणं द्वारि द्वाराणि शेषाणि ॥ ३५ ॥

सान्तःकरणा Sa-antaḥ-karaṇâ, together with the internal instruments of Ahaṃkâra and Manas, बुद्धिः Buddhiḥ, Buddhi, सर्वं Sarvaṃ, all. विषयम् Viṣayam, object. अवगाहते Avagâhate, adverts to, comprehends. यस्मात् Yasmât, since. तस्मात् Tasmât, therefore. त्रिविधं Tri-vidhaṃ, threefold. करणं Karaṇaṃ, instrument. द्वारि Dvâri, warders, gatemen, room. द्वाराणि Dvârâṇi, gates. शेषाणि Seṣâṇi, rest.

XXXV. Since Buddhi, together with Ahaṃkâra and Manas, comprehends all objects (at all times), therefore, the three Instruments are like a house of which the rest are gates.

Above continued.

एते प्रदीपकल्पाः परस्परविलक्षणा गुणविशेषाः ।
कृत्स्नं पुरुषस्यार्थं प्रकाश्य बुद्धौ प्रयच्छंति ॥ ३६ ॥

एते Ete, these, the ten external Indriyas, Manas, and Ahaṃkâra. प्रदीपकल्पाः Pradîpa-kalpâḥ, comparable to a lamp. परस्परविलक्षणाः Paraspara-vilakṣaṇâḥ, characteristically different from one another. गुणविशेषाः Guṇa-viśeṣâḥ, particular modifications of the Guṇas. कृत्स्नं Kṛitsnaṃ, whole. पुरुषस्य Puruṣa-sya, of, *i.e.*, to Puruṣa. अर्थं Arthaṃ, object. प्रकाश्य Prakâśya, manifesting. बुद्धौ Buddhau, to Buddhi. प्रयच्छंति Prayachchhanti, present, make over.

XXXVI. These particular modifications of the Guṇas, which are characteristically different from one another, and which are, therefore, in this matter, comparable to a lamp, present all their respective objects to Buddhi, so that these may be exhibited to Puruṣa.

ANNOTATION.

56. Comparable to a lamp : see Kârikâ XIII.

• Present......to Buddhi : for Puruṣa can experience objects, pleasure, etc., only such as are lodged in Buddhi. The process by which ideas are conveyed to Puruṣa is here described.

Above continued.

सर्वं प्रत्युपभोगं यस्मात् पुरुषस्य साधयति बुद्धिः ।
सैव च विशिनष्टि पुनः प्रधानपुरुषान्तरं सूक्ष्मम् ॥ ३७॥

सर्वं Sarvaṃ, all. प्रति Prati, in regard to. उपभोगं Upa-Bhogaṃ, experience through conjunction. यस्मात् Yasmât, since. पुरुषस्य Puruṣa-sya, of Puruṣa. साधयति Sâdhayati, effects, accomplishes. बुद्धिः Buddhiḥ, Buddhi. सा Sâ, it. एव Eva, the same. च Cha, and. विशिनष्टि Viśinaṣṭi, differentiates, discriminates. पुनः Punaḥ, again. प्रधानपुरुषान्तरं Pradhâna-puruṣa-antaram, difference between the Pradhâna and Puruṣa. सूक्ष्मम् Sukṣaṃ subtile, difficult to discern, not to be apprehended by those who have not practised religious austerities.

XXXVII. (The other Indriyas present all objects to Buddhi, so that they may be exhibited to Puruṣa), since it is Buddhi which accomplishes the experience of Puruṣa in regard to all (objects at all times). And it is that, again, which discriminates the subtile difference between the Pradhâna and Puruṣa.

ANNOTATION.

57. In these three Kârikâs it is established that Buddhi is supreme among the Indriyas. It is the principal means of accomplishing the apparently contradictory purposes of Puruṣa, *viz.*, experience and release. For Buddhi, through the adjacence of Puruṣa, by means of the falling of his shadow, becoming verily of his form, accomplishes Puruṣa's experience of all objects; for experience consists in the apprehension of pleasure and pain, and this exists in Buddhi, and Buddhi is verily of the form of Puruṣa; hence it causes experience to Puruṣa. And while, on the one hand, it is the cause of experience, it is, on the other hand, the cause of release as well, since it is Buddhi which causes discrimination between Prakṛiti and Puruṣa.

The Tan-mâtras and their products described.

तन्मात्राण्यविशेषास्तेभ्यो भूतानि पञ्च पञ्चभ्यः ।
एते स्मृता विशेषाः शान्ता घोराश्च मूढाश्च ॥ ३८ ॥

तन्मात्राणि Tan-mâtrâṇi, Tan-mâtras, subtile elements, the originals of atoms. अविशेषाः A-viśeṣâḥ, indistinguishables, indiscernibles, undifferentiated as pleasant, painful or dull. तेभ्यः Tebhyaḥ, from these. भूतानि Bhûtâni, the gross or great elements. पञ्च Pañcha, five. पञ्चभ्यः Pañchabhyaḥ, from the five. एते Ete, these. स्मृताः Smṛitâḥ, remembered. विशेषाः Viśeṣâḥ, the distinguishables, discernibles, differentiated as pleasant, painful and dull. शान्ताः Śântâḥ, pacific, causing pleasure, tranquil. घोराः Ghorâḥ, terrific, causing pain, disagreeable. च Cha, since. मूढाः Mûḍhâḥ, stupefic, dull. च Cha, and.

XXXVIII. The Tan-mâtras are the indiscernibles. From these five, proceed the five gross Elements which are remembered to be the discernibles; for they are pacific, terrific, and stupefic.

ANNOTATION.

58. Tan-mâtra: *lit.* That-merely or its measure. The Tan-mâtras are subtle forms of Sound, Touch, Form, Taste, and Smell which have

not yet come down to that degree of materialisation in which they cause pleasure, pain, and dulness, and thereby become capable of experience. Such is the force of the word *merely*, according to Vâchaspati's interpretation. They are, however, not properties or qualities but substances. Vijñâna Bhikṣu describes them as "fine substances, the undifferentiated originals of the Gross Elements, which form the substrata of Sound, Touch, Form, Flavour, and Smell, belonging to that class (that is, in that state of their evolution) in which the distinctions of Śânta, etc., do not exist." So we find from the Viṣṇu-Purâṇam and other sources, *e.g.*, that 'in them severally reside their parts (mâtrâ) wherefore the Smṛiti describes them as Tan (their)-mâtra (part). They are neither Śânta, pacific, nor Ghora, terrific, nor, again, Mûḍha, stupefying, but are indistinguishables.'

59. Pacific, etc. :—Every one of the five Gross Elements possesses the threefold characteristic of causing pleasure, pain, and dulness.

Subtile and Gross Bodies described and distinguished.

सूक्ष्मा मातापितृजाः सह प्रभूतैस्त्रिधा विशेषाः स्युः ।
सूक्ष्मास्तेषां नियता मातापितृजा निवर्तन्ते ॥ ३९ ॥

सूक्ष्माः Sûkṣmâḥ subtile Bodies. मातापितृजाः Mâtâ-pitṛi-jâḥ, Bodies produced from mother and father. सह Saha, together. प्रभूतैः Pra-bhûtaiḥ, with the Great Elements. त्रिधा Tri-dhâ, threefold. विशेषाः Viśeṣâḥ, distinguishables, specific objects. स्युः Syuḥ, will be. सूक्ष्माः Sûkṣmâh, subtile Bodies. तेषां Teṣâṃ, among them. नियताः Niyatâḥ constant, continuant. मातापितृजाः Mâtâ-pitṛi-jâḥ, Bodies produced from mother and father. निवर्तन्ते Nivartante, cease, perish.

XXXIX. The Subtile Bodies, Bodies produced from father and mother, together with the Great Elements, will be the Viśeṣas. Amongst them, the Subtile Bodies are continuant; Bodies produced from father and mother cease (to entangle after death.)

ANNOTATION.

60. Wilson's learned disquisition on the meaning of the present Kârikâ is misguided and misleading. The Sâṃkhya describes or displays the gradual materialisation of the Pradhâna from the highest degree of subtelity to the lowest form of grossness. In the series of evolutes, the Tan-mâtras and the Gross Elements may be said, loosely speaking, to occupy the same plane, that is, the plane of materiality in the current sense of the term, and to stand to each other as do atoms to earth, air,

etc. But though they are on the same plane, there is a marked difference between them; for the Tan-mâtras are indiscernible, while the Elements are discernible. A Viśeṣa is what contains a Viśeṣaṇa or qualification, something extra by means of which it is distinguished from others. In the present case the Viśeṣaṇa is the property of causing pleasure, pain and dulness. This is absent from the Tan-mâtras and is present in the Elements. It is clear, therefore, that the transition from the Tan-mâtras to the next succeeding form of evolution is marked by the development of the property of causing pleasure, pain and dulness. Similarly, the Subtile Body which is a combination of the Tan-mâtras and the Tattvas upward, and Indriyas which are pacific, terrific, and stupefic, contains the aroma of past experiences. So is it as well as the Elements and the Bodies formed of them classed among the Viśeṣas, as distinguished from the Tan-mâtras which are A-Viśeṣas.

How the Subtile Body migrates.

पूर्वोत्पन्नमसक्तं नियतं महदादिसूक्ष्मपर्यन्तम् ।
संसरति निरुपभोगं भावैरधिवासितं लिङ्गम् ॥ ४० ॥

पूर्वोत्पन्नं Pûrva-utpannam, primæval, produced at the beginning of creation by the Pradhâna, one for each Puruṣa. असक्तं A-saktam, unconnected, unconfined to any particular gross Body, and therefore unobstructed in its passage even through a mountain. नियतं Niyatam, continuant, constant, as it lasts from the beginning of creation to the time of the Great Dissolution. महदादिसूक्ष्मपर्यन्तम् Mahat-âdi-sûkṣma-paryantam, being the combination of the Tattvas beginning with Mahat and ending with the Subtile, *i.e.*, the Tan-mâtras. संसरति Samsarati, moves from Body to Body, transmigrates. निरुपभोगं Nir-upabhogam, free from, or without, experience. भावैः Bhâvaiḥ, dispositions, conditions, such as virtue, vice, etc. अधिवासितं Adhivâsitam, perfumed, affected, tinged. लिङ्गम् Liṅgam, mergent, that which suffers resolution, being a product, a combination of things.

XL. The Liṅga or mergent Body, the one primordially produced, unconfined, continuant, composed of the Tattvas beginning with Mahat and ending with the Tan-mâtras, transmigrates, free from Experience, tinged with the Bhâvas.

ANNOTATION.

61. Tinged with the Bhâvas: The Bhâvas reside in Buddhi which accompanies or is associated with the Subtile Body, and through such association, the Subtile Body is affected by the Bhâvas in the same manner, for instance, as a piece of cloth is perfumed with the sweet smell of a

Champaka flower from contact with it. And it is this affection by the Bhâvas which is the cause of the transmigration of the Subtile Body.

Necessity for Gross Creation shown.

चित्रं यथाश्रयमृते स्थाण्वादिभ्यो विना यथाच्छाया ।
तद्वद्विना विशेषैर्न तिष्ठति निराश्रयं लिङ्गम् ॥.४२ ॥

चित्रं Chitram, a painting or picture. यथा Yathâ, as. आश्रयम् Âśrayam, ground, support. ऋते Rite, without. स्थाण्वादिभ्यः Sthâṇu-âdi-bhyaḥ, a stake, etc. विना Vinâ without. यथा Yathâ, as. छाया Chhâyâ, shadow. तद्वत् Tat-vat, similarly to that. विना Viṇâ, without. विशेषैः Viśeṣaiḥ, Viśeṣas, Subtile Bodies (Vâchaspati), the Tan-mâtras (Goudapâda), Âtivâhika or Vehicular Bodies (Vijñâna Bhikṣu). न Na, not. तिष्ठति Tiṣṭhati, stands, subsists. निराश्रयं Nir-âśrayaṃ, supportless. लिङ्गम् Liṅgam, that which makes known, *viz.*, Buddhi, Ahaṃkâra, Manas and the other Indriyas (Vâchaspati, Gauḍapâda), the Subtile Body called Liṅga. (Vijñâna).

XLI. As a painting stands not without a support, nor is there a shadow without a stake or the like, so neither does the Liṅga subsist supportless, without the Viśeṣas.

ANNOTATION.

62. Viśeṣas : The difference of the interpretation of this word points to a difference of doctrine. Thus, according to Gauḍapâda and Vâchaspati, there are only two kinds of Body, as described above. But, according to Vijñâna Bhikṣu, there is also a third kind of Body, the Adhiṣṭhâna Śarira, which is formed of a finer form of the gross elements and which serves as the receptacle of the Liṅga Śarîra.

The activity of the Subtile Body further explained.

पुरुषार्थहेतुकमिदं निमित्तनैमित्तिकप्रसंगेन ।
प्रकृतेर्विभुत्वयोगान्नटवद्व्यवतिष्ठते लिङ्गम् ॥ ४२ ॥

पुरुषार्थहेतुकम् Puruṣa-artha-hetu-kam, which has the object of Puruṣa as motive. इदं Idaṃ, this. निमित्तनैमित्तिकप्रसंगेन Nimitta-naimittika-parasaṅgena, by association with instrumental causes such as virtue, vice, etc., and with their consequences such as the body of a god or a man or a beast. प्रकृतेः Prakṛiteḥ, of Prakṛiti. विभुत्वयोगात् Vibhu-tva-yogât, from conjunction or the universal supremacy of Prakṛiti. नटवत् Naṭa-vat, like a dramatic actor. व्यवतिष्ठते Vyavatiṣṭhate, appears in different roles. लिङ्गम् Liṅgam, the subtile body.

XLII. Impelled by the purpose of Puruṣa, this Subtile Body appears in different roles, like a dramatic performer, by means of association with instrumental causes and their consequences, through the universal supremacy of Prakṛiti.

ANNOTATION.

63. Like a dramatic performer: Just as, on the stage, one and the same person plays the parts of Paraśurâma, Ajâtaśatru and Vatsarâja, so the same Subtile Body may appear in the body of a god or an elephant or a man. The final and material causes of this transmigration of the Subtile Body in general are respectively the purpose of Puruṣa and Prakṛiti, and the formal and efficient causes which determine particular migrations, are respectively the consequences of the Nimittas and the Nimittas, namely, virtue, vice, and the like.

Bhâvas divided and described.

सांसिद्धिकाश्च भावाः प्राकृतिका वैकृतिकाश्च धर्माद्याः ।
दृष्टाः करणाश्रयिणः कार्याश्रयिणश्च कललाद्याः ॥४३॥

सांसिद्धिका : Sâṃsiddhikâḥ, produced from means already in existence, *viz.*, previous Karma; innate, instinctive. च Cha, and. भावाः: Bhâvâḥ, dispositions, conditions, circumstances. प्राकृतिकाः: Prâkṛitikâḥ, essential, natural, springing from Prâkṛiti direct. वैकृतिकाः: Vaikṛitikâḥ, acquired, due or relating to vikṛiti or transformations. च Cha, and. धर्माद्याः: Dharma-âdyâḥ, virtue and the rest. दृष्टाः: Dṛiṣṭâḥ, seen. करणाश्रयिणः: Karaṇa-âśrâyiṇaḥ, residing in the Karaṇa, *i.e*, Buddhi. कार्याश्रयिणः: Kârya-âsrayiṇaḥ, residing in the effect, *i.e*, body. च Cha, and. कललाद्याः: Kalala-âdyâḥ, the uterine germ and the rest.

XLIII. The Bhâvas or dispositions are instinctive, essential, and also acquired. Dharma and the rest are considered as residing in Buddhi, and the uterine germ and the rest as residing in the Body.

ANNOTATION.

64. *Sâṃsiddhika*: as, at the beginning of creation, when the Lord Kapila was to appear, the four Bhâvas, *viz.*, virtue, knowledge, dispassion, and power, were produced along with him. They are then the effects of causes appertaining to a former creation.

Prâkṛitika: These are equally innate or instinctive, but are the effects of causes appertaining to the present creation. Thus, from the very same causes, *i.e.*, highly purified form of Prakṛitic matter, from which the perpetually youthful Bodies of the four sons of Brahmâ, namely, Sanaka, Sanandana, Sanâtana, and Sanatkumâra, were produced, were also at the same time produced the Bhâvas of virtue and the rest in them.

Vaikṛitika: These are those acquired from a Vikṛiti or evolute, namely, a teacher whose Body is an evolute; thus the effect of tuition is knowledge, knowledge leads to dispassion, dispassion to virtue, and virtue to power. This is how ordinary human beings acquire the Bhâvas.

The Bhâvas, virtue, knowledge, dispassion, and power, grow when Sattva is dominant. Hence they are characterised as Sâttvic. Those that grow during the predominance of Tamas, are vice, ignorance, passion, and weakness. These are characterised as Tâmasic.

These eight Bhâvas are the Nimittas or efficient causes of particular migrations of the Liṅga Śarira. They operate through bringing about connection with their effects, the Naimittikas, from the first commingled blood and semen in the uterus up to the fully developed Body.

Effects of the Bhâvas described.

धर्मेण गमनमूर्ध्वं गमनमधस्ताद्भवत्यधर्मेण ।
ज्ञानेन चापवर्गो विपर्ययादिष्यते बन्धः ॥ ४४ ॥

धर्मेण Dharmeṇa, by means of virtue. गमनम् Gamanam, going. ऊर्ध्वं Urdhvaṃ, upward. गमनम् Gamanam, going. अधस्तात् Adhastât, downward. भवति Bhavati, is. अधर्मेण A-dharmeṇa, by means of vice. ज्ञानेन Jñânena, by means of knowledge. च Cha, and. अपवर्गः Apavargaḥ, release. विपर्ययात् Viparyayât, from the reverse, *i.e.*, of knowledge, that is, ignorance. इष्यते Iṣyate, considered. बन्धः Bandhaḥ, bondage.

XLIV. By virtue, is going upward; going downward is by vice; and by knowledge, is Release; from the reverse, Bondage is considered (to be.)

ANNOTATION.

65. Upwards: that is, to the worlds of Brahmâ, Prajâpati, Soma, Indra, the Gandharvas, the Yakṣas, the Râkṣasas, and the Piśâchas.

Downward: that is, into the Bodies of beasts, birds, reptiles, trees, etc.

Knowledge: that is, knowledge of the discrimination between Puruṣa and Prakṛiti.

Release: when the Subtile Body ceases and Puruṣa becomes Paramaâtmâ.

Bondage: it is either Prâkṛitika, or Vaikṛitika, or Dâkṣiṇaka. The first is of those who, mistaking either of the eight Prakṛitis, *viz.*, the Pradhâna, Mahat, Ahaṃkâra, and the five Tan-mâtras, to be Puruṣa, contemplate upon that, and not upon Puruṣa. After death, they are absorbed in the Prakṛitis, and are called Prakṛiti-layas. The second is of those who contemplate upon the transformations, *viz.*, the elements, the Indriyas, individual Ahaṃkâra and individual Buddhi, mistaking them for Puruṣa, and after death reach unto the archetypes of those transformations. The third is of those who, not knowing the Tattva, *i.e.*, Puruṣa, seek mundane and heavenly happiness through performance of acts of charity and public utility.

Above continued.

वैराग्यात् प्रकृतिलयः संसारो भवति राजसाद्रागात् ।
ऐश्वर्यादविघातो विपर्ययात्तद्विपर्यासः ॥ ४५ ॥

वैराग्यात् Vairâgyât, from dispassion, that is, from dispassion divorced from knowledge of the Tattvas. प्रकृतिलयः Prakṛiti-layaḥ, absorption into the eight Prakṛitis, which state of absorption lasts for full one hundred thousand Manvantaras. संसारः Saṃsâraḥ, transmigration, revolution of births and deaths. भवति Bhavati, is. राजसात् Râjasât, produced from, or appertaining to, Rajas. रागात् Râgât, from passion. ऐश्वर्यात् Aiśvaryât, from power. अविघातः A-vighâtaḥ, non-impediment *i.e.*, of desire. विपर्ययात् Viparyayât, from the reverse, *i.e.*, from weakness. तद्विपर्यासः Tat-viparyâsaḥ, the contrary thereof, *i e.* impediment.

XLV. From dispassion is absorption into the Prakṛitis, transmigration is from the passion of Rajas, from power is unimpediment, from the reverse is the contrary.

ANNOTATION.

66. In these two Kârikâs, the eight efficient causes and their eight effects have been declared. They are:

	CAUSE.	EFFECT.
Sattvic	1. Virtue.	2. Elevation to the higher worlds.
	3. Knowledge.	4. Release.
	5. Dispassion.	6. Dissolution into the Prakṛitis.
	7. Power.	8. Unimpediment to fulfilment of desire.
Tamasic	9. Vice.	10. Degradation to the lower worlds.
	11. Ignorance.	12. Bondage.
	13. Passion.	14. Migration.
	15. Weakness.	16. Impediment to fulfilment of desire.

The creations of Buddhi classified and explained.

एषो प्रत्ययसर्गो विपर्ययाशक्तितुष्टिसिद्ध्याख्यः ।
गुणवैषम्यविमर्दात्तस्य च भेदास्तु पञ्चाशत् ॥ ४६ ॥

एषः Esaḥ, this. प्रत्ययसर्गः Pratyaya-sargaḥ, the creation of that by which intuition of things is made, that is, Buddhi. विपर्ययाशक्तितुष्टिसिद्ध्याख्यः viparyâya-aśakti-tuṣti-siddhi-âkhyaḥ, called ignorance, incapacity, complacency, and perfection.

गुणवैषम्यविमर्दात् Guṇa-vaiṣamya-vimardât, from the conflict of the Guṇas in unequal degrees of strength, from the combination of the Guṇas in different proportions, and consequent predominance of one over others. तस्य Tasya, its, of the creation of Buddhi. च Cha and. भेदाः Bhedâḥ, sorts, divisions. तु Tu, again. पञ्चाशत् Pañchâśat, fifty.

XLVI. This is the creation of Buddhi, termed ignorance, incapacity, complacency, and perfection. And from the conflict of the Guṇas in unequal degree of strength, its sorts, again, are fifty.

ANNOTATION.

67. This: that is, the sixteenfold cause and effect mentioned in the preceding Kârikâ. They are all modifications or products of Buddhi. Their minor divisions are legions. To attempt some classification, they are primarily of four sorts, and secondarily of fifty sorts.

The creations of Buddhi subdivided.

पञ्च विपर्ययभेदा भवन्त्यशक्तिश्च करणवैकल्यात् ।
अष्टाविंशतिभेदा तुष्टिर्नवधाष्टधा सिद्धिः ॥ ४७ ॥

पञ्च Pañcha, five, *viz.*, A-vidyâ, Asmitâ, Râga, Dveṣa, and Abhiniveṣa. विपर्ययभेदाः Viparyaya-bhedâḥ, divisions of mistake or ignorance. भवन्ति Bhavanti, are. अशक्तिः A-śaktiḥ, incapacity. च Cha, and. करणवैकल्यात् Karaṇa-vaikalyât, according to the impairment of the Instruments or Indriyas. अष्टाविंशतिभेदा Aṣṭâviṃśati-bhedâ, having twenty-eight divisions. तुष्टिः Tuṣṭiḥ, complacency. नवधा Nava-dhâ, ninefold. अष्टधा Aṣṭa-dhâ, eightfold. सिद्धिः Siddhiḥ, perfection.

XLVII. Five are the divisions of ignorance; and according to the impairment of the instruments, incapacity has twenty-eight varieties; while complacency is ninefold; perfection, eightfold.

Divisions of Error subdivided.

भेदस्तमसोऽष्टविधो मोहस्य च दशविधो महामोहः ।
तामिस्रोऽष्टादशधा तथा भवत्यन्धतामिस्रः ॥ ४८ ॥

भेदाः Bhedâḥ, distinctions, divisions. तमसः Tamasaḥ, of Tamas, which is a technical term for A-Vidyâ or false knowledge. अष्टविधः Aṣṭa-vidhaḥ, eightfold. मोहस्य Mohasya, of Moha, which is technical for Asmitâ or Am-ness or egotism. च Cha-and. दशविधः Daśa-vidhaḥ, tenfold. महामोहः Mahâ-mohaḥ, Mahâmoha, which is technical for Râga or passion. तामिस्रः Tâmisraḥ, Tâmisra, which is technical for Dveṣa or aversion. अष्टादशधा Aṣṭâdaśa-dhâ, eighteenfold. तथा Tathâ, so. भवति Bhavâti, is. अन्धतामिस्रः Andha-tâmisraḥ. Andhatâmisra, which is technical for Abhiniveśa or blind attachment to life.

XLVIII. The distinctions of A-Vidyâ are eightfold, as also of Asmitâ ; tenfold is Râga ; Dveṣa is eighteenfold ; so also is Abhiniveśa.

Incapacity subdivided.

एकादशेन्द्रियवधाः सह बुद्धिवधैरशक्तिरुद्दिष्टा ।
सप्तदश वधा बुद्धेर्विपर्ययात्तुष्टिसिद्धीनाम् ॥ ४९ ॥

एकादशेन्द्रियवधाः Ekâdaśa-indriya-badhâḥ, injuries of the eleven Indriyas. सह Saha, together. बुद्धिवधैः Buddhi-badhaiḥ, with injuries of Buddhi. अशक्तिः A-śaktiḥ incapacity. उद्दिष्टा Uddiṣṭâ, pronounced. सप्तदशवधाः Saptadaśa-badhâḥ, seventeen injuries. बुद्धेः Buddheḥ, of Buddhi. विपर्ययात् Viparyayât, from inversion. तुष्टिसिद्धीनाम् Tuṣti-siddhînâm, of complacencies and perfections.

XLIX. Injuries of the eleven Indriyas, together with injuries of Buddhi, are pronounced to be Incapacity. The injuries of Buddhi are seventeen, through inversion of complacencies and perfections.

Complacency subdivided.

आध्यात्मिकाश्चतस्रः प्रकृत्युपादानकालभाग्याख्याः ।
बाह्या विषयोपरमात् पञ्च नव तुष्टयोऽभिमताः ॥ ५० ॥

आध्यात्मिकाः Âdhyâtmikâḥ, self (soul)-regarding, it is that form of complacency in which there is belief in the existence of a Self, as distinct from Prakriti, but in which the Self is identified with the Not-Self. चतस्रः Chatasra, four. प्रकृत्युपादानकालभाग्याख्याः Prakṛiti-upâdâna-kâla-bhâgya-âkhyâḥ, called after Prakṛiti or Root, Upâdâna or Material, Kâla or Time, and Bhâgya or Luck. बाह्याः Bâhyâḥ, external, Not-Self-regarding. विषयोपरमात् Viṣaya-uparamât, through abstinence from objects. पञ्च Pañcha, five. नवधा Nava-dhâ, ninefold. तुष्टयः Tuṣṭayaḥ, complacencies. अभिहिताः Abhihitâḥ, propounded.

L. The nine Complacencies are propounded : the four Self-regarding ones called after Prakṛiti, Material, Time, and Luck ; the external five, through abstinence from objects.

Perfection subdivided.

ऊहः शब्दोऽध्ययनं दुःखविघातास्त्रयः सुहृत्प्राप्तिः ।
दानं च सिद्धयोऽष्टौ सिद्धेः पूर्वोऽङ्कुशस्त्रिविधः ॥ ५१ ॥

ऊहः Ûhaḥ, reasoning, argumentation. शब्दः Śabdaḥ, word, verbal instruction. अध्ययनं Adhyayanaṃ, study. दुःखविघाताः Duḥkha-vighâtâḥ, preventions of pain. त्रयः Trayaḥ, three. सुहृत्प्राप्तिः Suhṛit-prâptiḥ, acquisition of friend, intercourse with friend. दानं Dânaṃ, charity, purity. च Cha, and. सिद्धयः Siddhayaḥ, perfections. अष्टौ Aṣṭau, eight. सिद्धेः Siddheḥ, of perfection. पूर्वः Pûrvaḥ, preceding, first. अङ्कुशः Aṅkuśaḥ, goad, curb, restrainer. त्रिविधः Tri-Vidhaḥ, threefold.

LI. Argumentation, Word, Study, the three Preventions of Pain, Acquisition of friends, Charity or Purity are the eight Perfections. Those mentioned before Perfection are the threefold goad to (Ignorance and suffering).

ANNOTATION.

68. Those mentioned before Perfection are Ignorance, Incapacity, and Complacency.

Aṅkuśa :—This word may also be rendered by curb, meaning that Ignorance and the rest curb, *i.e.*, impede or obstruct the means to Perfection.

69. Vijñâna Bhikṣu has interpreted this Kârikâ in a different manner and has criticised unfavourably the exposition of Gauḍapâda and Vâchaspati. See our Sâṃkhya-Pravachana-Sûtram, Sacred Books of the *H*indus, Vol. XI, page 321.

70. The above details of the creations of Buddhi have been fully explained in the commentaries on the Tattva-Samâsaḥ and the Sâṃkhya Pravachana-Sûtram. The reader is accordingly referred to Vol. XI of the Sacred Books of the *H*indus.

71. Now, if it be questioned that when any one of the two, *viz.*, creations of Buddhi and creations of the Tan-mâtras, is enough for the accomplishment of the purpose of Puruṣa, what need is there for a twofold creation? so it is declared in the succeeding Kârikâ.

Twofold creation, of Buddhi and of Tanmâtra, upheld.

न विना भावैर्लिङ्गं न विना लिङ्गेन भावनिर्वृत्तिः ।
लिङ्गाख्यो भावाख्यस्तस्माद्द्विविधः प्रवर्तते सर्गः ॥ ५२ ॥

न Na, not. विना Vinâ, without. भावैः Bhâvaiḥ, dispositions, the creations of Buddhi mentioned above. लिङ्गं Liṅgaṃ, the creation of the Tan-mâtras. न

Na, not. विना Vinâ, without. लिङ्गेन Liṅgena, the creation of the Tan-mâtras. भावनिर्वृत्तिः Bhâva-nirvrittiḥ, cessation or pause of the dispositions. लिङ्गाख्यः Liṅga-âkhyaḥ, termed Liṅga. भावाख्यः Bhâva-âkhyaḥ, termed Bhâva. तस्मात् Tasmât, hence. द्विविधः Dvi-vidhaḥ, twofold. प्रवर्तते Pravartate, proceeds. सर्गः Sargaḥ, creation.

LII. Without the Bhâvas, there would be no Liṅga, without the Linga, there would be no surcease of the Bhâvas; wherefrom a twofold creation proceeds; the one called after the Liṅga, the other called after the Bhâvas.

ANNOTATION.

72. Vâchaspati explains the necessity for a twofold creation and their interdependence thus: Experience which is the object of Puruṣa, cannot be possible in the absence of the objects of experience, such as sound and the rest, as well as of the twofold Body which is the Âyatana or house of experience: wherefore the creations of the Tan-mâtras are necessary. In the same manner, the very same Experience is not possible without the Indriyas and the Antaḥ-karaṇa which are the instruments of Experience; these, again, cannot be possible without the Bhâvas, virtue and the rest. Neither is the manifestation of Discrimination, which is the cause of Release, possible in the absence of the twofold creation. *Hence* the twofold creation is established.

The succession of the two kinds of creation as mutually cause and effect is no fault, as it is from eternity, like that of the seed and the sprout. Even in the beginning of a Kalpa the production of the Bhâvas and the Liṅga under the influence of the Saṃskâra or impression of the Bhâvas and the Liṅga produced in a previous Kalpa, is not unproved.

Gross Creation subdivided.

अष्टविकल्पो दैवस्तैर्यग्योनश्च पञ्चधा भवति ।
मानुष्यश्चैकविधः समासतोऽयं भौतिकः सर्गः ॥ ५३ ॥

अष्टविकल्पः Aṣṭa-vikalpaḥ, having eight specific kinds, *viz.*, Brâhma, Prâjâpatya, etc. दैवः Daivaḥ, divine, celestial, supernatural, super-human. तैर्यग्योनः Tairyak-yonaḥ, the grovelling-born. च Cha, and. पञ्चधा Pañcha-dhâ, fivefold. भवति Bhavati, is. मानुष्यः Mânuṣyaḥ, human. च Cha, and, while. एकविधः Eka-vidhaḥ, uniform, of one kind. समासतः Samâsa-taḥ, briefly. अयं Ayaṃ, this. भौतिकः Bhautikaḥ, of the Bhûtas or beings. सर्गः Sargaḥ, creation.

LIII. The superhuman is of eight kinds; and the grovelling species is of five kinds; and the human is of a single kind ; this, briefly, is the Bhautika Sarga or Creation of Beings.

Higher, Lower, and Intermediate Worlds characterised.

ऊर्द्ध्वं सत्त्वविशालस्तमोविशालश्च मूलतः सर्गः ।
मध्ये रजोविशालो ब्रह्मादिस्तम्बपर्यन्तः ॥ ५४ ॥

ऊर्द्ध्वं Urddhvam, above, in the higher worlds of Brahma and the rest. सत्त्वविशालः Sattva-viśâlaḥ, abundant in Sattva, in which Sattva is dominant and Rajas and Tamas are dormant. तमोविशालः Tamaḥ-viśâlaḥ, abundant in Tamas, in which Tamas is dominant and Sattva and Rajas are dormant. च Cha, and. मूलतः Mûla-taḥ, at the bottom, below.

सर्गः Sargaḥ, creation. मध्ये Madhye, in the middle, in the world of man. रजोविशालः Rajaḥ-viśâlaḥ, abundant in Rajas, in which Rajas is dominant and Sattva and Tamas are dormant. ब्रह्मादिस्तम्बपर्यन्तः Brahma-âdi-stamba-paryantaḥ, beginning with Brahmâ and ending with a stock.

LIV. Above, the creation is abundant in Sattva; below, it is abundant in Tamas; in the middle, it is abundant in Rajas; such is the creation from Brahmâ down to a stock.

Universality of pain demonstrated.

तत्र जरामरणकृतं दुःखं प्राप्नोति चेतनः पुरुषः ।
लिङ्गस्याविनिवृत्तेस्तस्माद्दुःखं स्वभावेन ॥ ५५ ॥

तत्र Tatra, therein, in the three worlds, in the bodies of the superhuman, human and grovelling species. जरामरणकृतं Jarâ-maraṇa-kṛitam, caused by decay and death. दुःखं Duḥkham, pain. प्राप्नोति Prâpnoti, experiences. चेतनः Chetanaḥ, intelligent. The force of this word is to exclude experience of pain from Prakṛiti and her products which are all non-intelligent. पुरुषः Puruṣaḥ, that which lies (*Sete*) in the *Puri* or the Liṅga Śarîra or Subtile Body, Puruṣa. लिङ्गस्य Liṅga-sya, of the Liṅga Śarîra. अविनिवृत्तेः A-vinivṛitteḥ, owing to the non-cessation, or till the cessation of the Liṅga Śarîra which is continuant (see Kârikâ XL). and does not cease till the development of discriminative knowledge. तस्मात् Tasmât, therefore. दुःखं Duḥkham, pain. स्वभावेन Sva-bhâvena, by nature.

LV. Therein does intelligent Puruṣa experience pain caused by decay and death, on acount of the non-cessation of, or till the cessation of, the Subtile Body : wherefore pain is the natural order of things.

Object of Prakriti's creation explained.

इत्येषः प्रकृतिकृतो महदादिविशेषभूतपर्यन्तः ।
प्रतिपुरुषविमोक्षार्थं स्वार्थ इव परार्थ आरम्भः ॥ ५६ ॥

इति Iti, thus then. एषः Eṣaḥ, this. प्रकृतिकृतः Prakriti-kritaḥ, originated by Prakriti. महदादिविशेषभूतपर्यन्तः Mahat-âdi-viśeṣa-bhûta-paryantaḥ, beginning with Mahat and ending with the particular, *i.e.*, gross elemental creations. प्रतिपुरुषविमोक्षार्थं Pratipuruṣa-artham, for the release of each individual Puruṣa. स्वार्थे Svâ-arthe, in her own interest. इव Iva, as. परार्थे Para-arthe, in the interest of another, *i.e.*, of Puruṣa. आरम्भः Ârambhaḥ, creation.

LVI. Thus then is this creation beginning with Mahat and ending with specific entities, originated by Prakriti in the interest of another as in her own interest, for the release of each individual Puruṣa.

ANNOTATION.

73. Originated by Prakriti: Creation by Prakriti is not guided, directed, and controlled by Îśvara or Âdi Puruṣa, for this is impossible, inasmuch as no activity can belong to him. Neither can Brahman be the material of creation, for, being the power or energy of Consciousness, it can undergo no transformation or modification.

For the release of each individual Puruṣa: This explains why, on the release of one Puruṣa, the release of others does not result, and how the activity of Prakriti whose nature is to energise, can cease in regard to a particular Puruṣa, and how creation does not ever continue, making release of any one impossible. Vâchaspati explains the passage thus: As a man who desires food, being engaged in the cooking of food, rests after the food has been cooked, so does Prakriti, who is engaged in activity with a view to release every individual Puruṣa, cease from energising again in regard to that Puruṣa whom she releases.

Spontaniety of Prakriti explained and illustrated.

वत्सविवृद्धिनिमित्तं क्षीरस्य यथा प्रवृत्तिरज्ञस्य ।
पुरुषविमोक्षनिमित्तं तथा प्रवृत्तिः प्रधानस्य ॥ ५७ ॥

वत्सविवृद्धिनिमित्तं Vatsa-vivriddhi-nimittam, for the sake of, or due to the nourishment of, the calf. क्षीरस्य Kṣîra-sya, of milk. यथा Yathâ, as. प्रवृत्तिः Pravrittiḥ, activity, *i.e.*, secretion. अज्ञस्य A-jña-sya, of the unintelligent. पुरुषविमोक्षनिमित्तं Puruṣa-vimokṣa-nimittam, due to the release of Puruṣa. तथा Tathâ, so. प्रवृत्तिः Pravrittiḥ, activity, *i.e.*, creation. प्रधानस्य Pradhâna-sya, of the Pradhâna.

LVII. Just as is the secretion of milk, which is unintelligent, for the sake of nourishment of the calf, so is the creation of the Pradhâna for the sake of the release of Puruṣa.

ANNOTATION.

74. This Kârikâ gives an answer to those who entertain doubts as to how an unintelligent substance such as Prakṛiti is represented here to be, can engage in activity for an altruistic end. It cannot be maintained that the secretion of milk takes place under the superintendence of Îśvara. For all intelligent activity such as, for instance, as is here attributed to Îśvara, proceeds either from selfish motives or from compassion. Now, in the case of Îśvara, who is *exhypothesi* all-full, having all desires fulfilled, wanting in nothing whatever, can possibly have no selfish ends to accomplish. Compassion also is impossible; for compassion implies the desire to alleviate, remove or prevent suffering, but prior to creation there is no existence of the Jîvas, Indriyas, Bodies, and Objects, and consequently no pain, no suffering. Compassion, therefore, cannot be the motive for creation. Further, were creation an act of compassion on the part of Îśvara, one would expect to find in it only happy beings, but such is not the case, but just the opposite. The anomaly cannot be explained by reference to diversity of Karma, as in that case the alleged superintendence of Karma by an omniscient and omnipotent Being falls to the ground. Prakṛiti, on the other hand, being unintelligent, has no selfish motive nor any motive of compassion to impel her to activity. Her activity is directed simply by the end of the other; she exists for his sake. Her action is of the nature of a sympathetic response, of harmonical variation or correspondence, like the secretion of the mother's milk, in response to the requirement of the baby.

Above continued.

औत्सुक्यनिवृत्त्यर्थं यथा क्रियासु प्रवर्तते लोकः ।
पुरुषस्य विमोक्षार्थं प्रवर्तते तद्वदव्यक्तम् ॥ ५८ ॥

औत्सुक्यनिवृत्त्यर्थं Autsukya-nivṛitti-artham, for the sake of relieving or gratifying desire or curiosity. यथा Yathâ, as. क्रियासु Kriyâsu, in acts. प्रवर्तते Pravartate, engages. लोकः Lokaḥ, man. पुरुषस्य Puruṣa-sya, of Puruṣa. विमोक्षार्थं Vimokṣa-artham, for the sake of release. प्रवर्तते Pravartate, energises. तद्वत् Tat-vat, similarly to this. अव्यक्तम् A-Vyaktam, the Unmanifest, Prakṛiti.

LVIII. Just as people engage in acts to relieve

anxiety or desires, so does the Unmanifest energise for the purpose of the release of Puruṣa.

How Prakṛiti's creation ceases spontaneously.

रङ्गस्य दर्शयित्वा निवर्तते नर्तकी यथा नृत्यात् ।
पुरुषस्य तथात्मानं प्रकाश्य निवर्तते प्रकृतिः ॥ ५६ ॥

रङ्गस्य Ranga-sya, to the stage, *i.e.*, the spectators. दर्शयित्वा Darśayitvâ, having exhibited. निवर्तते Nivartate, ceases, desists. नर्तकी Nartaki, fair dancer. यथा Yathâ, as. नृत्यात् Nṛityât, from dance. पुरुषस्य Puruṣa-sya, to Puruṣa. तथा Tathâ, similarly. आत्मानं Âtmânaṃ, herself. प्रकाश्य Prakâśya, having exhibited. निवर्तते Nivartate, ceases. प्रकृतिः Prakṛitiḥ, Prakṛiti.

LIX. Just as a fair dancer, having exhibited herself to the spectators, desists from the dance, so does Prakṛiti desist, having exhibited herself to Puruṣa.

Unselfishness of Prakṛiti demonstrated.

नानाविधैरुपायैरुपकारिण्यनुपकारिणः पुंसः ।
गुणवत्यगुणस्य सतस्तस्यार्थमपार्थकं चरति ॥ ६० ॥

नानाविधैः Nânâ-vidhaiḥ, manifold. उपायैः Upâyaiḥ, by means. उपकारिणी Upa-kâriṇi, generous, beneficent. अनुपकारिणः An-upakâriṇah, non-beneficent, ungrateful. पुंसः Puṃsaḥ, of Puruṣa. गुणवती Guṇa-vatî, possessing the Guṇas, possessing qualities, virtuous. अगुणस्य A-guṇa-sya, devoid of the Guṇas, devoid of qualities, worthless. सतः Sataḥ, as he is. तस्य Tasya, his. अर्थं Artham, object. अपार्थकं Ap-artha-kaṃ, objectless. चरति Charati, pursues.

LX. By manifold means does benevolent Prakṛiti, possessed of the Guṇas, pursue, in a manner in which she has no interest of her own, the object of Puruṣa who makes no return, being devoid as he is of the Guṇas.

How activity of Prakṛiti ceases for ever, in regard to the released Puruṣa.

प्रकृतेः सुकुमारतरं न किञ्चिदस्तीति मे मतिर्भवति ।
या दृष्टास्मीति पुनर्न दर्शनमुपैति पुरुषस्य ॥ ६१ ॥

प्रकृतेः Prakṛiteḥ, than Prakṛiti. सुकुमारतरं Sukumâra-taraṃ, more gentle or delicate. न Na, not. किञ्चित् Kiṃ chit, anything. अस्ति Asti, exists. इति Iti, such. मे Me, my. मतिः Matiḥ, opinion. भवति Bhavati, is. या Yâ, who. दृष्टा Driṣṭâ, seen.

अस्मि Asmi, I am. इति Iti, so. पुनः Punaḥ, again. न Na, not. दर्शनम् Darśanam, seeing, gaze, sight. उपैति Upaiti, approaches. पुरुषस्य Puruṣa-sya, of Puruṣa.

LXI. My opinion is that nothing exists which is more delicate than Prakṛiti who, knowing that, "I have seen," comes no more within the sight of Puruṣa.

ANNOTATION.

75. This Kârikâ explains and illustrates how Prakṛiti does not energise, over again, in regard to the released Puruṣa.

Bondage, Transmigration and Release are all of Prakṛiti, and not of Puruṣa.

तस्मान्न बध्यतेऽद्धा न मुच्यते नापि संसरति पुरुषः ।
संसरति बध्यते मुच्यते च नानाश्रया प्रकृतिः ॥ ६२ ॥

तस्मात् Tasmât, therefore. न Na, not. बध्यते Badhyate, is bound. अद्धा Addhâ, any, whatever. न Na, not. मुच्यते Muchyate, is released. न Na, not. अपि Api, also. संसरति Saṃsarati, transmigrates. पुरुषः Puruṣaḥ, Puruṣa. संसरति Saṃsarati, transmigrates. बध्यते Badhyate, is bound. मुच्यते Muchyate, is released. च Cha, and. नानाश्रया Nânâ-âśrayâ, the support of manifold creations or beings. प्रकृतिः Prakṛitiḥ, Prakṛiti.

LXII. Wherefore, verily, no Puruṣa is ever bound, nor is released, nor transmigrates. Prakṛiti, being the support of manifold creations, is bound, is released, and transmigrates.

How Prakṛiti binds and releases herself.

रूपैः सप्तभिरेव तु बध्नात्यात्मानमात्मना प्रकृतिः ।
सैव च पुरुषार्थं प्रति विमोचयत्येकरूपेण ॥ ६३ ॥

रूपैः Rûpaiḥ, by forms, modes, conditions, dispositions. सप्तभिः Saptabhiḥ, seven, *viz.* virtue, vice, dispassion, passion, power, weakness, and ignorance. एव Eva, verily. बध्नाति Badhnâti, binds. आत्मानम् Âtmânam, herself, आत्मना Âtmanâ, by herself. प्रकृतिः Prakṛitiḥ, Prakṛiti. सा Sâ, she. एव Eva, it is. च Cha, and. पुरुषार्थं Puruṣa-artham, object of Puruṣa. प्रति Prati, in regard to. विमोचयति vimochayati, releases. एकरूपेण Eka-rûpeṇa, by one form, *i. e.*, of Knowledge.

LXIII. By seven forms does Prakṛiti bind herself by herself; and it is she who, by one form, releases herself for the sake of Puruṣa.

How discriminative knowledge is fully developed.

एवं तत्त्वाभ्यासान्नास्मि न मे नाहमित्यपरिशेषम्।
अविपर्ययाद्विशुद्धं केवलमुत्पद्यते ज्ञानम्॥ ६४॥

एवं Evam, so, in the manner taught above. तत्त्वाभ्यासात् Tattva-abhyâsât, through cultivation of the knowledge of the Tattvas or twenty-five Principles. न Na, not. अस्मि Asti, is. न Na, not. मे Me, mine. न Na, not. अहम् Aham, I. इति Iti, thus. अपरिशेषम् Apariśeṣam, beyond which there remains nothing to know, final. अविपर्ययात् A-viparyayât, from the absence of error and doubt. विशुद्धं Viśuddham, purified, free. केवलम् Kevalam, single, unsullied. उत्पद्यते Utpadyate, is produced. ज्ञानम् Jñânam, knowledge.

LXIV. So, through cultivation of the knowledge of the Tattvas, is produced the final, pure, because free from error and doubt, and one single knowledge that neither does agency belong to me, nor is attachment mine, nor am I identical with the Body, etc.

Relation of Prakriti and Puruṣa after Release.

तेन निवृत्तप्रसवामर्थवशात् सप्तरूपविनिवृत्ताम्।
प्रकृतिं पश्यति पुरुषः प्रेक्षकवदवस्थितः स्वस्थः॥ ६५॥

तेन Tena, thereby, by means of knowledge of the Tattvas, as described in the preceding Kârikâ. निवृत्तप्रसवाम् Nivṛitta-prasavâm, whose prolificness has come to cease through creation of all that was to be created for the sake of Puruṣa. अर्थवशात् Artha-vaśât, through the influence of the object, *viz.*, knowledge of the Tattvas. सप्तरूपविनिवृत्ताम् Sapta-rûpa-vinivṛittâm, desisting from the seven forms, virtue and the rest, by which she binds herself and which are no longer required for the sake of Puruṣa, both of whose objects, experience and release, are accomplished. प्रकृतिं Prakritim, Prakṛiti. पश्यति Paśyati, looks at. पुरुषः Puruṣaḥ, Puruṣa. प्रेक्षकवत् Prekṣaka-vat, like a spectator in a theatre. अवस्थितः Avasthitaḥ, seated, standing by. स्वस्थः Sva-sthaḥ, self-reposed, undisturbed, freed from the reflection of Buddhi rendered impure by means of the modifications of Rajas and Tamas.

LXV. Thereby having her prolific energy stopped, and desisting from the seven forms under the influence of knowledge, Prakṛiti is looked at by Puruṣa just like a spectator, standing by, self-reposed.

Conjunction of Prakriti and Puruṣa is not, as such, the cause of creation.

दृष्टा मयेत्युपेक्षक एको दृष्टाहमित्युपरमत्यन्या ।
सति संयोगेऽपि तयोः प्रयोजनं नास्ति सर्गस्य ॥ ६६ ॥

दृष्टा Driṣtâ, seen. मया Mayâ, by me. इति Iti, so. उपेक्षकः Upekṣakaḥ, regardless, indifferent, unaffected. एकः Ekaḥ, the one, Puruṣa. दृष्टा Driṣtâ, seen. अहम् Aham, I. इति Iti, so. उपरमति Uparamati, desists. अन्या Anyâ, the other, Prakriti. सति Sati, existing, continuing. संयोगे Saṃyoge, conjunction, existence side by side. अपि Api, even. तयोः Tayoḥ of the two. प्रयोजनं Prayojanaṃ, purpose, motive. न Na, not. अस्ति, Exists. सर्गस्य Sarga-sya, of creation.

LXVI. "She has been seen by me,"—so the one stands indifferent; "I have been seen,"—so the other desists. Though their conjunction still remains, there does not exist any motive for creation.

Jîvan-Mukti explained.

सम्यग्ज्ञानाधिगमाद्धर्मादीनामकारणप्राप्तौ ।
तिष्ठति संस्कारवशाच्चक्रभ्रमवद्धृतशरीरः ॥ ६७ ॥

सम्यक् Samyak, perfect. ज्ञानाधिगमात् Jñâna-adhigamât, from attainment of knowledge. धर्मादीनाम् Dharma-âdînâm, of virtue and the rest. अकारणप्राप्तौ A-kâraṇa-prâptau, on reaching or being reduced to the state in which they lose their power of causing effects. तिष्ठति Tiṣthati, remains. संस्कारवशात् Saṃskâra-vaśât, from the influence of Saṃskâra or impression or the effect of the impulse previously given to it. चक्रभ्रमवत् Chakra-bhrama-vat, like the whirling of the potter's wheel. धृतशरीरः Dhrita-śarîraḥ, invested with a Body.

LXVII. Through attainment of perfect knowledge, virtue and the rest coming to be deprived of their power as causes, Puruṣa yet continues invested with body under the influence of previous Dharma and A-Dharma, as the potter's wheel continues whirling (from momentum).

ANNOTATION.

76. This Kârikâ explains the fact of Jîvan-Mukti or release in life, as in the case of Kapila, Vâmadeva, and others. Jîvan-Mukti consists in the release of an incarnate Puruṣa from the entanglement of Prakriti prior to his separation from the Body. These two things, *viz.*, release from bondage and continuance of the Body, are compatible with each other, as they are dependent upon independent causes. For, universally, release

takes place on the manifestation of discriminative knowledge between Prakṛiti and Puruṣa, in other words, it does not imply the acquisition of a new state or condition, but consists merely in the removal of a veil or a shadow, as it were; whereas the Body is the positive result of positive causes and depends for its existence or non-existence upon those very causes. These causes are Dharma and A-Dharma, or merit and demerit, collectively termed Karma. Now, 'Karma is distinguished as Prârabdha or operative, Sañchita or stored or potential, and Agamika, or to come, or future. On the attainment of discriminative knowledge, Sañchita Karma or Karma in seed-form is burnt up and rendered infructuous, and Âgamika Karma also is necessarily precluded. Only the Prârabdha then remains. It is Karma acquired by acts performed in a previous life and which has become operative in the present life, that is to say, it is the cause of conjunction with the present Body and of all the experiences of the present incarnate existence. It is not affected by discriminative knowledge, and it goes on sustaining the Body till it is exhausted or works itself out, in its natural course, when the Body which was supported by it, automatically drops down. It is hence, therefore, that when discriminative knowledge is perfectly developed before the Prârabdha has worked itself out, the incarnate Puruṣa in question, is released, but remains awhile burdened with the Body. This is what is called Jîvan-Mukti or the state of release during life.

When a Jîvan-Mukto is finally released.

प्राप्ते शरीरभेदे चरितार्थत्वात् प्रधानविनिवृत्तौ ।
ऐकान्तिकमात्यन्तिकमुभयं कैवल्यमाप्नोति ॥ ६८ ॥

प्राप्ते Prâpte, come to pass, that is, on the exhaustion of Prârabdha Karma by experience. शरीरभेदे Śarîra-bhede, on separation from the body. चरितार्थत्वात् Charita-artha-tvât, for the reason that she has fulfilled her purpose, *viz.*, Creation for the experience and release of Puruṣa. प्रधानविनिवृत्तौ Pradhâna-vinivṛittau, on the cessation of the activity of the Pradhâna. ऐकान्तिकम् Aikântikam, certain, absolute. आत्यन्तिकम् Âtyantikam, final, imperishable. उभयं Ubhayaṃ, both. कैवल्यम् Kaivalyam, singleness, pureness, freedom from the reflection of the threefold pain. आप्नोति Âpnoti, attains.

LXVIII. When (in due course) separation from the Body takes place, and there is cessation of the activity of the Pradhâna from her purpose having been fulfilled Puruṣa attains both absolute and final Kaivalya.

Origin of the Sâṃkhya declared.

पुरुषार्थज्ञानमिदं गुह्यं परमर्षिणा समाख्यातम्।
स्थित्युत्पत्तिप्रलयाश्चिन्त्यन्ते यत्र भूतानाम् ॥ ६९ ॥

पुरुषार्थज्ञानम् Puruṣa-artha-jñânam, knowledge for the accomplishment of the end of Puruṣa, *i.e.*, release. इदं Idaṃ, this. गुह्य Guhyaṃ, secret, abstruse, unintelligible to the dull. परमर्षिणा Parama-ṛiṣiṇâ, by the great Ṛiṣi or Seer, namely Kapila. समाख्यातम् Sam-âkhyâtam, thoroughly expounded, expounded in all details. स्थित्युत्पत्तिप्रलयाः Sthiti-utpatti-pralayâḥ, duration, production, and dissolution. चिन्त्यन्ते Chintyante, are considered, discussed. यत्र Yatra, wherein. भूतानाम् Bhûtânâm, of created things, beings.

LXIX. This abstruse knowledge, adapted to the end of Puruṣa, wherein the production, duration, and dissolution of beings are considered, has been thoroughly expounded by the great Ṛiṣi.

ANNOTATION.

77. Vâchaspati construes the second line of the Kârikâ in a different manner. It is thus: Yatra, wherein, that is, in which knowledge, that is to say, for which knowledge, the origin, duration and destruction of living beings are considered by the Śrutis. Hereby he wants to bring out the sense that the Sâṃkhya is connected with, and is supported by, the Veda.

Traditional succession of the Sâṃkhya stated.

एतत् पवित्रमग्र्यं मुनिरासुरयेऽनुकम्पया प्रददौ।
आसुरिरपि पञ्चशिखाय तेन च बहुधाकृतं तन्त्रम् ॥७०॥

एतत् Etat, this. पवित्रम् Pavitram, purifying, *i.e.*, from the sin causing the threefold pain. अग्र्यं Agryaṃ, first in order, principal among all purifying things, foremost. मुनिः Muniḥ, Muni, sage Kapila. आसुरये Âsuraye, to Âsuri. अनुकम्पया Anukampayâ, through compassion. प्रददौ Pradadau, taught, imparted. आसुरिः Âsuriḥ, Âsuri. अपि Api, again. पञ्चशिखाय Pañchaśikhâya, to Pañchaśikha. तेन Tena, by him. च Cha, and. बहुधाकृतं Bahu-dhâ-kṛitaṃ, extensively propagated, elaborated in manifold ways. तन्त्रम् Tantram, the system.

LXX. This foremost purifying knowledge the Muni, through compassion, imparted to Asuri; Âsuri, again, to Pañchaśikha, by whom the System was elaborated in manifold ways.

ANNOTATION.

78. In this and the succeeding Kârikâ the traditional succession of the Sâṃkhya doctrine is recorded with a view to establish its authentic character and thereby to inspire reverence towards it.

79. According to Gauḍapâda, the Sâṃkhya-Kârikâ ends with this Kârikâ. "For the Sâṃkhya which is the cause of release from transmigration, was declared by the Muni Kapila, wherein or in regard to which," as he says, "there are these seventy verses in the Ârya metre." This is supported by the other traditional name for the Sâṃkhya-Kârikâ, which is Sâṃkhya-Saptati or the Seventy (Verses) on the Sâṃkhya. Vâchaspati, on the other hand, has not questioned the genuineness, or the claim to authority, of the additional two Kârikâs and has added his comment to them.

Above continued.

शिष्यपरम्परयागतमीश्वरकृष्णेन स चैतदार्याभिः ।
संक्षिप्तमार्यमतिना सम्यग् विज्ञाय सिद्धान्तम् ॥ ७१ ॥

शिष्यपरम्परया Śiṣya-paramparayâ, by tradition of disciples. आगतम् Âgatam, descended, received. ईश्वरकृष्णेन Îśvarakṛiṣṇena, by Îśvarakṛiṣṇa, the author of the Sâṃkhya-Kârikâ. सः Saḥ, this. च Cha, and. एतत्, this. आर्याभिः Âryâbhiḥ, by Ârya verses. संक्षिप्तम् Saṃkṣiptam, abridged, summarised, compendiously written. आर्यमतिना Ârya-matinâ, whose intelligence reached to the Tattvas; holy-minded. सम्यक् Samyak, thoroughly. विज्ञाय Vijñâya, understanding, realising. सिद्धान्तम् Siddhântam, domonstrated truth, established tenet, doctrine.

LXXI. And this doctrine, descended by tradition of disciples, to the holy-minded Iśvarakṛiṣṇa, having been thoroughly understood by him, has been summarised by means of these Âryâs.

Relation of the Sâṃkhya-Kârikâ to the Sâṃkya-Pravachana-Sûtram.

सप्तत्या किल येऽर्थास्तेऽर्थाः कृत्स्नस्य षष्टितन्त्रस्य ।
आख्यायिकाविरहिताः परवादविवर्जिताश्चापि ॥ ७२ ॥

सप्तत्या Saptatyâ, by the seventy-versed treatise. किल Kila, truly. ये Ye, what. अर्थाः Arthâḥ, subjects, topics. ते Te, those. अर्थाः Arthâḥ, subjects. कृत्स्नस्य Kritsna-sya, entire, whole. षष्टितन्त्रस्य Ṣaṣti-tantra-sya, of the system of sixty topics. आख्यायिकाविरहिताः Âkhyâyikâ-virahitâḥ, disjoined from the illustrative stories. परवादविवर्जिताः Para-vâda-vivarjitâḥ, omitting demolition of opposite doctrines. च Cha, and. अपि Api, also.

LXXII. The subjects which are treated by the Saptati, are the subjects of the entire Ṣaṣṭi-Tantra, exclusive of the illustrative stories, and omitting demolition of opposite doctrines.

ANNOTATION.

80. The term Ṣaṣṭi-Tantra alludes to the Sâṃkhya-Pravachana-Sûtram divided into the six Books, namely, of Topics, of the Evolutions of the Pradhâna, of Dispassion, of Fables, of the Demolition of Counter-Theories, and of Recapitulation of Teachings. It is thus constructive, illustrative and destructive in its method. In its constructive portions, it establishes the sixty topics of the Sâṃkhya System. The same is done by the Saptati as well. Inasmuch, however, as the latter omits the stories and controversies, and also does not deal with the topics in so much detail, it has, in the preceding Kârikâ, been described as a summary of the former.

The sixty topics alluded to above are: 1. the existence, that is, conjunction with, and disjunction from, Puruṣa, of the Pradhâna, 2. her unity or singleness, 3. her objectiveness, 4. her subservience, 5. the distinctness of Puruṣa, 6. his manifoldness, 7. his inactivity, 8. his conjunction, 9. his disjunction, and 10. the duration of the rest,—these are the ten radical topics.

According to another enumeration, the ten radical categories are 1. Puruṣa, 2. Prakṛiti, 3. Mahat, 4. Ahamkâra, 5-7. Sattva, Rajas, and Tamas, 8. the Tan-Mâtras, 9. the Indriyas, and 10. the Elements.

A third enumeration specifies them as, 1. the eternality of Puruṣa and Prakṛiti, 2. the reality of experience and discriminative knowledge in Prakṛiti, 3. the unity of Prakṛiti and of Puruṣa, throughout transmigration, 4. the subservience of Prakṛiti, 5. the difference between Puruṣa and Prakṛiti, 6. the inactivity of Puruṣa, 7. the multiplicity of Puruṣa, 8. the conjunction of Puruṣa and Prakṛiti at the time of creation, 9. the disjunction of Puruṣa and Prakṛiti at the time of release, and 10. the pre-existence of Mahat and the other Tattvas in their respective causes.

Add to them, the five kinds of error, nine of complacency, twenty-eight of incapacity, and eight of perfection. Thus the number sixty is obtained.

Alphabetical Index of Karikas.

	PAGE.
अतिदूरात् सामीप्यात्, vii ...	7
अध्यवसायो बुद्धिर्धर्मो ज्ञानम्, xxiii	22
अंतःकरणं त्रिविधम्, xxxiii ...	29
अभिमानोऽहंकारः, xxiv ...	23
अविवेक्यादेः सिद्धिः, xiv ...	14
अष्टविकल्पो दैवः, liii ...	42
असदकरणात् उपादानग्रहणात्, ix	8
आध्यात्मिकाश्चतस्रः, l ...	40
इत्येषः प्रकृतिकृतः, lvi ...	44
उभयात्मकमत्र मनः, xxvii ...	25
ऊर्ध्वं सत्वविशालः liv ...	43
ऊहः शब्दोऽध्ययनम्, li ...	41
एकादशेन्द्रियवधाः, xlix ...	40
एतत् पवित्रमग्र्यम्, lxx ...	51
एते प्रदीपकल्पाः, xxxvi ...	31
एवं तत्वाभ्यासात्, lxiv ..	48
एष प्रत्ययसर्गो, xlvi ...	38
औत्सुक्यनिवृत्त्यर्थम्, lviii ...	45
करणं त्रयोदशविधं, xxxii ...	29
कारणमस्त्यव्यक्तम्, xvi ...	15
चित्रं यथाऽऽश्रयमृते, xli ...	35
जननमरणकरणानाम्प्रतिनियमात्, xviii ...	17
तत्र जरामरणकृतम्, lv ...	43
तन्मात्राण्यविशेषाः, xlviii ...	39
तस्माच्च विपर्यासात्, xix ...	18
तस्मात् तत्संयोगात्, xx ...	19
तस्मान्न बध्यतेऽद्धा, lxii ...	47
तेन निवृत्तप्रसवाम्, lxv ...	48
त्रिगुणमविवेकि विषयः, xi ...	10
दुःखत्रयाभिघातात्, i	1
दृष्टवदानुश्रविकः, ii	2
दृष्टमनुमानमाप्तवचनम्, iv ...	4
दृष्टा मयेत्युपेक्षक एको, lxvi ...	49
धर्मेण गमनमूर्ध्वम्, xliv ...	37
न विना भावैर्लिङ्गम्, lii ...	41
नानाविधैरुपायैः, lx	46
पञ्च विपर्ययभेदाः, xlvii ...	39
पुरुषस्य दर्शनार्थम्, xxi ...	20
पुरुषार्थज्ञानमिदम्, lxix ...	51
पुरुषार्थहेतुकमिदम्, xlii ...	35
पूर्वोत्पन्नमसक्तम्, xl	34
प्रकृतेर्महांस्ततोऽहङ्कारः, xxii ...	21
प्रकृतेः सुकुमारतरम्, lxi ...	46
प्रतिविषयाध्यवसायो दृष्टम्, v ...	4
प्राप्ते शरीरभेदे, lxviii	50
प्रीत्यप्रीतिविषादात्मकाः, xii ...	11
बुद्धीन्द्रियाणि तेषाम्, xxxiv ...	30
बुद्धीन्द्रियाणि चक्षुःश्रोत्रघ्राण, xxvi	24
भेदस्तमसोऽष्टविधः, xlviii ...	39
भेदानाम्परिमाणात्, xv ...	15
मूलप्रकृतिरविकृतिः, iii	3

		PAGE.
युगपत्चतुष्टयस्य तु वृत्तिः, xxx	...	27
रङ्गस्य दर्शयित्वा, lix	...	46
रूपैःसप्तभिरेव तु, lxiii	...	47
वत्सविवृद्धिनिमित्तम्, lvii	...	44
वैराग्यात् प्रकृतिलयः, xlv	...	38
शब्दादिषु पञ्चानां, xxviii	..	26
शिष्यपरम्परयागतम्, lxxi	...	52
सत्वं लघु प्रकाशकमिष्टम्, xiii	...	13
सप्तत्या किल येऽर्थाः lxxii	...	52
सम्यग्ज्ञानाधिगमात्, lxvii	...	49
सर्वम् प्रत्युपभोगम्, xxxvii	...	31

		PAGE.
सांसिद्धिकाश्च भावाः, xliii	...	36
सान्तःकरणा बुद्धिः, xxxv	...	30
सात्विक एकादशकः, xxv	...	24
सामान्यतस्तु दृष्टात्, vi	...	6
सूक्ष्मा मातापितृजा, xxxix	...	33
सौक्ष्म्यात् तदनुपलब्धिः viii	...	7
संघातपरार्थत्वात्, xvii	...	17
स्वां स्वाम्प्रतिपद्यन्ते, xxxi	...	28
स्वालक्षण्यं वृत्तिः xxix	...	27
हेतुमदनित्यमव्यापि, x		9

Words Index of the Karikas.

PAGE.

अकर्तृभावः xix ... 18
अकारण lxvii ... 49
अंकुशः li ... 41
अगुणस्य lx ... 46
अग्र्य lxx ... 51
अचेतनं xi, xx ...11, 19
अज्ञस्य lvii ... 44
अतिशय ii 2
अतीन्द्रियाणां vi ... 6
अत्यन्ततः i ... 1
अत्र xxvii ... 25
अदृष्टे xxx 27
अधर्मेण xliv ... 37
अधस्तात् xliv ... 37
अधिगमात् lxvii ... 49
अधिवासितं xl ... 34
अधिष्ठानात् xvii ... 17
अद्धा lxii ... 47
अध्ययनं li ... 41
अध्यवसायः v, xxiii ... 4, 22
अनवस्थानात् vii ... 7
अनित्यं x .. 9
अनुकम्पया lxx 51
अनुपकारिणः lx ... 46
अनुमानात् vi ... 6
अनुमानम् iv, v ... 4, 4
अनेकं x ... 9
अन्तरं xxxvii ... 31
अन्तःकरणं xxxiii ... 29
अन्ध xlviii ... 39
अन्धतामिस्रः xlviii ... 39

PAGE.

अन्धवत् xxi 20
अन्या lxvi 49
अन्योन्य xii 11
अपवर्गः xliv ... 37
अपरिशेषम् lxiv 48
अपार्थकं lx ... 46
अपि vi, xiv, xxi, xxii, xxx, lxii, lxvi, lxx, lxxii 6, 14, 20, 21, 27, 47, 49, 51, 52
अप्रीति xii ... 11
अभावात् i, viii, ix, xiv ... 1, 7, 8, 14
अभिघातात् i ... 1
अभिभव xii 11
अभिभवात् vii 7
अभिमताः l 40
अभिमानः xxiv 23
अभिहारात् vii 7
अभ्यन्तरं xxxiii 29
अभ्यासात् lxiv 48
अयं liii ... 42
अयुगपत् xviii 17
अर्थ lxix 51
अर्थतः xiii 13
अर्थवशात् lxv ... 48
अर्थं xxxvi, lx ...31, 46
अर्थाः xii, lxxii, ...11, 52
अवगाहते xxxv ... 30
अवघातके i 1
अवस्थितः lxv 48
अविकृतिः iii 3

	PAGE.
अविघातः xlv ...	38
अविदूरात् vii ...	7
अविनिवृत्तेः lv ...	43
अविपर्ययात् lxiv ...	48
अविभागात् xv ...	15
अविवेकि xi ...	11
अविवेक्यादेः xiv ...	14
अविशुद्धि ii ...	2
अविशुद्धिक्षमातिशययुक्तः ii ...	2
अविशेषाः xxxviii ...	32
अव्यक्तम् x, xiv, lviii	9, 14, 45
अव्यक्तञ्च ii ...	2
अव्यवतिष्ठते xlii ...	35
अव्यापि x ...	9
अशक्ति xlvi ...	38
अशक्तिः xlvii, xlix	...39, 40
अष्टधा xlvii ...	39
अष्टविकल्पः liii ...	42
अष्टादशधा xlviii ...	39
अष्टाविंशति xlviii ...	39
अष्टाविंशतिभेदाः xlvii ...	39
अष्टौ li ...	41
असक्तं xl ...	34
असदकरणात् ix ...	8
असामान्या xxix ...	27
असिद्धं vi ...	6
अस्ति xvii, lxi, lxiv, lxvi	17, 46, 48, 49
अस्मात् xxiii ...	22
अस्य xvi, xix	...15, 18
अहं lxiv lxvi	...48, 49
अहङ्कारः xxii, xxiv	...21, 23
अहङ्कारात् xxv ...	24
आकूत xxxi ...	28
आख्याः xlvi l	...38, 40

	PAGE.
आख्यातम् v	4
आख्यानि xxvi ...	24
आख्यायिका lxxii	52
आत्मकत्वात् xiv ...	14
आत्मकं xxvii	25
आत्मकाः xii	11
आत्मना lxiii ...	47
आत्मानं lix, lxiii	...46, 47
आत्यन्तिकं lxviii ...	50
आदान xxviii ...	26
आदि viii, xvii, xl, lvi	7, 17, 34, 44
आदिभ्यः xli	35
आद्याः iii	3
आध्यात्मिकाः l	40
आनन्दाः xxviii	26
आनुश्राविकः ii .	2
आप्तवचनं iv, v .	4, 4
आप्तश्रुति v	4
आप्तागमात् vi ...	6
आप्नोति lxviii ...	50
आयूपस्थान् xxvi ...	24
आरंभः lvi ...	44
आर्याभिः lxxi ...	52
आर्यमतिना lxxi ...	52
आलोचनमात्रं xxviii ...	26
आश्रय xii, xvi	...11, 15
आश्रया lxii	47
आश्रयिणः xliii ...	36
आश्रयं xli ...	35
आश्रितं x ...	9
आसीनः xx ...	19
आसुरये lxx	51
आसुरिः lxx ...	51
आहरण xxxii	29
आहुः xxvi	24

PAGE.

इति lvi, lxi, lxiv, lxvi ... 44, 46, 48, 49
इदं xlii, lxix ...35, 51
इन्द्रियघातात् vii ... 7
इन्द्रियत्वं xxvii ... 25
इन्द्रियवधा xlix ... 40
इन्द्रियाणि xxvi, xxxiv ...24, 30
इव xx, lvi 19, 44
इष्टं iv, xiii 4, 13
इष्यते xxviii 26
ईश्वर lxxi 51
ईश्वरकृष्णेन lxxi ... 51
उत्पत्ति lxix 51
उत्पद्यते lxiv 48
उत्पन्नं xl 34
उत्सर्गं xxviii ... 26
उद्दिष्टा xlix 40
उपकारिणी lx ... 46
उपरमति lxvi ... 49
उलपब्धेः viii ... 7
उपष्टम्भकं xiii ... 13
उपादान ix, l ... 8, 40
उपादनकालभाग्यल्या l. 40
उपादानग्रहणात् ix ... 8
उपायैः lx 46
उपेक्षकः lxvi ... 49
उपैति lxi 46
उभय xxvii 25
उभयं xxv, lxviii ...24, 50
उभयोः xxi 20
ऊर्ध्वं xliv, liv ...37, 43
ऊहः li 41
ऋषिणा lxix 51
ऋते xli 35
एकः lxvi 49
एकरूपेण lxiii ... 47

PAGE

एकविधः liii 42
एकादश xlix ... 40
एकादशकः xxiv, xxv ...23, 24
एकान्त i 1
एकान्तात्यन्ततोऽभावात् i ... 1
एतत् xxiii, lxx, lxxi ... 22, 51, 52
एते xxxvi, xxxviii ...31, 32
एव xiii, xviii, xxiv, xxxi, xxxvii, lxiii ... 13, 17, 23, 28, 31, 47
एवं lxiv 48
एषः xlvi, lvi ...38, 44
एषा xxix 27
ऐकान्तिकं lxviii 50
ऐश्वर्यम् xxiii 22
ऐश्वर्यात् xlv 38
औत्सुक्य lviii 45
औत्सुक्यनिवृत्त्यर्थं lviii 45
करण xxix, xliii, xlvii 27, 36, 39
करणं xxxi, xxxii, xxxv 28, 29, 30
करणवैकल्यात् xlvii ... 39
करणानां xviii 17
करणाश्रयिणः xliii ... 36
कर्ता xx 19
कर्तृत्वे xx 19
कर्म xxvi 24
कलभाद्याः xliii 36
कारण ix, xiv, xv ... 8, 14, 15
कारणं xvi ... 15
कारणगुणात्मकत्वात् xiv ... 14
कारणभावात् ix ... 8
कार्यं xv, xliii ...15, 36

PAGE.

कार्यं viii, ix, xxxii ... 7, 8, 29
कार्यतः viii ... 7
कार्यते xxxi ... 28
कार्यस्य xiv ... 14
काल l ... 40
किंचित् lxi ... 46
किल lxxii ... 52
कुतः xxi ... 20
कृत्स्नस्य lxxii ... 52
कृत्स्नं xxxvi ... 31
कुशीन lxxi ... 52
केनचित् xxxi ... 28
केवलं lxiv ... 48
कैवल्यं xix, lxviii ...18, 50
कैवल्यार्थं xvii, xxi ...17, 20
क्षय ii 2
क्षीरस्य lvii 44
क्रमशः xxx 27
क्रियासु lviii 45
गणः xxii, xxiv ...21, 58
गमनं xliv 37
गुण xiv, xx, xxvii, xxxvi, xlvi 14, 19, 25, 31, 38
गुणाः xii 11
गुणकर्तृत्वे xx ... 19
गुणवति lx 46
गुणविशेषाः xxx ... 27
गुरु xiii 13
गुह्यं lxix 51
ग्रहणात् ix 8
घोरा xxxviii ... 32
च iv, vi, vii, viii, ix, xi, xii, xiii, xv, xvi, xvii, xviii, xix, xx, xxii, xxiv, xxvii, xxviii, xxx, xxxii, xxxvii, xxxviii, xliii, xliv, xlvi, xlvii, xlviii, li, liii, liv, lxiii, lxx, lxxi, lxxii 4, 6, 7, 7, 8, 11, 11, 13, 15, 15, 17, 17, 18, 19, 21, 23, 25, 26, 27, 29, 31, 32, 36, 37, 38, 39, 39, 41, 42, 43, 47, 51, 52, 52

PAGE.

चक्रभ्रमवत् lxvii ... 49
चक्षुः xxvi ... 24
चतस्रः l ... 40
चतुष्टयस्य xxx 27
चरति lx ... 46
चरितार्थत्वात् lxviii ... 50
चलं xiii ... 13
चित्रं xli ... 35
चिन्त्यन्ते lxix ... 51
चेत् i ... 1
चेतनः lv ... 43
चेतनावत् xx 19
छाया xli 35
जनन xii xviii ...11, 17
जनन मरणकरणानां xviii ... 17
जरा lv, ... 43
जरामरणकृतं lv 43
जिज्ञासा i 1
ज्ञानं xxiii, lxiv, lxvii, lxix 22, 48, 49, 51
ज्ञानेन xliv 37
तत् i, ii, v, viii, xi, xiv, xx, xxi, xxxii, xlv ... 1, 2, 4, 7, 11, 14, 19, 20, 29, 38
ततः xxii 21
तत्व lxiv ... 48
तत्कृतः xxi ... 55
तत्पूर्विका xxx 27
तत्र lv ... 43

PAGE.

तंत्रम् lxx 51
तंत्रस्य lxxii 52
तथा xi, xx, xxi, xxx, xlviii lvii, lix ... 11, 19, 20, 27, 39, 44, 46
तदनुपलब्धिः viii ... 7
तदवघातके i ... 1
तद्वत् xli, lviii ...35, 45
तद्विपर्यासैः xlv ... 38
तन्मात्र xxiv ... 23
तन्मात्रः xxv ... 24
तन्मात्राणि xxxviii ... 32
तमः xiii, liv ... 13, 43
तामसः xlviii ... 39
तयोः lxvi 49
तस्य xxx, xxxii xlvi, lx... 27, 29, 38, 46
तस्मात् vi, xix, xx, xxii, xxiv, xxxv, lii, lv, lxii 6, 18, 19, 21, 23, 30, 41, 43, 47
तामसं xxiii 22
तामसः xxv 24
तामिश्रः xlviii ... 39
तिष्ठति xli, lxvii ... 35, 49
तु iii, v, vi, xxx, xxxiv, xlvi, lxiii ... 3, 4, 6, 27, 30, 38, 47
तुष्टयः l 40
तुष्टि xlvi, xlvii, xlix ... 38, 39, 40
तुष्टिसिद्धानां xlix ... 40
ते lxxii 52
तेन lxv, lxx ... 48, 51
तेभ्यः xxxviii ... 32
तेषां xiv, xxxix 30, 33
तैः liii 42

PAGE.

तैजसात् xxv 24
त्रय i ... 1
त्रयः li ... 41
त्रयोदशविधं xxxii ... 29
त्रयस्य xxix, xxx, xxxiii ... 27, 27, 29
त्रिकालं xxxiii ... 29
त्रिगुण xvii ... 17
त्रिगुणतः xvi 15
त्रिगुणं xi 11
त्रिगुणादिविपर्ययात् xvii ... 17
त्रिधा xxxix 33
त्रिविधं iv, v, xxxiii, xxxv 4, 4 29, 30
त्रिविधः li 41
त्रैगुण्य xviii ... 17
त्रैगुण्यात् xiv 14
त्रैगुण्य विपर्ययात् xviii ... 17
दर्शनं lxi ... 46
दर्शनार्थं xxi 20
दर्शयित्वा lix ... 46
दशधा xxxii, xxxiii ... 29, 29
दशविधः xlviii ... 39
दानं li 41
दुःख i, li, lv 1, 41, 43
दुःखत्रयाभिघातात् i ... 1
दृष्ट lxi 46
दृष्टम् iv, v 4, 4
दृष्टवत् ii 2
दृष्टा lxvi 49
दृष्टाः xliii ... 36
दृष्टात् vi 6
दृष्टे i, xxx 1, 27
दैवः liii 42
द्रष्टृत्वं xix ... 18

	Page.
द्वाराणि xxxv ...	30
द्वारि xxxv	30
द्विविधः xxiv, lii	23, 41
धर्म्म xxiii	22
धर्माद्याः xliii	36
धर्म्मादीनां lxvii ...	49
धर्मेण xliv	37
धारण xxxii	29
धार्य्य xxxii	29
धृत lxvii	49
न i, iii, viii, xxxi, xli, xlii, lxi, lxii, lxiv, lxvi ...	1, 3, 7, 28, 35, 35, 46, 47, 48, 49
नटवत् xlii	35
नर्त्तकी lix	46
नव l	40
नवधा xlvii	39
नाना lxii	47
नानात्वं xxvii ...	25
नानाविधैः lx	46
निमित्त xlii	35
निमित्तं lvii	44
निमित्त नैमित्तिक प्रसंगेन xlii ...	35
नियता xxxix ...	33
नियतं xl	34
नियम xii	11
निराश्रयं xli	35
निर्दिष्टा xxx	27
निरुपभोगम् xl ...	34
निवर्तते lix	46
निवर्तन्ते xxxix ...	33
निवृत्त lxv	48
निवृत्ताम् lxv	48
निवृत्यर्थं lviii ...	45
निवृत्तिः lii	41
नृत्यात् lix	46

	Page.
नैमित्तकः xlii ..	35
परम lxix	51
परतन्त्रं x ...	9
परम्परमागतं lxxi ...	52
परमात् l	40
परमार्षिणा lxix ...	51
परवाद lxxii... ...	52
परस्पर xxxi, xxxvi	28, 31
परार्थ lvi ...	44
परार्थत्वात् xvii ...	17
परिणाम xxvii	25
परिणामतः xvi	15
परिणामात् xv	15
परोक्षात् vi	6
पर्यन्त lvi	44
पर्यन्तम् xl	34
पवित्रं lxx ...	51
पश्यति lxv ...	48
पाणि xxvi	24
पादप xxvi ...	24
पितृजाः xxix ...	33
पुनः xxxvii, lxi	31, 46
पुमान् xi	11
पुरुष xviii, xxxvii, lvii, lxix ...	17, 31, 44, 51
पुरुषः iii, xvii, lv, lxii, lxv	3, 17, 43, 47, 48
पुरुषस्य xix, xxi, xxxvi, xxxvii, lviii, lix, lxi ...	18, 20, 31, 31, 45, 46, 46
पुरुषबहुत्वं xviii ...	17
पुरुषविमोक्ष lvii ...	44
पुरुषार्थ xxxi, xlii, lxiii ...	28, 37, 47
पुरुषार्थज्ञानं lxix	50
पुरुषार्थहेतुकं xlii ...	35

PAGE.

पुंसः lx ... 46
पूर्व xl, li ... 34, 41
पूर्वोत्पन्नं xl 34
पंगु xxi, ... 20
पंच xxii, xxix, xxxiv, xxxviii, xlvii, l ... 21
27, 30, 32, 39, 40
पंचकं xxiv 23
पंचधा liii 42
पंचभ्यः xxii, xxxviii ... 21, 32
पंचशिखाय lxx ... 51
पंचानां xxviii ... 26
पंचाशत् xlvi... ... 38
प्रकाश xii 11
प्रकाशकं xiii 13
प्रकाशकरं xii ... 19
प्रकाश प्रवृत्तिनियमार्थाः xii ... 11
प्रकाश्य xxxii ...36, 59
प्रकाश्यं l 29
प्रकृति lxv 40
प्रकृतिं lvi 48
प्रकृतिः iii, lix, lxii, lxiii 3, 46, 47, 47
प्रकृतिकृतः xlv ... 44
प्रकृतिंलयः iii ... 8
प्रकृतिविकृतयः viii ... 3
प्रकृतिस्वरूपं xviii ... 7
प्रकृतेः xxii, xlii, lxi 21, 35, 46
प्रतिनियमात् xxxi ... 17
प्रतिपद्यन्ते lvi ... 28
प्रतिपुरुष xvi ... 44
प्रतिप्रतिगुण lxiii ... 15
प्रतिमोचयति v ... 7
प्रतिविषय v ... 4
प्रतिविषयाध्यवसायः v... ... 4

PAGE.

प्रतीतिः vi 6
प्रत्ययसर्गः xlvi ... 38
प्रत्युपभोगं xxxvii ... 31
प्रददौ lxx 51
प्रदीपकल्पाः xxxvi ... 31
प्रदीपवत् xiii ... 13
प्रधान xxxvii, lxviii 31, 32
प्रधानस्य xxi, lvii 20, 44
प्रधानविनिवृत्तौ lxviii ... 50
प्रधाने xi 11
प्रभूतैः xxix ... 33
प्रमाण iv . . 4
प्रमाणं iv ... 4
प्रमाणात् iv 4
प्रमेय iv ... 4
प्रमेयसिद्धिः iv 4
प्रयच्छन्ति xxxvi ... 31
प्रयोजनं lxvi 49
प्रवर्तते xvi, xxiv, xxv, lii, lviii 15, 23, 24, 41, 45,
प्रवृत्ति xii 11
प्रवृत्तिः lvii 44
प्रवृत्तेः xv, xvii, xviii 15, 17, 17
प्रलयाः lxix ... 51
प्रसवधर्मि xi 11
प्रसवां lxv ... 48
प्रसंगेन xlii ... 35
प्राकृतिका xliii 36
प्राण xxvi 24
प्राणाद्या xxix 27
प्राप्तिः li ... 41
प्राप्तेः lxviii 50
प्राप्तौ lxvii 49
प्राप्नोति lv 43
प्रीति xii 11
प्रीत्यप्रीतिविषयात्मकाः xii ... 11

PAGE.

प्रेक्षकवत् lxv 48
वचन xxviii 26
बध्यते lxii 47
बधैः xlix 40
बन्ध्यति xliv ... 37
बन्धः lxiii 47
बहुत्वं xviii 17
बहुधाकृतं xliv ... 51
बुद्धि xxvi, xxxiv, xlix 24, 30, 40
बुद्धिः xxiii, xxxv, xxxvii 22, 30, 31
बुद्धेः xlix 40
बुद्धौ xxxvi 31
ब्रह्मादिभ्यः liv ... 43
भवति xx, xxix, xxxiv, xliv, xlv, xlviii, liii, lxi 19, 27, 30, 37, 38, 39, 42, 46
भवन्ति xlvii ... 39
भाग्य l 40
भाव lii 41
भवानिर्वृत्तिः lii ... 41
भावाः xliii 36
भावाख्याः lii 41
भावात् ix 8
भावैः xl, lii ... 34, 41
भूत lvi 44
भूतादेः xxv 24
भूतानां lxix 51
भूतानि xxii, xxxviii 21, 32
भेदः xlviii 39
भेदा xlvii 39
भेदाः xlvi 38
भेदानां xv 15
भेदे lxviii 50

PAGE.

भोक्तृभावात् xvii ... 17
भौतिकः liii ... 42
मतिः lxi ... 46
मध्ये liv 43
मनः vii, xxvii ... 7, 25
मया lxvi 49
मरण xviii 17
मरणकृतं lv 43
महत् iii, viii, xl, lvi 3, 7, 34, 44
महदादि viii 7
महदाद्याः iii ... 3
महान् xxii ... 21
महामोहः xlviii ... 36
मातः xxxix ... 33
मातापितृजाः xxxix 33
माध्यस्थ्यं xix 18
मानुष्यः liii 42
मिथुन xii ... 11
मुच्यते lxii ... 47
मुनिः lxx 51
मूढाः xxxviii ... 32
मूल iii ... 3
मूलतः liv ... 43
मूलप्रकृतिः iii ... 3
मे lxi, lxiv 46, 48
मोहस्य xlviii ... 39
यगूयोनः liii ... 42
यत्र lxix 51
यथा xli, lvii, lviii, lix 35, 44, 45, 46
यस्मात् xxxv, xxxvii ...30, 31
या lxi 46
युक्त ii ... 2
युगपत् xxx ... 27
ये lxxii 52

PAGE.

रंगस्य lix 40
रजः xiii, liv ...13, 43
रजोविशालः liv ... 43
रसनत्वक् xxvi ... 24
रागात् xlv 38
राजसात् xlv ... 38
रूप lxv 48
रूपैः lxiii 47
रूपं xxiii 22
लघु xiii 13
लिंगम् x, xx, xl, xli, xlii, lii 9, 19, 34, 35, 35, 41
लिंगिलिंगिपूर्वकम् v ... 4
लिंगस्य lv 43
लिंगाख्यः lii 51
लिंगेन lii 51
लोकः lviii 45
वत्स lvii 44
वधा xlix 40
वरणकं xiii 13
वशात् lxvii 49
वाक् xxvi, xxxiv ...24, 30
वायवः xxix 27
वाह्यभेदाः xxvii ... 25
वाह्याः l 40
वाह्यं xxxiii ... 29
विकारः iii 3
विकृतिः iii 3
विकृतयः iii 3
विज्ञाय lxxi 52
विज्ञानात् ii 2
विघाताः li 41
विना xli, lii... ...35, 41
विनिवृत्तौ lxviii ... 50
विपरीतं x 9
विपरीतः ii, xi ... 2, 11

PAGE.

विपर्यय xiv, xlvi, xlvii ...14, 38, 39
विपर्ययभेदा xlvii ... 39
विपर्ययात् xvii, xviii, xlv, xlix 17, 17, 38, 40
विपर्ययादिष्यते xliv ... 37
विपर्यासः xlv ... 38
विपर्यासात् xix ... 18
विपर्यस्तम् xxiii 22
विभागात् xv 15
विभुत्वयोगात् xlii ... 35
विमर्दात् xlvi ... 38
विमोक्ष lvii 44
विमोक्षार्थ lvi 44
विमोक्षार्थं lviii 45
विरहिताः lxxii 52
विराग xxiii ... 22
विरूपं viii ... 7
विलक्षणा xxxvi 31
विवर्जिताः lxxii 52
विवृद्धि lvii ... 44
विशालः liv ... 43
विशिनष्टि xxxvii 31
विशुद्धं lxiv 48
विशेष xxxiv, lvi ... 30, 44
विशेषा xxxiv ... 30
विशेषाः xxxvi, xxxix ... 31, 33
विशेषात् xvi, xxvii ... 15, 25
विशेषैः xlvii ... 35
विषय l 40
विषया xxxiv ... 30
विषयाख्य xxxiii ... 29
विषयाणि xxxiv ... 30
विषयं xxxv 30
विषयः xi 11

PAGE.

विषाद xii 11
विहरण xxviii ... 26
वैकल्यात् xlvii ... 39
वैकृतात् xxv... ... 24
वैकृतिकाः xliii ... 36
वैराग्यात् xlv ... 38
वैश्वरूपस्य xv ... 15
वैषम्य xlvi 38
वृत्तिः xiii, xxviii, xxix, xxx 13,26, 27, 27
वृत्तिं xxxi 28
वृत्तयः xii 11
व्यक्त ii 2
व्यक्ताव्यक्तज्ञविज्ञानात् ii ... 2
व्यक्तं x, xi, xvi ... 9, 11, 15
व्यवधानात् vii ... 7
शक्तस्य ix 8
शक्तितः xv 15
शक्यकरणात् ix ... 8
शब्द xxxiv 30
शब्दः li 41
शब्दविषया xxxiv ... 30
शब्दादिषु xxviii ... 26
शरीर lxviii ... 50
शरीरः lxvii 49
शरीरभेदे lxviii ... 50
शान्ता xxxviii ... 32
शिष्य lxxi 52
शेषाणि xxxiv, xxxv ... 30, 30
श्रयान् ii 2
श्रोत्र xxvi 24
षष्टि lxxii 52
षोडशकः iii 3
स xxv, lxxi ... 24, 52
सः ii 2

PAGE.

सत् ix 8
सतः lx 46
सति lxvi 49
सत्व liv ... 43
सत्वं xiii 13
सत्क्रियं x 9
सप्त iii, lxv 3, 48
सप्तत्या lxxii 52
सप्तदश xlix 40
सप्तभिः lxiii ... 47
समन्वयात् xv 15
समाख्यातं lxix 51
समान vii 7
समानाभिहारात् vii ... 7
समासतः liii ... 42
समुदयात् xvi ... 15
सम्यक् lxvii, lxxi ... 49, 52
संयेागात् xx 19
संयेागः lxvi, xxi ... 49, 20
सर्गः xxi, xxiv, lii, liii, liv... 20, 23, 41, 42, 43
सर्गस्य lxvi 49
सर्व iv, ix 4, 8
सर्वं xxxv, xxxvii ... 30, 31.
सर्वप्रमाणसिद्धत्वात् iv ... 4
सलिलवत् xvi ... 15
सह xxxix, xlix ... 33, 40
सा xxix, xxxvii, lxiii ... 27, 31, 47
साक्षित्वं xix... 18
सत्विक xxv ... 24
सात्विकं xxiii 22
साधर्म्यात् xxvii 25
साधयति xxxvii ... 31
सान्तःकरण xxxv 30
सापार्था i ... 1

	PAGE.
सामान्य xxix ...	27
सामान्यं xi	10
सामान्यकरणवृत्तिः xxix ...	27
सामान्यतः vi ...	6
सामीप्यात् vii ...	7
साम्प्रतकालं xxxiii ...	29
सावयवं x	9
सिद्धत्वात् iv ...	4
सिद्धम् vi, xiv ...	6, 14
सिद्धयः li	41
सिद्धान्तं lxxi ...	52
सिद्धि xlvi	38
सिद्धिं xviii, xix ...	17, 18
सिद्धिः iv, xiv, xlvii ...	4, 14, 39
सिद्धिनां xlix ...	40
सिद्धेः li	41
सुकुमारतरं lxi ...	46
सुहृत् li	41
सूक्ष्म xl	34
सूक्ष्मपर्यन्तम् xl ...	34
सूक्ष्यम् xxxvii ...	31
सूक्ष्मया xxxix ...	33
सौक्ष्मात् vii, viii ...	7, 7
संकल्पकं xxvii. ...	25
संस्कार lxxi... ...	49
संक्षिप्त lxxi	52
संघात xvii ...	17
संघातपरार्थत्वात् xvii ...	17
संभव ix	8
संसरति xl, lxii ...	34, 47
संसारः xlv	38
सांसिद्धिकाः xliii	36
स्तम्बपर्यन्तः liv	43
स्थाणु xli ...	35
स्थिति lxix ...	51
स्मृता xxxviii	32
स्युः xxxix ...	33
स्वभावेन lv	43
स्वास्थः lxv	48
स्वार्थ lvi ...	44
स्वालक्षण्यं xxix	27
स्वां स्वां xxxi	28
षोडशकः xxii	21
षोडशकात् xxii	21
हार्यं xxxii	29
हि ii, iv	2, 4
हेतुः xxxi	28
हेतुकं xlii ...	35
हेतुकां xxxi ...	28
हेतुमत् x ...	9
हेतौ i ...	1

APPENDIX VII.

PANCHAS'IKHA SÛTRAM

OR

A FEW OF THE APHORISMS OF PANCHAS'IKHA.

PANCHASIKHA-SUTRAM.

INTRODUCTORY.

1. Páñchaśikha is one of the few earliest writers on the Sâṃkhya. He is an authority on the subject, and is mentioned as an Âchârya or Professor of the School. According to Īśvarakṛiṣṇa, the author of Sâṃkhya-Kârikâ, the original Sâṃkhya which descended from its founder Kapila to Pañchaśikha (through Âsuri, see Sâṃkhya-Kârikâ, No. LXX), was elaborated by him in manifold ways. But not a single one of his works is amongst the current coins of the Sâṃkhya literature. "He is known, by scanty fragments, as the author of a collection of philosophical aphorisms. One other performance, if not two, is likewise imputed to him; and he, perhaps, descanted on the theistic (sic) Sâṃkhya as well as on the atheistic (sic.)" (F. E. Hall). It would appear, from Vijñâna Bhikṣu's Commentary on the Vedânta-Sûtram, that Pañchaśikha wrote a commentary on the Tattva-Samâsa.

2. The only source, as yet discovered, so far as we know, from which a few of the aphorisms of Pañchaśikha can be recovered, is Vyâsa's Commentary on the Yoga-Sûtram of Patañjali. In the Preface to his edition of the Sâṃkhya-Pravachana-Bhâṣyam of Vijñâna Bhikṣu, Mr. Fitz-Edward Hall has collected eleven aphorisms of Pañchaśikha quoted by Vyâsa in his said Commentary. Another collection of extracts from the same source has been published, under the title of Pañchaśikha-âchârya-praṇîta Sâṃkhya-Sûtra, by Paṇḍita Râjâ Ram, Professor of Sanskrit, D. A. V. College, Lahore, in Nos. 4 and 5, Vol. VIII, 1912, of the series entitled Ârṣa-Granthâvali, Lahore. This collection contains twenty-one aphorisms including one of Vârṣagaṇya. Quite recently, again, we had a peculiar opportunity of examining the MS. of another collection of aphorisms attributed to Pañchaśikha, prepared by Svâmî Hariharânanda Araṇya of the Kâpila Âśrama in the District of Hooghli. This was obviously not an original compilation, but a reproduction of the Lahore publication, with a few additions, one of which was taken from the Veda without acknowledgment! As regards the collection of Mr. Fitz-Edward Hall and the collection of Paṇḍita Râja Râm, we have found that the one is, in certain respects, more complete and correct than the other, while the paternity of some of the aphorisms attributed in it to Pañchaśikha

is not free from suspicion. These will be noticed more in detail in the subsequent pages.

3. "Little can safely be conjectured," as rightly observes Mr. Fitz-Edward Hall, "with regard to the character of the work or works from which these sentences were collected by Vyâsa. They may be text; and they may be commentary. Probably they are Sâṃkhya; but, possibly, they pertain to the Yoga. That Pañchaśikha treated of other subjects than the Sâṃkhya, may be inferred from a remark of Vijñâna Bhikṣu's:

Svaprayojana-abhâve'pi viduṣâṃ pravṛittau Pañchaśikha-âchârya-vâkyaṃ sâṃkhya-sthaṃ pramâṇayati.—*Yoga-Vârtika*, I. 25."

आदिविद्वान् निर्माणचित्तमधिष्ठाय कारुण्याद्भगवान् परमर्षिरासुरये जिज्ञासमानाय तन्त्रं प्रोवाच ॥

4. आदिविद्वान् Âdi-Vidvân, the primeval Seer. "Primeval" means produced at the beginning of Creation. "Seer" means Darśana-kâra or one who has had direct vision of Puruṣa as distinct from Prakṛiti. In its primary significance, the term "Âdi-Vidvân" is applicable to Viṣṇu alone. Here it refers to Kapila, the reputed founder of the Sâṃkhya Tantra, because "it is the self-existent Viṣṇu who appeared as the first Wise Man, Kapila, at the beginning of the current cycle of Cosmic Evolution, endowed with virtue, knowledge, dispassion, and infallible will" (Vâchaspati Miśra).

5. निर्माणचित्तमधिष्ठाय Nirmâṇa-chittam adhiṣṭhâya, presiding over, ensouling, or through the medium of, a self-made mental vehicle. These words explain how Viṣṇu became incarnated as Kapila. He, by an act of will, reproduced Himself as the mighty sage Kapila. Kapila was not a developed man, but an enveloped Divinity. This artificial creation of bodies, ensouled by artificial emanations of the mind, which is one of the most wonderful discoveries of the Hindu Spiritual Science, is not expected to make any deep impression on the minds of the majority of Western Scholars in the present age, nor to engage them in the investigation or in an examination of the truth in this matter, in a true scientific spirit. Neither do we here propose to enter into a discussion with them on this subject. We shall simply mention, for the information of readers at large, that this subject of the creation of artificial bodies and minds is dealt with in the Yoga-Sûtram of Patañjali, IV. 4, 5, and 6 (See the Sacred Books of the Hindus, Vol IV., 272-273). And to make the words of our text a little more illuminating to them, we may take the following extract from the Introduction to the above volume :—

"A Yogî, having attained the power of Samâdhi, sets about destroying his past Karmas. All Karmas may be divided into three classes :—(1) The acts done in the past, the consequences of which the man *must* suffer in the present life; the Karmas to expiate which he has taken the present birth or incarnation. They are the *ripe* Karmas (Prârabdha). (2) The Karmas done in the past, but which are not ripe, and will have to be expiated in some future life. They are the *stored* Karmas, or *unripe* (Sañchita). (3) The Karmas which a man creates in his present life, and which have to be expiated in a future or the present life. This last kind of act,—the fresh Karmas, can be stopped. By devotion to the Lord and doing everything in a spirit of service, no *fresh* Karmas are generated. The incurring of debt is stopped. The man, however, has to pay off past debts—the ripe and unripe Karmas. The ripe Karmas will produce their effects in the present life. The Yogî does not trouble himself about this. But the *unripe* or *stored* Karmas require a future birth. It is here that the Yoga is of the greatest practical importance. The Yogî is not bound to wait for future lives in order to get an opportunity to pay off the debt of Sañchita Karmas. He simultaneously *creates* ALL the bodies that those Sañchita Karmas require,—through those bodies expiates all his Karmas simultaneously. Every one of such bodies has a Chitta or mentality of his own. This is the Nirmâṇa-chitta or the Artificial mind—like the Pseudo-Personalities of hypnoptic trance. These artificial minds arise simultaneously like so many sparks from the Âhaṃkâric matter of the Yogî's Self, and they ensoul the artificial bodies created for them. These artificial bodies, with artificial minds in them, walk through the earth in hundreds,—they are distinguished from ordinary men by the fact that they are perfectly methodical in all their acts, and automatic in their lives. All these artificials are controlled by the consciousness of the Yogî,—one consciousness controlling hundred automatons. Every one of these automatons has a particular destiny, a particular portion of the Sañchita Karma to exhaust. As soon as that destiny is fulfilled, the Yogî withdraws his ray from it, and the "man" dies a sudden death,—a heart-failure generally.

"Now, what is the difference between the ordinary mind and the Yoga-created mind,—the natural Chitta and the artificial Chitta? The natural mind by experience gains a habit, the impressions are stored in it, and they, as Vâsanâs, become the seeds of desires and activities. The artificial mind is incapable of storing up impressions in it. It has no Vâsanâs and consequently it disintegrates as soon as the body falls down."

6. कारुण्यात् Kâruṇyât, through compassion. This word, according to Vyâsa, tells us what the teaching of the text is. It is this that Îśvara, out of the abundance of His compassion towards all Puruṣas, incarnates Himself, from time to time, in order to teach them knowledge and virtue, whereby they may be delivered from bondage. The passage of the text is quoted by Vyâsa in his Commentary on the Yoga-Sûtram, I. 25, and Vâchaspati explains the purpose of the quotation thus: "This theory that the compassionate Lord teaches knowledge and virtue is also common to the teaching of Kapila:—So has it been said by Pañchaśikha." *Râma Prasâda's translation.*

7. भगवान् Bhagavân, divine. This term connotes the possession of

virtue, knowledge, dispassion, and infallible will. And we know that these were cognate with Kapila.

8. परमर्षिः: Parama-ṛiṣiḥ, the mighty sage. Viṣṇu appeared on earth as Kapila, in the highly purified and richly developed body of a saint who held communion with the gods. The necessity for such bodies for divine manifestations has been admirably explained and illustrated by the late Babu Sisir Kumar Ghosh in his *Lord Gaurâṅga.*

9. आसुरये Âsuraye, to Âsuri, a disciple of Kapila and the first recipient of the Sâṃkhya.

10. जिज्ञासमानाय Jijñâsamânâya, who wished to know Âsuri approached the divine man Kapila and desired to know from him the means for the accomplishment of the Supreme Good, namely, the permanent prevention of pain.

11. तन्त्रं Tantraṃ, the systematic teaching, the Sâṃkhya doctrine.

12. प्रोवाच Pra-uvâcha, declared fully, revealed. Such, then, is the origin of the Sâṃkhya.

I. The primeval Seer, (incarnated), through the medium of an artificial mind, (as) the mighty divine sage (Kapila), out of compassion (towards all entangled Puruṣas), revealed the (Sâṃkhya) doctrine, in a systematic way, to Âsuri, who desired to know them.

13. Now, what is this Sâṃkhya Darśana? "Darśana" etymologically means the act or the result of seeing, from the root √Dṛiś, to see. Here it stands for Sâkṣâtkâra or immeditae vision, that is, intuition of the Self. And "Sâṃkhya" means that by which something is perfectly revealed, from the root √Khyâ, to manifest. The "Sâṃkhya Darśana," therefore, is that form of Spiritual Intuition of the Self, whereby the nature of the Self is perfectly revealed. So declares Pañchaśikha :—

एकमेव दर्शनं ख्यातिरेव दर्शनम् ॥

एकम् Ekam, one, single. एव Eva, only, there is no second. दर्शनं Darśanaṃ, intuition, knowledge. ख्यातिः Khyâtiḥ, coming to light, shining, manifestation, illumination. एव Eva, alone. दर्शनम् Darśanam, intuition, knowledge.

II. There is but one Spiritual Intuition of the Self; it is nothing but manifestation which is the Spiritual Intuition of the Self.

14. The word 'Khyâti' is suggestive in more respects than one. Now, manifestation is declared to be the means of accomplishing Mokṣa or Release. (1) What, then, must be its nature? It cannot obviously be of the nature of the attainment of some advanced state or development from a state less advanced or less developed; for Manifestation itself cannot accomplish this. It will also be repugnant to the Sâṃkhya conception of the Self; for the Self is kûṭastha, unchangeable; it ever *is*, never *becomes*. It follows, therefore, that Mokṣa consists merely in the removal of a shadow, as it were, that is, of something which casts its reflection on the Self and thereby overshadows it and causes obstruction to its shining out in the fullness of its own light. (2) This shadow, this obstruction, is not of, or from, the Self, but is a creation of the Not-Self. And what is the cause of its origin, the same is also the cause of its removal. It fades or deepens, it contracts or expands, it exists or ceases to exist, and for this depends entirely on the activity or non-activity of the Not-Self. (3) The Self is altogether passive and inert. Shadow or no shadow, it is ever there, all-full, ever shining, unaffected, unsullied. In ignorance, men speak of the Bondage of the Self which is never bound, ever released. Bondage, in reality, is this supreme ignorance, this veil of the Not-Self,—the non-discrimination of the principle of Becoming and the principle of Being,—to which alone is due all the suffering in the world,—not exactly suffering, for actual suffering there can be, and is, nothing in the Self, but the Abhimâna or assumption or attribution of it to the Self. Replace non-discrimination by Discrimination, the veil is gone, and gone with it is the Shadow—the obstruction—and see the ever pure, ever constant, ever shining Self.

15. This Aphorism of Pañchaśikha has been quoted by Vyâsa in his Commentary on the Aphorism I. 4 of Patañjali's Yoga-Sûtram in the following context: Yoga is the inihibition of the modifications of the mind (chitta) (Yoga-Sûtram I. 2). Then the Seer (Puruṣa) stands in his own nature (*Ibid* I. 3), that is, is established in his own intrinsic form, as in the state of kaivalya or absolute abstractedness. Elsewhere (there takes place in him) similarity of form with the modifications (*Ibid* I. 4). How does it take place? Because objects are presented to him. Whatever, therefore, be the modifications of the mind, with the same is Puruṣa invested, so long as the mind remains up and doing. That is to say, Puruṣa, with the light of his intelligence, illuminates the manifold modifications of the active mind, which, consequently, are mistaken as being the manifestations of Puruṣa. It is thus this mistake, the failure to distinguish between the unintelligent modifications of

the unintelligent mind and the intelligence of the inert, immutable Puruṣa, which is the cause of all the mental phenomena so universally attributed to Puruṣa. In reality, however, the manifestation of Puruṣa is one and one only, the same at all times and in all circumstances. And so there is the Aphorism : " There is but one Spiritual Intuition of the Self ; it is nothing but Manifestation, which is the Spiritual Intuition of the Self."

16. The Self is most difficult to know. It is inscrutable. Only a steady, pure, and peaceful mind can reflect it as it is in itself. Steadiness of the mind implies a long and arduous process of Yogic practice. The stepping-stone to it is what is called Jyotiṣmatî or the state of lucidity, or the activity which causes illumination. This activity of the mind is twofold, according as it is painless objective (viśoka-viṣayavatî) or is purely egoistic (asmitâ-mâtrâ). It is described by Vyâsa in his Commentary on Yoga-Sûtram, I. 36, in the following manner: "It is the consciousness of thought-forms (Buddhi), on the part of one who practises concentration upon the Lotus of the Heart. For, the substance of Buddhi is refulgent and is like Âkâśa, *i.e.*, all-pervading. Through success in concentration upon that, the activity of the mind modifies by the forms having the colour of the light of the sun, the moon, the planets and precious stones. Likewise, the mind concentrated upon Asmitâ, I-aṃ-ness or egoism, becomes pure egoism, calm and infinite, like a waveless ocean." And he supports his exposition by quoting the following Aphorism of Pañchaśikha :

तमणुमात्रमात्मानुविद्यास्मीत्येवं तावत् संप्रजानीते ॥

तम् Tam, that. अणुमात्रम् Aṇu-mâtram, of the size of an atom, small as an atom, difficult to understand, inscrutable. आत्मानम् Âtmânam, Self. अनुविद्य Anu-vidya, knowing at last. अस्मि Asmi, am. इति Iti, that. एवं Evaṃ, in this form. तावत् Tâvat, for certain. संप्रजानीते Saṃ-pra-jânîte, fully and accurately knows.

III. Knowing, at last, that inscrutable Self, his consciousness mainfests as " I am " only.

17. It has been mentioned above that the identification of the Principle of Being with the Principle of Becoming, of the Self with the Not-Self, is the cause of all the suffering in the Universe. This identification is called A-vidyâ. Its nature is declared by Pañchaśikha in the following two Aphorisms :

व्यक्तमव्यक्तं वा सत्त्वमात्मत्वेनाभिप्रतीत्य तस्य संपदमनुनन्दत्यात्मसंपदं मन्वानस्तस्य व्यापदमनुशोचत्यात्मव्यापदं मन्वानः स सर्वोऽप्रतिबुद्धः ॥

व्यक्तम् Vyaktam, unfolded, sentient substances or existences. such as wife, son, animals, etc. अव्यक्तं A-vyaktam, not unfolded, insentient objects, such as riches, house, couch, etc. वा Vâ, or. सत्त्वम् Sattvam, existence, substance, object. आत्मत्वेन Âtma-tvena, under the characteristic of the Self, as being the Self. अभिप्रतीत्य Abhi-pratîtya, approaching towards in mind, thinking, believing, taking up. तस्य Tasya, its, of the object. संपदम् Sampadam, prosperity, well-being. अनुनन्दति Anu-nandati, rejoices at or according to. आत्मसंपदं Âtma-Sampadam, well-being of the Self. मन्वानः Manvânaḥ, imagining. तस्य Tasya, its, of the object. व्यापदम् Vyâpadam, adversity. अनुशोचति Anu-Śochati, grieves according to. आत्मव्यापदं Âtma-vyâpadam, adversity of the Self. मन्वानः Manvânaḥ, imagining. सः Saḥ, he. सर्वः Sarvaḥ, all. अप्रतिबुद्धः A-prati-buddhaḥ, unawakened in regard to the truth.

IV. They are all unawakened who, believing the objective entities, whether they be sentient or insentient, to be the Self, rejoice at their prosperity, imagining it to be the prosperity of the Self, and grieve at their adversity, imagining it to be the adversity of the Self.

18. This Aphorism has been quoted by Vyâsa in his Commentary on Yoga-Sûtram II. 5 which describes A-vidyâ as being "the manifestation of the non-eternal, the impure, the painful, and the Not-Self to be the eternal, the pure, the pleasant, and the Self."

बुद्धितः परं पुरुषमाकारशीलविद्यादिभिरपश्यन् कुर्यात्तत्रात्म-बुद्धिं मोहेन ॥

बुद्धितः Buddhi-taḥ, from Buddhi. परं Param, different. पुरुषम् Puruṣam, Puruṣa. आकारशीलविद्यादिभिः Âkâra-Śîla-vidyâ-âdibhiḥ, by nature, character, knowledge, etc. The nature of Puruṣa is constant purity. Indifference is his character. By knowledge is denoted his being intelligent. Whereas Buddhi is impure, not indifferent, and non-intelligent. अपश्यन् A-paśyan, not seeing. कुर्यात् Kuryât, is led to form. तत्र Tatra, therein, in respect of Buddhi. आत्मबुद्धिं Âtma-buddhim, the notion of the Self. मोहेन Mohena, by reason of the dullness (of Tamas).

V. Not knowing Puruṣa to be different from Buddhi in nature, character, knowledge, etc., a man is led, by reason of the dullness born of Tamas, to form the notion of the Self in respect of Buddhi.

19. The above has been quoted by Vyâsa in his Commentary on the Yoga-Sûtram II. 6 which describes Asmitâ or Egoism as being "the apparent identity of the subjective power of seeing (*i.e.*, Puruṣa) and the instrumental power of seeing (*i. e.*, Buddhi)."

20. It follows, therefore, that there is Bondage as long as this notion of the Self in respect of the Not-Self remains, and that there is Release when this notion is destroyed by the knowledge of the Self as being distinct and different from the Not-Self in all essential particulars.

स्यात् स्वल्पः संकरः सपरिहारः सप्रत्यवमर्शः कुशलस्य नापकर्षायालम् ॥

स्यात् Syât, can be. स्वल्पः Svalpaḥ, little. संकरः Saṃkaraḥ, mixture. सपरिहारः Sa-parihâraḥ attended with, *i.e.*, capable of, avoidance or removal. सप्रत्यवमर्शः Sa-prati-avamarśaḥ, attended with, *i.e.*, capable of, being borne easily. कुशलस्य Kuśalasya, of the good. न Na, not. अपकर्षाय Apakarṣâya, for damage or impairment or lessening the effect. अलम् Alam, sufficient, strong or powerful enough.

VI. A little mixture (of evil entailed, for instance, by the killing of animals) which is capable of removal (by expiation) or is easy to bear, cannot prevail for the diminution of the (greater) good (produced by the performance of sacrifices such as the Aśvamedha and the like).

21. The above bears reference to the vexed question as to the consequences of the acts of sin necessarily committed in the course of the performance of sacrifices which are calculated to produce merits of far-reaching consequences. For instance, an Aśvamedha sacrifice cannot be performed without the killing of a horse, and killing is a sinful act. So that, while the performance of the Aśvamedha produces its desirable consequences, the killing of the horse cannot, at the same time, fail to produce its undesirable consequences. The question, therefore, arises whether what is acquired through the sacrifice, be not lost through the sin. This is an important issue arising in the discussion of the Law of Karma as a whole.

22. Now, "the killing of animals, etc., has," as Vâchaspati explains, "two effects. The first is that, being ordained as part of the principal action, it helps in its fulfilment. The second is that, the causing of pain to all living beings being forbidden, it results in undesirable consequences. Of these, when it is performed only as subsidiary to the principal action, then, for that very reason, it does not manifest its result all at once, independently of the principal action. On the contrary, it keeps its position of an accessory only, and manifests only when the fruition of the principal ruling action begins. 'It is said to be tacked on to the ruling action, when, while helping the ruling action, it exists as the seed of its own proper effect. Pañchaśikha has said the following on the subject: A, little mixture.'

"When the ruling factor of the present karma, born from the sacrifice of Jyotiṣṭoma, etc, is mixed up with the present cause of evil, it may be easily removed. It is possible of removal by a small expiatory sacrifice. Even if an expiatory sacrifice be not performed by carelessness, the subsidiary action would ripen at the time of the ripening of the principal only, and, in that case, the evil generated thereby would be easy to bear. The wise who are taking their baths in the great lake of the nectar of pleasure brought about by a collection of good actions, put up easily with a small piece of the fire of pain produced by a small evil. It is not, therefore, capable of diminishing, *i.e.*, appreciably lessening the effect of the good, *i.e.*, of his large virtues."—*Râma Prasâda's translation.*

23. This Aphorism of Pañchaśikha has been quoted by Vyâsa in his Commentary on the Yoga-Sûtram II. 13. "So long as the cause remains, the fruition of Merit and Demerit is in the kind of birth, length of life and experience."

24. Pandit Raja Ram is wrong in reading the next sentence in the Commentary as part of the present Aphorism. For both Svapneśvara and Vâchaspati are against this reading.

25. But the fact remains that even a highly meritorious act is tainted with sin, and with consequent pain. It is even as Patañjali declares that "to the discriminative, all is pain" (Yoga-Sûtram II. 15). And pain is the thing which every mortal seeks to get rid of: not merely present pain, but pain not-yet-come is the thing to be avoided (Yoga-Sûtram II. 16). Accordingly, both in the Sâṃkhya and in the Yoga Śâstra, enquiries have been instituted into the cause of its origin as well as into the means of its removal. In the Yoga-Sûtram II. 17, Patañjali declares that the conjunction of Buddhi and Puruṣa is the cause of pain. And on this subject, also says Pañchaśikha:

तत्संयोगहेतुविवर्जनात् स्यादयमात्यन्तिको दुःखप्रतीकारः ॥

तत्संयोगहेतुविवर्जनात् Tat-Saṃyoga-hetu-vivarjanât, through abandonment of the cause, namely, Non-discrimination, of the conjunction thereof, *i.e.*, of Buddhi. स्यात् Syât, will be. अयम् Ayam, this, *i.e.*, the desired prevention of pain not-yet-come. आत्यन्तिकः Âtyantikaḥ, final, permanent. दुःखप्रतीकारः Duḥkha-pratîkâraḥ, prevention or remedy of pain.

VII. Through the abandonment of the cause thereof, there can be the permanent prevention of pain, which is desired.

26. The above has been quoted by Vyâsa in his Commentary on the Yoga-Sûtram II. 17.

27. Pain is due to conjunction. Rajas gives rise to pain in Sattva, which reflects it on Puruṣa, through conjunction. In this reflection consists the experience (Bhoga) of Puruṣa from which emancipation (Apavarga is sought. To describe them more correctly, Bhoga is the ascertainment of the essential nature of the Guṇas, as desirable and undesirable, in their undifferentiated form ; and Apavarga is the ascertainment of the essential nature of the Experiencer, through the withdrawal of the influence of Prakṛiti upon him. To accomplish both these objects, namely, Bhoga and Apavarga, is the creation of the world. Creation is the exhibition of Prakṛiti to Puruṣa. Puruṣa regards or looks at Prakṛiti from these points of view only ; and there is no third point of view. So declares Pañchaśikha also :

अयंतु खलु त्रिषु गुणेषु कर्तृष्वकर्तरि च पुरुषे तुल्यातुल्यजातीये तत्क्रियासाक्षिण्युपनीयमानान्त्सर्वभावाननुपश्यन्नदर्शनमन्यच्छंकते ॥

अयं Ayam, this Puruṣa. तु Tu, but. खलु Khalu, surely. त्रिषु Triṣu, in the three. गुणेषु Guṇeṣu, in the Guṇas, Sattva, Rajas, and Tamas. कर्तृषु Kartṛiṣu, which are the actors, agents. अकर्तरि A Kartari, who is not the actor. च Cha, and. पुरुषे Puruṣe, in Puruṣa. तुल्यातुल्यजातीये Tulya-a-tulya-jâtîye, who is of a like and unlike kind. चतुर्थे Chaturthe, the fourth. तत्क्रियासाक्षिणि Tat-kriyâ-sâkṣiṇi, who is the witness of the action thereof, *i.e.*, of the Guṇas. उपनीयमानान् Upanîyamânân, that are being presented. सर्वभावान् Sarva-bhâvân, all objects. उपपन्नान् Upapannân, established, known. अनुपश्यन् Anupaśyan, knowing. न Na, not. दर्शनम् Darśanam, view. अन्यत् Anyat, other. शंकते Śaṅkate, suspects.

VIII. This one, however, seeing all things explained as these are being presented to the three Guṇas as the actors and to the fourth, *viz.*, Puruṣa, of a like and unlike kind, as the non-actor and as the witness of their action, does not suspect (the existence of) any other point of view, or object of knowledge.

28. " Of a like and unlike kind":—For instance, the Guṇas are eternal, so is Puruṣa ; Puruṣa is intelligent, but the Guṇas are non-intelligent.

29. " The above has been quoted by Vyâsa in his Commentary on Yoga-Sûtram II 18: The object (Dṛiśya) which possesses the nature of illumination (Sattva), activity (Rajas), and inertia (Tamas) and consists

of the elements and of the powers of cognition and action, exists for the purpose of experience and of emancipation.

30. "But these two, experience and emancipation, which are effected by Buddhi, reside in Buddhi alone; how are they, then," asks Vyâsa, "predicated of Puruṣa?" He next gives the answer: "Just as victory or defeat, which lies in the army, is predicated of the owner of the army, as he is the experiencer of its consequences, so too are Bondage and Release, residing in Buddhi alone, are predicated of Puruṣa, as he is the experiencer of their consequences. Of Buddhi alone are Bondage in the shape of the non-accomplishment of the object of Puruṣa, and Release in the shape of the fulfilment thereof. Similarly, are perception, memory, reasoning, doubt, knowledge of the truth, and blind attachment to life, which reside in Buddhi, are attributed as existing in Puruṣa, as he is the experiencer of their consequences, by having their reflections thrown upon him from Buddhi, through proximity."

31. Puruṣa, then, is neither quite similar to Buddhi nor quite dissimilar to it. He is not quite subject to Bondage and Release, nor is quite free from them. On this subject, Pañchaśikha further declares:

अपरिणामिनी हि भोक्तृशक्तिरप्रतिसंक्रमा च परिणामिन्यर्थे प्रतिसंक्रान्तेव तद्वृत्तिमनुपतति । तस्याश्च प्राप्तचैतन्योपग्रहरूपाया बुद्धिवृत्तेरनुकारमात्रतया बुद्धिवृत्त्याऽविशिष्टा हि ज्ञानवृत्तिरित्याख्यायते ॥

अपरिणामिनी A-pariṇâminî, not subject to transformation, unchangeable. हि Hi, for. भोक्तृशक्तिः Bhoktṛi-Śaktiḥ, the power of the experiencer, intelligence, consciousness. अप्रतिसंक्रमा A-prati-Saṇkramâ, not moving towards objects, inert, actionless, inactive. च Cha, and. परिणामिनी Pariṇâminî, subject to transformation, changeful. अर्थे Arthe, into the object, *i e.*, Buddhi. प्रतिसंक्रान्ता Pratisaṃkrâṇtâ, transferred, moved to. इव Iva, as if. तद्वृत्तिम् Tat-vṛittim, the modifications thereof, *i e.*, of Buddhi. अनुपतति Anu-patati, imitates, modifies according to तस्याः Tasyâḥ, its, *i.e*, of Buddhi. च Cha, and. प्राप्तचैतन्योपग्रहरूपायाः Prâpta-chaitanya-upagraha-rûpâyâḥ, transformed by receiving the reflection of intelligence. बुद्धिवृत्तेः Bûddhi-vṛitteḥ, of the modification of Buddhi. अनुकारमात्रतया Anu-kâra-mâtra-tayâ, by reason of mere imitation. बुद्धिवृत्त्या Buddhi-vṛittyâ, by the modification of Buddhi अविशिष्टा A-viśiṣṭâ, unqualified. हि Hi, verily. ज्ञानवृत्तिः Jñâna-vṛittiḥ, modification of consciousness. इति Iti, thus. आख्यायते Âkhyâyate, called, described.

IX. For the power of the Experiencer which is unchangeable as well as inert, as if running into the changeful object (*i.e.*, Buddhi), imitates its modifications. And by reason of the mere imitation of the modifications of Buddhi, while that is transformed by receiving the reflection of intelligence, it (the imitation) is described as the modification of intelligence unqualified by the modification of Buddhi.

32. The above has been quoted by Vyâsa in his Commentary on Yoga-Sûtram II. 20: "The seer is the power of seeing merely: though pure, he sees ideas by imitation," and he thereby supports the proposition that "though pure, he sees ideas by imitation; because he sees, by imitation, ideas belonging to Buddhi, and, though he is not of the same nature as Buddhi, as he sees by imitation, because he looks as if he were of the nature of Buddhi." This is further explained by Vâchaspati in the following manner:

"Although the moon is not, as a matter of fact, transferred into pure water, yet, inasmuch as its reflection passes into water, it is, as it were, transferred into it. So also, the power of consciousness, although not actually transferred into the Buddhi, yet is, as it were, transferred into it, because it is reflected into it. By that fact, consciousness becomes, as it were, of the very nature of the will-to-be (Buddhi). It accordingly follows the modifications of the will-to-be. This explains the words "by imitation." It is said, it cognises by imitation, as it cognises by following the modifications of the will-to-be."—*Ram Prasâda's translation.*

33. Conjunction has been stated to be the cause of Bhoga. The objective world owes its existence to it. But when, in the case of a Puruṣa whose objects have been fulfilled, the objective world no longer exists for him, it does not at the same time altogether vanish out of existence, because there are other Puruṣas whose Bhoga and Apavarga still remain to be accomplished. (*Vide* the Yoga-Sûtram II. 22). Thus is the continuity of creation established. Hereby is also established that, whereas the Subject and the Object exist from eternity, their conjunction must, in the form of a stream of successive conjunctions, be without beginning. On this subject there has been quoted by Vyâsa, in his Commentary on the above Yoga-Sûtram, the following Aphorism of Pañchaśikha:

धर्मिणामनादिसंयोगात् धर्ममात्राणामप्यनादिः संयोगः ॥

धर्मिणाम Dharmiṇâm, of the containers, that is, the Guṇas, Sattva, Rajas, and Tamas. अनादिसंयोगात् An-âdi-saṃyogât, because conjunction with Puruṣa is without beginning. धर्ममात्राणाम् Dharma-mâtrâṇâm, of all the contained, that is, the products

Mahat and the rest. अपि Api, also. अनादिः An-âdiḥ, without beginning. संयोगः Saṃyogaḥ, conjunction.

X. Because the conjunction of the Guṇas (with Puruṣa) is without beginning, the conjunction also of the products thereof, taken as a class, is without beginning.

34. "It is for this reason that, although the conjunction of one Puruṣa with one manifestation of the principle of Mahat has ceased to exist, the conjunction of another Puruṣa with another manifestation of the Mahat has not become a thing of the past."—*Ram Prasada's translation of Vâchaspati.*

35. In the Yoga-Sûtram III. 13, Patañjali declares: "By this are described the changes of characteristic (dharma), of secondary quality (lakṣaṇa), and of condition (avasthâ) in the objective and instrumental phenomena."—*Ram Prasada's translation.*

36. In the course of his Commentary on the above, Vyâsa observes: "The change of secondary quality is the moving of the characteristic along the paths of being (past, present, and future). The past characteristic joined to the past secondary quality, is not devoid of the future and the present secondary quality. Similarly, the present (characteristic) joined to the present secondary quality, is not devoid of the past and the future secondary quality. Similarly, the future (characteristic) joined to the future secondary quality, is not devoid of the present and past secondary qualities. For example, a man who is attached to one woman, does not hate all the others.

"Others find a fault in this change of secondary qualities They say that all the qualities being in simultaneous existence, their paths of being must be confused, (and thus overlapping one another, cannot be considered as distinct and different).

"This is thus met: That the characteristics do exist as such, requires no proof. When there is such a thing as a characteristic, the differences of the secondary qualities also must be posited. It is not only in the present time that the characteristic characterizes. If it were so, the mind would not possess the characteristic of attachment, seeing that attachment is not in manifestation at the time of anger. Further, the three (peaceful, fearful, and dull) secondary qualities are not possible of existence in one individual simultaneously. They may, however, appear in succession, by virtue of the operation of their several (exciting) causes. Therefore, there is no confusion. For example, attachment being in the height of manifestation with reference to some object, it does not, for that reason, cease to exist with reference to all other objects. On the contrary, it is then ordinarily in existence with reference to them."—*Ram Prasada's translation.*

And in support of the above view, Vyâsa quotes the following Aphorism of Pañchaśikha:

रूपातिशयाः वृत्त्यतिशयाश्च विरुध्यन्ते सामान्यानि त्वति-शयैः सह प्रवर्तन्ते ॥

रूपातिशयाः Rûpa-atiśayâḥ, intensities of nature or characteristic. वृत्त्यतिशयाः Vṛitti-atiśayâḥ, intensities of function or manifestation. च cha, and. विरुध्यन्ते Virudhyante, are opposed. सामान्यानि Sâmânyâni, ordinary ones. तु Tu, but. अतिशयैः Atiśayaiḥ, with the intense ones. सह Saha, with. प्रवर्तन्ते Pravartante, co-exist, co-operate.

XI. Intensities of characteristic and intensities of manifestation are opposed to each other, but the ordinary ones co-exist with the intense ones.

37. This simple Aphorism of Pañchaśikha embodies the discovery of the important doctrine of the sub-conscious mind.

38. As to the relation between Âkâśa and the Power of Hearing, there is the following Aphorism of Pañchaśikha:

तुल्यदेशश्रवणानामेकदेशश्रुतित्वं सर्वेषां भवति ॥

तुल्यदेशश्रवणानाम् Tulya-deśa-śravaṇânâm, of those having their powers of hearing similarly located, that is, equally in Âkâśa or soniferous ether. एकदेशश्रुतित्वं Eka-deśa-śruti-tvaṃ, to have the power of hearing in the same situation. सर्वेषां Sarveṣâm, of all. भवति Bhavati, is.

XII. In the case of all, having their powers of hearing equally located in Akâśa, hearing takes place in the same situation.

39. The above has been quoted by Vyâsa in his Commentary on the Yoga-Sûtram III. 40: "By Saṃyama over the relation between Âkâśa and the power-of-hearing, comes the higher power hearing."

40. And Vâchaspati explains its sense and significance in the following manner: "This sense of hearing, then, having its origin in the principle of egoism, acts like iron, drawn as it is by sound originating and located in the mouth of the speaker, acting as loadstone, transforms them into its own modifications in sequence of the sounds of the speaker, and thus senses them. And it is for this reason that for every living

creature, the perception of sound in external space is, in the absence of defects, never void of authority. So says the quotation from Pañchaśikha: "To all those whose organs of hearing are similarly situated, the situation of hearing is the same." "All those" are Chaitras and others whose powers of hearing are similarly situated in space. The meaning is, that the powers of hearing of all are located in Âkâśa. Further, the Âkâśa in which the power of hearing is located, is born out of the Soniferous Tanmâtra, and has therefore the quality of sound inherent in itself. It is by this sound acting in unison, that it takes the sound of external solids, etc. Hence the hearing, *i.e.*, the sound, of all is of the same class.

"This, then, establishes that Âkâśa is the substratum of the power of hearing, and also possesses the quality of sound. And this sameness of the situation of sound is an indication of the existence of Âkâśa. That which is the substratum of the auditory power (Śruti) which manifests as sound of the same class, is Âkâśa."—*Ram Prasada's translation.*

41. In his Pañchaśikha—Âchârya-praṇîta Sâṃkhya-Sûtra, Paṇḍita Râja Râm includes the following quotations by Vyâsa:

प्रधानं स्थित्यैव वर्तमानं विकाराकरणादप्रधानं स्यात् तथा गत्यैव वर्तमानं विकारनित्वत्यादप्रधानं स्यात् उभयथा चास्य प्रवृत्तिः प्रधानव्यवहारं लभते नान्यथा कारणान्तरेष्वपि कल्पितेष्वेष समानश्चर्चः ॥

XIII. The Pradhâna, the material cause of all manifestation, would become what it is not, if it tended only to rest, because in that case there would not be any manifestation into phenomena; nor would it be what it is, if it were to remain in constant motion, because in that case, the phenomena would become eternal and never disappear. It is only when it tends to both these states, that it can be called the Pradhâna (the cause of manifestation), not otherwise. The same considerations apply to any other causes that might be imagined.—*Vide* Vyâsa's Commentary on Yoga-Sûtram II. 23.

मूर्तिव्यवधिजातिभेदाभावान्नास्ति मूलपृथक्त्वम् ॥

XIV. On account of the absence of the difference of form, intervening space and time, and genus, there is no separation in the Root (*i.e.*, the Pradhâna.)—*Vide* Vyâsa's Commentary on Yoga-Sûtram III. 52.

जलभूम्योः पारिणामिकं रसादिवैश्वरूप्यं स्थावरेषु दृष्टं तथा स्थावराणां जङ्गमेषु जङ्गमानां स्थावरेषु ॥

XV. All the diverse forms of juice, etc., caused by the transformation of earth and water, is seen in immobile objects; similarly of the immobile, in the mobile, and of the mobile, in the immobile.—*Vide* Vyâsa's Commentary on Yoga-Sûtram III. 14.

एकजातिसमन्वितानामेषां धर्ममात्रं व्यावृत्तिः ॥

XVI. Of these which possess the same genus, the differences are in (specific) properties only.—*Vide* Vyasa's Commentary on Yoga-Sûtram III. 43.

महामोहमयेनेन्द्रजालेन प्रकाशशीलं सत्त्वमावृत्य तदेवाकार्ये नियुङ्क्ते ॥

XVII. By the magic panorama of Mahâmoha (desire and ignorance), overshadowing the Sattva which is luminous by nature, the very same is employed in acts of vice.—*Vide* Vyâsa's Commentary on Yoga-Sûtram II. 52.

तपो न परं प्राणायामात्ततो विशुद्धिर्मलानां दीप्तिश्च ज्ञानस्य ॥

XVIII. There is no penance greater than Prâṇâyâma: whence are the purification from dirts and the brightness of knowledge.—*Vide* Vyâsa's Commentary on Yoga-Sûtram II. 52.

स्वभावं मुक्त्वा येषां पूर्वपक्षे रुचिर्भवति अरुचिश्च निर्णये भवति ॥

XIX. (In the case of those who do not possess the curiosity to know the nature of the Self), giving up, through faults (*i. e.*, demerits), the nature, there arises a liking for *primâ facie* contrary views, and dislike for the ascertainment of the truth.—*Vide* Vyâsa's Commentary on Yoga-Sûtram, IV 25.

स खल्वयं ब्राह्मणो यथा यथा व्रतानि बहूनि समादित्सते तथा तथा प्रमादकृतेभ्यो हिंसानिदानेभ्यो निवर्तमानस्तामेवावदातरूपामहिंसां करोति ॥

XX. As a Brâhmaṇa undertakes many a vow, one after another, he turns away successively from acts of injury due to inadvertence, and thereby makes the virtue of non-injury (ahiṃsâ) gradually purer and purer.—*Vide* Vyâsa's Commentary on Yoga-Sûtram II. 30.

ये चैते मैत्र्यादयो ध्यायिनां विहारास्ते बाह्यसाधननिरनुग्रहात्मानः प्रकृष्टं धर्ममभिनिर्वर्तयन्ति ॥

XXI. And what are these activities of the Dhyâyins, namely, friendliness (maitri), etc., being, by nature, independent of external means, accomplish the highest virtue.—*Vide* Vyâsa's Commentary on Yoga-Sûtram IV. 10.

42. And to them, the Kâpila Âśrama reproduction adds:

प्रधानस्यात्मख्यापनार्था प्रवृत्तिः ॥

XXII. The activity of the Pradhâna is for the sake of the exhibition of herself.—*Vide* Vyâsa's Commentary on Yoga-Sûtram II. 23.

43. But Vâchaspati tells us that No. XIII is a doctrine of an opposite school, and Nos. XVII—XX are the teachings of the Âgamins (Śaiva Darśana); while Vyâsa himself tells us that No. XIV is an aphorism of Vârṣagaṇya and No. XXII is a text of the Veda. Both of them, again, are silent as to the paternity of Nos. XV and XVI. The remaining one, No. XI, is referred by Vâchaspati to the Âchâryas or older teachers of the Sâṃkhya School. In these circumstances, we do not feel we should be justified in affiliating these aphorisms to Pañchaśikha.

44. Paṇḍita Râja Râm has, we observe, arranged *his* aphorisms of Pañchaśikha in a particular order, and has explained them in a connected form. This may mislead the unwary in thinking that this collection of aphorisms is a complete treatise composed by Pañchaśikha which, however, it is not, and can, by no means, pretend to be. To avoid any such misconception, we have, with the single exception of the first one,—and this, for obvious reasons—presented the aphorisms just in the order of their quotation by Vyâsa; for there is no more reason known to us for placing them in one particular order than in any other.

45 It may also be just mentioned here that some other views, not aphorisms or sayings, of Pañchaśikha have been referred to in the Sâṃkhya-Pavrachana-Sûtram also. See *Ibidem* V. 32 and VI. 68; and Vijñâna Bikṣu's Commentary on I. 127.

WS - #0022 - 010825 - C0 - 229/152/11 [13] - CB - 9780331603187 - Gloss Lamination

God With Us

A 17th Century Family in War and Peace

by

John Longworth

"If God be for us, who can be against us?"
Epistle to the Romans Chapter 8 Verse 31

Published in 2012

Cover image from an original digital painting by
Slavyan Dimitrov Stoyanov *'The English Soldier'*

Contents

PART ONE: FROM PEACE TO WAR

1. A ROYAL VISIT 9
2. WHITE SALT 24
3. GOD'S PROVIDENCE 35
4. ST. GEORGE'S DAY 51
5. DUMB AND DARK IMAGES 58
6. THE CHESHIRE PROPHET 68
7. THE BLACK SCOURGE 75
8. SOLDIER IN GOD'S CAUSE 93
9. LYNETTE 108
10. AT WAR IN HIGH GERMANY 116
11. STRUGGLE FOR SURVIVAL 127
12. THE PROMISED HAVEN 138
13. LUKE BLACKSHAW 150
14. CALL TO ARMS 159
15. THE RETURN 171

PART TWO: FROM WAR TO PEACE

16. CROMWELL AND FAIRFAX 185
17. A SPRIG OF HOLLY 195
18. THE SINS OF THE FLESH 212
19. AMALIA 222
20. GOD IS OUR STRENGTH 243
21. APOTHECARY SURGEON 253
22. CAPTAIN MYNTON 263
23. SEALS OF LOVE 284
24. A NEW SON FOR THOMAS 296
25. DARWEN STREAM 307
26. THAT MAN OF BLOOD 318
27. DUNBAR FIELD 333
28. TEMPTATION 345
29. A BROKEN ARMY 362
30. SWORDS INTO PLOUGHSHARES 373

PART ONE: FROM PEACE TO WAR

1617—1642

"The Lord gave the word;
great was the company of those that published it. "
Psalm 68